Lars von Trier |

Contemporary Film Directors

Edited by James Naremore

The Contemporary Film Directors series provides concise, well-written introductions to directors from around the world and from every level of the film industry. Its chief aims are to broaden our awareness of important artists, to give serious critical attention to their work, and to illustrate the variety and vitality of contemporary cinema. Contributors to the series include an array of internationally respected critics and academics. Each volume contains an incisive critical commentary, an informative interview with the director, and a detailed filmography.

A list of books in the series appears
at the end of this book.

Lars von Trier |

Linda Badley

**UNIVERSITY
OF
ILLINOIS
PRESS**
URBANA
CHICAGO
SPRINGFIELD

Frontispiece: Lars von Trier, *Antichrist*.
© 2009, Zentropa Entertainments ApS.

© 2010 by Linda Badley
All rights reserved
Manufactured in the United States of America
1 2 3 4 5 C P 5 4 3 2 1
∞ This book is printed on acid-free paper.

Library of Congress Cataloging-in-Publication Data
Badley, Linda.
Lars von Trier / Linda Badley.
p.   cm. — (Contemporary film directors)
Includes bibliographical references and index.
ISBN-13: 978-0-252-03591-3 (hardcover : alk. paper)
ISBN-10: 0-252-03591-7 (hardcover : alk. paper)
ISBN-13: 978-0-252-07790-6 (pbk. : alk. paper)
ISBN-10: 0-252-07790-3 (pbk. : alk. paper)
1. Trier, Lars von, 1956–
—Criticism and interpretation. I. Title.
PN1998.3.T747B34   2011
791.4302'33092—dc22   2010040241

Contents |

The manuscript for this project was in its final stages as the controversy over *Antichrist* broke at Cannes, months before the film was to become available in the United States. Although I managed to see it shortly before submitting the final draft, constraints of time and space required that the book end with a brief, in-the-moment analysis of the film's origins, inspirations, and critical and popular reception as the story emerged from the surrounding publicity and the two interviews that Trier granted during crucial stages of the film's development. During those discussions (ostensibly about other subjects), Trier (and I) invariably returned to the film-in-progress, the horror genre, and topics such as fear, cruelty, and depression. Together, the "Epilogue" on *Antichrist* and the interviews should be understood as a provisional and somewhat risky experiment intended in the spirit in which Trier's most recent film was made.

Spatial constraints also precluded any sustained analysis of Trier and Jørgen Leth's extraordinary and acclaimed "Dogumentary" film/provocation/event *The Five Obstructions* (2003), which adapted the game strategy of Dogme95—the imposition of "arbitrary" rules and limitations—within a more personal and experimental environment. Interested readers should see Mette Hjort's *Dekalog¹: On* The Five Obstructions (Wallflower, 2008) for comprehensive coverage from several disciplinary approaches.

Like many Americans, I was introduced to Lars von Trier by way of the controversy surrounding *Breaking the Waves* in 1996. Prepared by my feminism for an onslaught of misogyny, I was instead transfixed, stunned, and moved to see more of his films. I began to think about writing a book on his work only several years later while writing the article "Danish Dogme: 'Truth' and Cultural Politics," for *Traditions in World*

Cinema (Edinburgh University Press, 2006), portions of which the press has graciously permitted me to use in the discussions of Dogme and *The Idiots.* To Barton Palmer, who encouraged me to propose this volume, I owe special thanks. Jim Naremore, Joan Catapano, and the excellent staff at the University of Illinois Press have been infinitely patient and helpful, and I thank them for their support and guidance throughout this process.

Many kind, energetic, and efficient people at Zentropa and Filmbyen deserve my gratitude, notably Trier's producer Meta Louise Foldager, Ulrik Krapper at Station Next, Signe Iarussi, and Jonas Jørgensen—and most especially Trier's assistant Katrine Sahlstrøm, for her gracious assistance in arranging interviews and obtaining information and permissions. I cannot thank Lars von Trier and Peter Aalbæk Jenson enough for devoting their time and energy to the interviews that are included, quoted, and reflected throughout the book. I also thank the Danish Film Institute for arranging for me to screen Trier's student films. Finally, I am indebted to Mette Hjort and Peter Schepelern for their inspiration and assistance.

Middle Tennessee State University generously provided release time through an academic year grant and funded travel to Copenhagen to conduct firsthand research at the Danish Film Institute and Filmbyen, interview Trier and Jensen, and attend the Copenhagen International Film Festival for the premiere of *The Boss of It All* in September 2006. I am grateful to graduate assistants Jessica McKee, Michael Morris, Lisa Williams, and especially James Francis for their hard work and astute responses to Trier's films. Kirsten Boatwright, who proved a tireless and invaluable reader at several points in this process, deserves special mention. Without her support and assistance, I would have been hard put to get the manuscript through these final stages. I also owe special thanks to the students in my fall 2006 Horror Film class whom, at Trier's request, I polled for information about their favorite Asian horror titles and scenes. To these and many other students who, in my Contemporary World Cinema and Women and Film classes, have screened and responded to Trier's films, I am indebted for too many insights to account for. Finally, I thank my husband Bill Badley for his patience throughout these many months of preoccupation on my part and for his companionship, insight, and unfailing encouragement throughout this process.

Quotations from Trier's films on DVD as well as from supplementary materials (commentaries, featurettes, interviews, and press conferences) are taken from the (typically definitive) Region 2 DVDs, and when the language is other than English, from their subtitles. I refer to von Trier's third feature (1991) as *Europa*, its original title and the one listed on the 2008 Criterion Collection DVD. (In 1991, the film was released in North America as *Zentropa* to avoid marketing confusion with Agnieszka Holland's international hit of the same year, *Europa, Europa*, but is no longer available in that version.) Illustrations, unless otherwise noted, are frame enlargements.

Lars von Trier |

Making the Waves
Cinema as Performance

"Lars von Trier—genius or fraud?" asks a May 2009 *Guardian Arts Diary* poll. Its subject is arguably world cinema's most confrontational and polarizing figure, the results: 60.3 percent genius, 39.7 percent fraud. Trier takes risks no other filmmaker would conceive of, mounting projects that somehow transcend the grand follies they narrowly miss becoming, and willfully devastates audiences. Scandinavia's foremost auteur since Ingmar Bergman, the Danish director has premiered all but one of his ten features at Cannes and reigns, as *IndieWIRE* would have it, "the unabashed prince of the European avant-garde" (qtd. in *"Trier"*). Challenging conventional limitations and imposing his own rules (changing them with each film), he restlessly reinvents the language of cinema.

Personally he is as challenging as his films. After having written some of the most compelling heroines in recent cinema and elicited stunning, career-topping performances from Emily Watson, Björk, Nicole Kidman, and Charlotte Gainsbourg, he is reputed to be a misogynist who bullies actresses and abuses his female characters in cinematic reinstatements of depleted sexist clichés. He is notorious at Cannes for his provocations and insults, as in 1991, when he thanked "the midget" (Jury President Roman Polanski) for awarding his film *Europa* third, rather than first, prize. At home in Denmark, his uncensored, frequently petty outbursts are regularly reported in the tabloids. In 2005, for instance, he referred to Zentropa colleagues Susanne Bier and Anders Thomas Jensen's collaborations (*Open Hearts,* 2002, *Brothers,* 2005), which had outperformed him critically and at the box office, as "crap" (Pedersen). Just as often, his outbursts have political import, as in February 2006, via video broadcast, he sarcastically thanked Danish Minister of Culture Brian Mikkelsen (who had selected *The Idiots* [1998] for an official Danish "canon") for "nationalising our culture" (McGwin). The previous year at Cannes, in a scene worthy of Michael Moore, he called U.S. President George W. Bush an "idiot" and an "asshole," lending vituperation to the already divisive *Manderlay* (2005), his film about an Alabama plantation practicing slavery into the 1930s, by claiming to be "60% American" (Higgins)—an assertion made more offensive by his celebrated refusal or inability (he has a fear of flying) to set foot in the United States. (In other words, coming from a small country infiltrated by America's media-driven cultural imperialism, he has found it not merely his right or duty to make films about the United States but impossible to do otherwise.) A similar effrontery had provided the catalyst for Dogme95, the Danish collective and global movement that took on Hollywood in the 1990s and continues to be well served by the punk impertinence of the Dogme logo, a large, staring eye that flickers from the rear end of a bulldog (or is it a pig?).

Dogme shows where the provocateur and auteur come together. Claiming a new democracy in which (in the manifesto's words) "anybody can make films," Trier and the Dogme "brothers" marked out a space for independent filmmaking beyond the global mass entertainment industry. Similarly working out of Zentropa, his production company, the lynchpin of a collaborative "Film Town" near Copenhagen, he situates his own projects outside the pale, further marking them off within trilogies: the obsessively stylized Europe Trilogy, the raw and radically unironic Gold Heart Trilogy, and the drippingly sardonic (two-thirds-completed) USA—Land of Opportunities Trilogy. The political Trier reflects enduring philosophical and aesthetic allegiances and extends the important impulses of his work as a whole, having emerged out of the defiantly transnational outlook of his early films, through which he set himself off from all things Danish. Although he rarely leaves Denmark, he has cultivated a European and uniquely global cinema. Making his first features primarily in English, he quickly found a niche in the international festival circuit. At odds with the Danish industry's preference for heritage films, social realism, and native language, he drew inspiration from a wide swath—from the genius of Andrei Tarkovsky to movements such as Italian neorealism and the international new waves of the 1960s-1970s to American auteurs Stanley Kubrick and David Lynch. Trier's long-term affinity with German culture—from expressionism and New German cinema to the writings of Karl Marx, Franz Kafka, and Friedrich Nietzsche—extends to equal passions for Wagnerian opera and anti-Wagnerian (Brechtian) theater, enhancing a central dichotomy in his practice. Similar contradictions emerge between his modernist identification with European high art and a fascination with American genres. These are united in a passion for postmodern bricolage; thus in 1983, he compared filmmaking to "a supermarket, where you go around with your little cart and pick things up" (Schwander 16) and described his first feature *The Element of Crime* (1984) as "a bastard child of a mating of American with German film" (Larsen 39). However different, these German and American mythologies afforded a diversity and range—geographical, political, and emotional—that Danish culture lacked. Similarly, he draws on "low" and exploitation genres: from horror/science fiction to the "woman's picture," pornography, and even propaganda.

From the outset, Trier has presented himself as a contradictory, eclectic, European, and transnational figure within a global postmodern (as opposed to Danish) context. For this reason, and to account for Trier's larger impact, this book assumes a broadly comparative framework. Intended to supplement Peter Schepelern's and Jack Stevenson's groundbreaking studies, which emphasize the Danish context and reception of his career, it also draws on Mette Hjort's essential work on small-nation cinemas and Trier's catalytic role in their resurgence within an increasingly transnational environment.[1]

In spite or because of his flaunted internationalism, Trier has become the standard-bearer for Nordic cinema. Like Bergman and Carl Th. Dreyer, whose visions transcended nationality, he has exploited the Scandinavian "imaginary"—bleak landscapes, Lutheran austerity and self-denial, the explosive release of repressed emotions—to project it elsewhere: on the harshly photogenic seacoast community of *Breaking the Waves*'s (1996) Hebrides or in *Dogville*'s (2003) bare-stage minimalism. He has similarly appropriated the Northern European *Kammerspiel* (chamber play) that Henrik Ibsen and August Strindberg had condensed into a charged medium. Reincarnating Dreyer's martyrs (*The Passion of Joan of Arc*, 1928; *Ordet*, 1955) and the anguished female performances of Bergman's films for the present era, he has invented a form of psychodrama that traumatizes audiences while challenging them to respond to cinema in new ways.

Along the way, Trier's provocations have revolutionized the Danish film industry. In its exotic mélange of sources, *The Element of Crime* could not have been more different from Danish social realism. Made in English, set in a festering, postapocalyptic Europe, it challenged Danish Film Institute policies that funded only native-language films about Danish subjects. Its international success led to a 1989 Film Act that expanded the definition of a Danish film to include any film produced by a Danish company that contributed to film art and culture (Hjort, *Small Nation* 12–13), essentially denationalizing the industry. In 1992, to fund *Breaking the Waves* and assume control over his films, Trier and producer Peter Aalbæk Jensen founded Zentropa Productions. In accommodating Trier's eccentric strengths, Zentropa's business model offered other filmmakers an independent alternative both to the state-supported Danish Film Institute and the commercial Hollywood model (Ostrowska), becoming what *Screen* in 2002 called "the creative and business powerhouse" that "reinvigorated an industry" (Hjort, *Small Nation* 8) and eventually stimulated a renaissance in Nordic cinema.

Dogme's international success marked the beginning of Trier's direct engagement with cultural politics. It was launched on March 20, 1995, in Paris's Odéon Théâtre at an international symposium marking cinema's first century when Trier pronounced recent cinema "rubbish," read from a manifesto, and showered the astonished audience with red leaflets before abruptly departing. Dogme (*dogma* in French) required abstinence from Hollywood-style high-tech "cosmetics," calling for an oppositional movement with its own doctrine and ten-rule "Vow of Chastity." In contrast to the *Cahiers du Cinéma* critics, who created an opening for fresh, personal films and, in the process, generated the French New Wave, Trier invented Dogme as a performative space. *Europa's* technical virtuosity had proved a dead end, and he had found working "imperfectly" with an ensemble on his television miniseries *The Kingdom* (1994) a joy. As Peter Schepelern comments, Dogme "might have been augured from the start" (Schepelern and Björkman), and it continues to inform his *oeuvre*. Coming up with the infamous rules was "easy," claims their cowriter Thomas Vinterberg: "We asked ourselves what we most hated about film today, and then we drew up a list banning it all." The idea was "to put a mirror in front of [the movie industry] and say we can do it another way as well" (*Name of This Film*). Coinciding with the digital revolution and offering a recipe for low-budget films, the initiative took on a revolutionary, anti-Hollywood stance whose all-important side effect, Mette Hjort has shown, was to stimulate an oppositional form of globalization, "a network of audiences with a genuine global reach" through which individual directors and small countries could compete ("Globalisation" 155).

Since Dogme, Trier's aesthetic choices, themes, and aims have followed this logic—even when displaying a brazenly un-Dogmatic artifice. Filmed in Denmark, Sweden, and Germany and financed as international coproductions, *Dancer in the Dark* (2000), *Dogville, Manderlay,* and *Antichrist* were made "as if" American—in English with star-studded international casts with (often) a cacophony of accents. In their defiant inappropriateness, they might also be viewed as "accented" in the sense that Hamid Naficy uses the term to denote filmmakers and cinemas positioned in a marginal and antagonistic relation to the norms of Hollywood entertainment, which pretends to be ideologically neutral or lacking accent (Naficy 23; Penner and Stichele 14). Claiming to be "occupied" by American mediatized culture, dispossessed and exiled, culturally and ideologically, from his country and himself, he thus set four (of six) of his post-Dogme films in America, flaunted his use of American genre stereotypes, and deployed a European ideological aesthetic in the service of critique. Filmed on an empty stage with chalk marks for streets and buildings (while reflecting America's "true" face in its minimalist, European mirror), *Dogville* and *Manderlay* culminate Trier's quest as outlined in the Dogma manifesto for a "pure" cinema of emotion and provocation. Even the titular (if nonexistent) character of *The Boss of It All*, his Danish satire on empty-suit capitalism shot by a computerized "cinematographer" called Automavision, resides in America. But there is yet another sense in which Trier found himself "American" or at least other than "Danish."

More than any auteur in recent memory, Trier's personal life is a public myth featured in the elaborate metatextual apparatus that accompanies nearly all his productions. His manifestos, rule making, and interrogations of the medium emerge from what he claims are profoundly personal needs, and interviewers are hard pressed to steer him from subjects such as his childhood, phobias, and medications. Speculation about authorial intentions, always risky, is especially so when Trier's image is so overtly self-constructed and publicly staged, and when contradicting previous statements is integral to his game. A demonstration model of the intentional fallacy, he is an auteurist critic's dream subject and worst nightmare.

The issue gets trickier when considering the role of psychoanalysis in the myth of Lars von Trier. A long-term therapy patient, he uses therapeutic language to explain himself to himself and others, speaking of creativity as "a means of survival" beyond any mere "need" or "desire" and claiming that "your driving force is connected to your psychological insecurities" (Björkman, *Trier* 16). The psychoanalytic model is ubiquitous in his oeuvre. Regressive hypnosis is the key narrative device and metaphor of the Europe Trilogy, physical and psychic trauma haunts the hospital miniseries *The Kingdom,* and mental impairment is central to Gold Heart Trilogy whose heroines, along with *The Idiots'* titular protagonists, achieve a sublime schizophrenic transcendence. The Europe and USA trilogies re-expose the scars of the Holocaust, the American Depression, and slavery.

Trauma is not only his inevitable subject but also, as Caroline Bainbridge has stressed, his films' affect ("Making"; *Cinema* 114–19, 135–37) and primary aim: to induce emotional, ethical, and intellectual distress in audiences, other filmmakers, and himself. Think of *Antichrist*'s culminating shock/schlock effects, for instance, or *The Five Obstructions* (2003), Trier's "Dogumentary" challenge to former mentor Jørgen Leth to remake his too-"perfect" short film *The Perfect Human* (1967) five times according to perversely counterintuitive rules such as "#2: Bombay," which requires him to film himself experiencing his own personal hell. (When the imperturbable Leth makes a poignantly multilayered metafilm, Trier snaps: "This is therapy, not a film competition with yourself!") The notion of "therapeutic trauma" is attached to the metacinematic apparatus surrounding Trier's collaborations and films, adding yet another level of performativity and self-construction to what are already psychodramas or confessions. Freud may be dead, but Trier's practice brings psychotherapeutic myths and methods to the creative act, which he portrays as inseparable from self-fashioning—a process with crucial cultural and political ramifications.

What Roger Luckhurst and Mark Seltzer have called our current "trauma culture" helps contextualize Trier's case. As depth psychology has lost credibility, identity has shaped itself around the concept of trauma, and as Seltzer suggests, a mediatized trauma discourse has become our common language, whether through confession of psychological damage on television talk shows or in the public display of "torn and open bodies" (1). On one hand, in art and theory, as Hal Foster writes in *Return of the Real,*

> the discourse of trauma continues the poststructuralist critique of the subject by other means, for there is no subject of trauma; the position is evacuated. . . . On the other, in popular culture, trauma is treated as an event that guarantees the subject [which] . . . however disturbed, rushes back in as witness, testifier, survivor. Here is indeed a traumatic subject, and it has absolute authority, for one cannot challenge the trauma of another. . . . *In trauma discourse, the subject is evacuated and elevated at once.* (168)

Magically resolving contemporary culture's two opposing imperatives, deconstruction and identity politics, this "strange rebirth of the author, is a significant turn in contemporary art, criticism, and cultural politics" (Foster 168).

Trauma discourse goes some distance in explaining why Lars von Trier shapes his identity so publicly around personal crisis. His psychomythology offers a microcosm of the existential subject in our late or post-postmodern predicament. He portrays himself as a child in a world without borders, given complete freedom by his radical leftist mother, and forced to erect the structures of his identity. He was born "Lars Trier" in Copenhagen on April 30, 1956, the second child of Inger Høst and Ulf Trier. "Cultural radicals" (as he describes them) employed in the Social Ministry, both had master's degrees in political economics, progressive social views, and artistic tastes, and lived comfortably in the wooded suburb of Lundtofte (Stevenson, *Lars* 6–7). Ulf, who was Jewish, was a kind and tolerant social democrat. Inger, an ardent communist and prominent feminist who had fought in the Danish resistance and associated with various left-wing writers, nourished Lars's creative ego, charging him with complete autonomy while discouraging religion, emotion, and bourgeois pleasures. With freedom came a terrible burden of choice—of having to decide not simply when but whether to go to the dentist (Björkman, *Trier* 4–6). Thrown back on himself, he was persistently anxious. "I was forced to create an internal authority, and that isn't particularly easy for a child," he told Björkman. "I thought I was responsible for the whole world" (*Trier* 7). This lack also resulted in a compulsion to construct elaborate games and impose systems of rules on himself and others.

The lack of a metanarrative or Law of the Father became a full-fledged crisis when, on her deathbed in April 1989, Inger revealed that Ulf (who had died in 1979) was not his real father and the Jewish heritage that had been an identity marker, "a sense of belonging," he "didn't have any right to at all" (Björkman, *Trier* 9). Lars had been conceived with her employer Fritz Michael Hartmann (whose family included Johan Peter Emilius Hartmann, one of Denmark's most famous composers, and other distinguished musicians) out of her desire for a child with "artistic genes" (Schepelern, "Making" 123–24). Her plan succeeded to the degree that, as Schepelern suggests, Inger Høst might be seen as the author of a deliberate "artistic construction, a genetic project" that became Lars von Trier ("Making" 124). "My mother was unusually creative," Trier quipped to Björkman (*Trier,* 12). Her ideas of childcare were "based on a demand for complete openness. Everything was up for discussion . . . . [however] with therapy, I've come to the conclusion that my childhood wasn't as free as I used to think" (Björkman, *Trier* 11–12).

Trier has projected his mother's creative treachery backward as his foundational trauma or origin, the wound or gap around which his identity is constructed. Both radically open and rigidly deterministic, his upbringing was at odds with Danish values of discretion, moderation, and "hygge" ("coziness"). Instinctively he defied the *Jantelovn*, the unwritten law coined by Danish-Norwegian author Aksel Sandemose that no one is better than anybody else and that pride in exceptionality should be leveled, and this often got him into trouble. After a self-directed childhood, the "outside world" was an experience of "forever being knocked back" (Björkman, *Trier* 7), and school was especially difficult. At recess, Lars was often bullied; yet he was smart and articulate and among friends a natural leader who persuaded others to play his games (Björkman, *Trier* 6–7). Eventually dropping out, he experimented with painting and writing, studied privately, and passed an equivalency exam before enrolling in film studies classes at the University of Copenhagen and joining the filmmaking collective Gruppe 16. Three years later, in 1979, he was admitted to the exclusive Danish Film School (which he found useful primarily as a "workshop" [Björkman, *Trier* 32]) and graduated in 1982 with several prizes.

With youthful ideals shaped by Nietzsche and Strindberg (and in opposition to Sandemose), he fashioned himself into "Lars von Trier" the artist even before he had found a medium, as Schepelern relates. His first public use of the aristocratic "von" was in his 1976 newspaper article about Strindberg's period of creative psychosis (1894–97) accompanied by a photo of "writer and artist Lars von Trier" posed outside the estate in Holte where Strindberg wrote *Miss Julie* (Björkman, *Trier* 2)—"Strindberg's and Munch's madness were the height of romanticism for me then," he told Björkman (*Trier* 28). At the Danish Film School, he formally assumed the exotic "von" after an exasperated professor "baptiz[ed]" him with it (Michelsen 9), although he also mentions Sternberg and Stroheim, Austrian-Jewish directors who took the "von" along with aristocratic Germanic stage personas (Björkman, *Trier* 2). "You could call it a provocation on my part," Trier explained in 1982 to Ole Michelsen. "But I would very much like to see it as an inner aristocracy, one that I radiate, and besides, it's of course a no-no in Danish cinema and in Denmark in general to radiate anything whatsoever" (9).

Whether genius, fraud, or cinema's P. T. Barnum, he has perfected the art of self-promotion and cultivates the mystique of the international auteur. His films tell the same story—of a flawed, often betrayed and persecuted, idealist, and he has maintained complete creative control over his art, having written or cowritten all his films and operated the camera for most of them since 1998. He acted in many of his student films and in his first three features—starring in the 37-minute *The Orchid Gardener* (1977) as a cross-dressing Jewish painter in search of his artistic identity and in *Epidemic* in the dual role of the filmmaker and the ill-fated Dr. Mesmer in the film-within-the film. Most recently, in "Occupations" (2007), his contribution to Cannes's sixtieth anniversary tribute to the cinema, he performed a blackly humorous, axe-murdering version of himself. Since *The Kingdom* (1994), whose episodes he concluded with personally delivered Hitchcockian conundrums (figure 1), he has interjected himself into his productions—whether as the invisible interrogator of *The Idiots* or as himself as narrator in *The Boss of It All*. Or, he employs narrators as surrogates, as in Bergman icon Max von Sydow's hypnotic voiceover in *Europa* or John Hurt's sardonic rendering of the "sad tale" of *Dogville*. Yet perhaps most telling of all is the way he issues a manifesto every couple of years.

Like the legendary Werner Herzog, his only serious competitor in this field, he produces or collaborates on biographies, tell-all diaries,

Figure 1. *The Kingdom*. Trier in a Hitchcockian pose: "—for Satan's sake, be prepared to take the good with the evil."

and confessions in various media that simultaneously humanize and make him larger than life. Notoriously reclusive and "difficult," he is nevertheless the subject of countless published, televised, videocast, and filmed interviews, documentaries, and retrospectives. In facilitating the "film about the film," Trier is a virtuoso. One *Dogville* trailer, composed of clips from Sami Saif's *Dogville Confessions* (2003), consists of actors' "candid" revelations to the camera in a confession booth. Beginning with a nervously cryptic Nicole Kidman, culminating with Ben Gazzara ("I will never do another picture with an insane director—what's his name—funny name—Lars *van* Trier!"), and topped off with a sighing Trier, it played off publicity surrounding the director's struggle with his cast. Two recent Danish comedies are *films à clef* based on his life and work: *Clash of Egos* (2006) and *The Early Years: Erik Nietzsche Part 1* (2007), the latter written and narrated by Trier and featuring droll reenactments of his film school achievements with original footage. Gareth James and Gardar Eide Einarsson's *Lars von Trier,* a 2002 installation at New York City's American Fine Arts Gallery consisting of sculpture, drawing, and photography (including *Idioterne,* a portrait of the artists *sans* trousers), dismantles the director's legendary personal dilemma in an appropriately Trieresque fusion of admiration, ridicule, and reflexiveness.

In sum, unlike auteurs shaped by existing conditions, trends, or movements within or outside the mainstream industry, he is self-authorized, his career "a prototype auteurist initiative," as Schepelern puts it, a project "not primarily to make films but to construct Lars von Trier, the auteur filmmaker" ("Making" 111). "I've used my name a lot in promoting my films," he admits, "as David Bowie—whom I'm a great fan of—has allowed his person to fuse with his work" (Hjort and Bondebjerg 221). Bowie "managed to create an entire myth around himself" that was "as important as his music" (Björkman, *Trier* 167) and became an ongoing influence, particularly in his propensity for redefining himself for every decade. If his films are identified by auteurist trademarks as trilogies and movements, he systematically violates commandments like the lynchpin of continuity editing, the 180-degree rule. More characteristic yet, though, is his propensity for making 180-degree turns, whether between trilogies—from *Europa*'s rigorous mise-en-scène to the "spastic" *Breaking the Waves* and *The Idiots*—or within films, as in the final act of *Dogville,* in which, after 150 minutes of passive suffering, his heroine wreaks vengeance on an entire town. Fond of issuing paradoxes, he is known to assert that whatever he said was true when he said it, and when he tells a reporter that "Everything written about me is a lie" (*Tranceformer*) he means the same thing. His signature may well be his "punk" habit of breaking whatever rules he has laid out in previous manifestos.

If Trier's primary auteurist goal is beating himself at his own game, his role as Zentropa's co-owner/figurehead furnishes a surprisingly different portrait. As Scandinavia's largest film production company since 1994, its power base offers another stage for his self-fashioning—paradoxically through relinquishing (and advertising that relinquishment of) control. His name is associated with initiatives that disperse authorship through collaborative relationships and coproductions—local, pan-Scandinavian, and international—and by sponsoring educational, community, and international outreach programs with a workshop model. These range from *The Five Obstructions* collaboration, to the Advance Party initiative which jump-started the Scottish production company Sigma Films in 2007 and launched Andrea Arnold's feature film career, to "film towns" in Århus, Denmark; Trollhättan, Sweden; and Glasgow, Scotland.

The film towns are modeled on Zentropa's home base, Filmbyen ("Film Town"), in Hvidovre, a suburban ghetto southwest of Copenhagen that since 2000 has housed a large studio complex and twenty-odd production companies, initiatives, and facilities. As former communists (who nevertheless participate quite effectively in the capitalist system), Trier and Peter Aalbæk Jensen advertise their anticapitalist leanings, especially Zentropa's pseudocollectivist social activities (including nude swimming and Friday morning songfests). In 2006, Trier and Jensen sold half the company to their employees, standing by its claim, stated on the company homepage, to "a decentralised autonomous organisation structure which creates space for new ideas and alternative methods of productions" ("History"). Through such magnanimous yet self-reflexive gestures, Schepelern has commented, Trier counters a natural bent toward "solitary" auteurism with a quest (however qualified by postmodern relativism and irony) for ethics and "solidarity" ("Making" 122–245). Balancing the idealism is a pragmatic strain exemplified in Zentropa's 2008 sale of half its stocks to former rival Nordisk. The partnership has allowed the company to expand internationally and fund higher-risk projects (such as the $11 million *Antichrist*) in economically uncertain times. With companies in Sweden, Scotland, Norway, Holland, Germany, France, Poland, Italy (Nielsen), and more recently Spain, Estonia, Belgium, and Latvia, Zentropa leads Scandinavia if not Europe in the sheer number and variety of collaborations and coproductions it initiates.

Trier's relationship with the auteur theory, as with issues of control, is paradoxical. There is the über auteur who asserts that the only thing he is not afraid of is making films that offer him an arena for controlled play and a border for the performance that is Lars von Trier. Yet he is equally the filmmaker obsessed with giving up control. The Dogme Manifesto condemned the auteur concept as "bourgeois romanticism" and thereby "false," rule #10 prohibited crediting the director (Trier, "Dogme95"), and the rules collectively constituted "a punch in the face of all directors" (Hjort and Bondebjerg 221)—especially himself, as he claims that he wrote the rules first of all "for myself": "[W]here I have followed the line of least resistance, I have increased the resistance," he told *Politiken* in 2003, with rules like #10 constituting "my Super Ego" (Schepelern, "Making" 117). Yet Dogme almost immediately became a brand and a genre (of sorts) associated with its authors' names, the first being Lars von Trier.

Provocation "is always initially inwardly directed, and then it becomes other-directed as a side effect," he also explains (Hjort and Bondebjerg 221). The personal *becomes* political. Finding a source of his dilemma in Hollywood-inflected global postmodernism, Trier often makes Hollywood the backdrop against which he projects that dilemma in elaborate games and rules or in auteurist psychodramas set in allegorical and politicized frameworks. In short, it might be said that Trier's body of work is designed to lend an image and a context to the blank space he fears is truly "Lars." While such an assertion might seem to blunder into crude psychoanalysis and the intentional fallacy, it is made with the assumption that the psychoanalytic model is one—perhaps the primary one—of many structures or "obstructions" he has erected to support the oeuvre and the auteur.

One exit from this dilemma is suggested by Jan Simons, whose *Playing the Waves: Lars von Trier's Game Cinema* (2007) claims that Trier brings game structures and logistics to bear on cinema in new ways, outdistancing the methods of traditional media criticism. From *The Element of Crime* through *Manderlay,* Trier's films are psychological, social, and/or aesthetic experiments governed by externally imposed rules. The "Vow of Chastity" readily comes to mind along with his instinct for anticipating and ushering in trends and his increasing reference to video games such as *Tetris* (Björkman, *Trier* 15) and *Silent Hill.* The films are often presided over by an extradiegetic character—hypnotist/narrator/interrogator—or played out on gameboard-like sets (Odgen) as in *Dogville,* where he appropriates Brecht's V-effect to make film more interactive, to force audiences to "revirtualize" the empty space with their own mental images (Simons, "Von" 5). Beyond the films themselves, Trier obsessively constructs game environments: from Dogme to a version of *Pong* that (until 2008) challenged the Zentropa Web site's visitors with "Tennis, anyone?," to the pinball machines that, along with garden gnomes used as pissing targets, are Filmbyen fixtures. At the radical edge are the intermediary projects such as *Psykomobile #1: The World Clock* (1996) and *D-Dag* (*D-Day,* 2000) that occupy a space between cinema, theater, performance art, and game. *Psykomobile,* which he has called "a drama 'happening,'" assigned characters to fifty-nine actors in twenty rooms who changed moods (anger, melancholy, joy, lust) as dictated by signals controlled by the movements of an ant colony in Mexico (Trier and Albinus).

But game theory goes only so far in explaining Trier's filmmaking practice, as Simons admits (*Playing* 198–99). An equal interest in theater goes back to his youth, and his films are theatrical in several senses: stylized, emotionally intense, and provocative. Beginning with his second feature, they have invoked twentieth-century theatrical initiatives clustered under the heading of the performative: especially Antonin Artaud's Theatre of Cruelty, Allen Kaprow's "happenings," and Guy Debord's situationism, which reformulated Marxist-Brechtian aesthetics for the age of the "spectacle" in which power, concentrated in the media image, turns individuals into passive consumers. In 1952, Debord called for an art that would "*create* situations rather than reproduce already existing [ones]" (Jappe 6) and through the performance of "lived experience" disrupt and expose the spectacle. In 1996, Trier similarly explained his view of cinema-as-provocation: "A provocation's purpose is to get people to think. If you subject people to a provocation, you allow them the possibility of their own interpretation" (*Tranceformer*). Cultivating a perverse "cinema of cruelty" (as in *Antichrist,* for example), his films are reflexively performed "events" that, disturbing audiences, force them to salvage meaning out of distress—often (as in *The Idiots*) in conjunction with initiatives such as Dogme (or, on a larger scale, Zentropa and Filmbyen) attempt to confound a consumerist economy. In these ways, Hjort suggests, Trier creates a metaculture or public forum for controversy, debate, and creative engagement ("Globalisation" 133–57).

Trier's films, with or without manifestos, are best viewed as what J. L. Austin names performative (as opposed to representational or constative) speech acts, which depend for meaning upon audiences within social and institutional contexts (Gade and Jerslev, "Introduction" 9). Specifically they have *illocutionary* functions, Austin's term for utterances intended to effect, to do things. The films bear witness, make proclamations, issue commands, pose questions, and provoke responses, as when *Europa's* narrator literally compels the audience to "Listen to my voice" and puts us into a trance that becomes the film or when *The Five Obstructions,* invented as a "Help Jørgen Leth project," reinvigorated the veteran Danish director and brought him to international attention. Thus Trier's cinema is also *perlocutionary*, especially since 1996; his films have had an impact on their surrounding contexts, affecting audiences, producing controversies, and changing the aesthetic, cultural, and political climate of the late 1990s and the 2000s.

Trier figures centrally in another discussion of the performative associated with a "post-theory," post-postmodern "return to the Real." Heralded in the mid-1990s by Hal Foster and Raoul Eshelman, a "performatist" approach seeks a way out of postmodern irony, producing an affect, "an aesthetic experience of transcendence" in which subject, sign, and thing come together. Offering an alternative to poststructuralism's infinite regress and dispersal and the nihilistic "postmodern sublime," a performative film brackets off space for an ostensive narrative act, encouraging identification with the character who performs it, exhibiting it in such a way that it resists deconstruction.[2] Bess's self-sacrifice in *Breaking the Waves* thus insists on an "impossible" sincerity in the face of patently unbelievable events, alerting audiences to the film's refusal of an expected irony—to the point that Victoria Nelson heralds Trier as a progenitor of a "new expressionism" that attempts to recover a spiritual vitality otherwise extinct in the Western world (213–32). Nicholas Rombes similarly hails a "new sincerity" characteristic of the "new punk" cinema of directors and writers such as Paul Thomas Anderson (*Magnolia*, 1999) and Charlie Kaufman (*Adaptation*, 2002), whose films evoke an emotional response while allowing the audience to see the devices eliciting it ("Sincerity" 74). While attempting something more "'authentic'" than Hollywood material, this cinema is underwritten with "a deep awareness that authenticity is itself a construct," and the resulting tension is foregrounded as in the handheld camerawork of *The Celebration* (1998) or the documentary pretenses of *The Idiots* (Rombes, "Introduction" 16). Trier's cinema is therefore pivotal to a "new" double-voiced auteurism whose signature is uniquely self-aware, becoming "a *narration* of their signature" (Perkins 38).

Performatism clarifies a pivotal moment in Trier's career (the Gold Heart/Dogme films) and testifies to his role in the resurgence of melodrama in current American and transnational independent film, yet it hardly represents a way out of postmodernism. Rather, it is a mutation of postmodernism that erects, through aesthetics, a performative space for emotion, ethics, and politics. But neither performatism, in this sense, nor the "new sincerity" can account for Trier's long-term engagement with the ludic, the carnivalesque, or his decisive turn, in the twenty-first century, toward Brechtian satire and global politics, least of all his recent, purportedly therapeutic, revisitation/reinvention of genres such as comedy and horror. An approach mindful of the performative in a more inclusive sense allowing for the plethora of forced juxtapositions, shifts, and paradoxes that inform his vision may better account for the director and the work. Lars von Trier after all *is* a performance and his work a narration of his signature, however necessary to Lars Trier, and his career has accessed the performative in ways that reflect (and contribute to) the senses in which the term is increasingly used and theorized. Some of the most interesting are found in his earliest creative efforts.

Prescient Affects: The Student Films

A decade before his first feature, Trier made several short films that explored what he thought was his Jewish heritage. Riddled with the ambivalence that still plays throughout his oeuvre, they employed shocking juxtapositions to project issues of identity against a Holocaust-haunted screen, and Liliana Cavani's exploration of sadomasochism in *The Night Porter* (1974) was an obvious influence. Trier made the 37-minute *The Orchid Gardener* (1977) with Gruppe 16, submitting it in his application to the Danish Film School but later suppressing it out of embarrassment, calling it "exhibitionist" in the manner of David Bowie, his "role model" at the time (Björkman, *Trier* 24). Based on an unpublished novel, it featured Trier as a Jewish artist searching for identity in a series of role-play performances. Approaching a life-sized blank canvas, he attempts to create a self portrait and to please an "ideal" woman, Eliza, by posing as a Christ figure, a woman, and a Nazi in a series of tableaux. In one sequence, he is naked, trussed up in a harness, and assumes a crucifix position; in another, made up as a woman, with a shock of hair bizarrely covering one eye, he wrenches the head off a bird and smears his cheeks with its blood. In another, dressed as a Nazi officer, he approaches the camera, dipping a whip in honey and then salt. In a last, desperate pose, he wanders outside, hunched over in an overcoat, and approaches a child. Finally, collapsed naked in front of his canvas, he smears it with bloody hands. In the epilogue, we find the elderly orchid gardener of the title finding solace in nature, much as Trier did as a child (Stevenson, *Lars* 16), and signaling a secondary motif that runs through the early films and recurs in features as recent as *Antichrist:* the return to childhood and the unconscious, associated with Tarkovskian images of nature. *The Blissful* (1979), another short film with Gruppe 16, in French in the style of Marguerite Duras, was a variation on *The Story of O* (1954), a text that would inspire *Manderlay.*

At the Danish Film School Trier immediately caused a stir by winning prizes with two shockingly "un-Danish" films—that is, made in opposition to the norms of social realism—the seven-minute *Nocturne* (1980) and the substantial (57-minute) *Images of a Relief* (1982). He found Danish films "boring" and "insipid" and wary of "fascination," miracles, or "effects" (Michelsen 8)—taboos that he proceeded to make his trademarks. Photographed by Tom Elling and edited by Tómas Gislason, who collaborated with him through *The Element of Crime, Nocturne* was an angst-ridden mood piece about a light-sensitive woman plagued by insomnia who is booked on an early flight to Brazil. Awakened by a nightmare (a man [Trier] crashes through her window, filling the room with glass and blinding sunlight), she turns on a lamp that glows an alarming red, gets up, and calls a friend. After a sleepless night, arriving just in time to miss her plane, she gazes up at the muted dawn and watches a flock of birds fly overhead.

Nocturne marked a shift from text-based to what Gislason calls a "subconscious" narrative structure composed almost solely of images. Filmed in semidarkness with monochrome lighting, the film was geometrically storyboarded and governed by a set of framing rules that matched lines or centered images in one frame meticulously with the next (Trier and Gislason). In consecutive scenes, water dribbles down an interior wall with strong horizontal shadows; a tear trickles down a woman's cheek; and dew drops from a wildflower. A church dome in the frame's center is matched with a cut to the face of a watch. Inspired by Tarkovsky, *Nocturne* followed its own interior logic and, together with Trier's graduation film, *Images of a Relief* (1982), began to articulate the characteristics of "Europa," his vision of postwar Europe dominated by Germany.

As he explained to Björkman in terms of a map, "if you look down towards Europe, the first thing you see is Germany. Seen from Denmark, Germany is Europe" (*Trier* 70), and Nazism is "the great European trauma " (Tapper 73). Germany imagined as a map over- or underlying Europe appears throughout Trier's early films as a leitmotif and chronotope. Set in the final days of World War II, shortly after the German occupation of Denmark on May 4, 1945, *Images of a Relief* opens with previously unseen documentary footage (from Danmarks Radio archives) of Danish civilians beating and torturing suspected collaborators. The hellish first act is set in an abandoned factory where German soldiers are held and, one by one, shoot themselves in the darkness. The film depicts Nazi officer Leo Mandel (Edward Fleming) as a sacrificial victim betrayed by his Danish mistress Esther (Kirsten Olesen) and executed in the forest where, moments before his capture, he recapitulated idyllic moments of his childhood when he "talked" to birds (with the bird calls alerting his executioners). At the moment of death he ascends vertically through the pines in an unabashed deus ex machina.

The film's flagrant intertextuality would become typical in the Europe Trilogy. The simple literalism of the ascension suggested Dreyer's *Joan of Arc* and *Ordet* and put a provocative spin on already controversial content. The forest scenes echoed Bertolucci's *The Conformist* (1970) as well as Tarkovsky's *The Mirror* (1974)—the latter in the lack of conventional narrative structure, the alternation between documentary and subjective modes, the meditative tone drawn out in excruciatingly long takes, the use of selective color, and an emphasis on the consolations of nature. A peculiar artifice, the result of prioritizing personally imposed rules over a rudimentary narrative, would become signatural. Thus the color-coded three-act structure shifts from the hellish torchlit red and black of the detention camp scenes to the lurid yellow highlights of the garden party sequence to the misty/mystical greens of Leo's gethsemane.

Trier's trademarks are already fully evident: the theme of sacrifice and beauty in defeat, the priority of subjective experience, the Nietzschean inversion of normative values, the powerful gesture of an ending with its performative or "magic realist special effect," and the overwrought affect of the whole. Leo is, like many of Trier's protagonists, a misguided idealist who believes, as he writes Esther in the film's first moments, that "What you love stands above good or evil"—a sentiment supported by the final flourish. As 26-year-old Trier explained to Ole Michelsen, "passion is the lifeblood of the cinema, and it can assume many different forms"—adding that it might also "raise some moral questions" (6). The culminating "miracle" was meant to create "politically incorrect" empathy at a time when the view of Nazis was still quite one-sided, and it disturbed and angered audiences, split a jury, and yet won prizes. Fourteen years later, the bells pealing from heaven in *Breaking the Waves* would similarly affirm the transcendence of its "perverse" heroine, provoke controversy, and win prizes.

Images of a Relief is an early instance of the performative as Eshelman uses the term: to refer to the filmmaker's assertion, through aesthetic technique, of the reality and significance of a subjective event that is patently unbelievable—and politically discomforting as well. As Trier in 1982 explained its aim, what was important—indeed, "the definition of true art"—was "that you use an impeccable technique to tell people a story they don't want to be told" (Michelsen 10). Confronting Danish audiences with a repressed history, the film's "German heavy-handedness" (Michelsen 8) was all the more disturbing. Yet how could one dispute a crane shot in which a man rises twenty-eight meters (ninety-two feet) over the Gribskov Forest? "The idea is to elevate—here I go again with that word, it's very religious-sounding—elevate the effect" until it becomes the film's main point, he told Michelsen, noting that scenes were linked poetically rather than narratively: "You could say that there's a story," but "what we have desired is to create some moods and some images, meant to live their own lives" (8).

On another level the film was about voyeurism (Trier, qtd. in Michelsen 11). References to seeing, blinding, and oblivion abound. In the first scene, Leo, wearing wire-rimmed glasses with a fractured right lens, looks at the screen in unseeing, blank despair. Escaping the compound, he finds Esther entertaining Allies, and the camera shares his perspective as he watches her with a black American soldier. Becoming aware of his gaze, Esther visibly savors his jealousy and taunts him with her pleasure. Then, dismissing the soldier, she accuses him of watching/condoning Nazis torture and blind a partisan boy. Hissing, "You are so brilliant. You don't care what you see. You can be used. What kind of morality is that?" she damns him while damning herself as a brilliant woman consensually "used" by him. "When will you scream?" she asks, adding, "I could never see the reflection in your eyes. You haven't seen me. These eyes, they don't love. They despise"—whether his eyes or hers becomes ambiguous. "Don't look at me," she concludes, speaking simultaneously of Leo's objectifying/"Nazi" gaze and her shift to the partisan side, while foreshadowing the betrayal to culminate in her destruction of Leo's eyes. "I see [Leo] as some kind of voyeur" whose stance is "really a self-critical image," Trier explained, adding: "Cinema is very much about living off the passion of others" (Michelsen 11). The motif equally implicates the audience, first in Leo's gaze and Esther's exhibitionism and finally in the outrageous "effect" that constitutes the film, much as it would implicate and provoke audiences in later films.

Esther's character expresses the ambivalence Danes felt over their collusion under the German occupation and expressed with a vengeance at war's end. Offering to hide Leo, she drives him to a forest, tinted in cool, damp green, where he rests against a tree. Now dressed in trench coat and mannish hat, her back turned to the camera, Esther joins resistance forces waiting in ambush, and as they restrain him, sharpens a stick with relish and stabs first one eye and then the other. In such scenes, Olesen anticipates her rawly intense performance of Medea in Trier's 1987 television drama, Grace's execution-style shooting of Tom Edison in *Dogville,* and the genital mutilation sequences of *Antichrist.*

In the climactic scene, Trier cuts to a long shot of Leo kneeling on the ground, where he emits a protracted scream. This is followed by a medium shot of his face averted, eyes streaming blood as he ascends to the tops of the pines, then a slow zoom to the ground where moles are pushing up mounds, making signs of blind but fecund life. As in *Dancer in the Dark*, blindness is associated with innocence and transcendence and nature with childhood and with senses other than sight as bird sounds and forest greens convey an almost tactile image. "There's some sort of nature poetry in that ending," Trier explained (Michelsen 10). The final shot, accompanied by dim strains of choral music, cuts to Esther framed by the automobile's rear window as she weeps and moves her lips in prayer.

In an earlier scene, Leo's dissolution is prefigured on a geopolitical scale when a German soldier attempts to telephone Berlin and is told there is "no connection anymore." Subsequent attempts to "connect" are rendered ritualistically as a litany of the names of German cities that, having fallen one by one to Allied troops, are unreachable and in effect no longer "Germany": Berlin, Frankfurt am Main, Hamburg, Cracow, and so on. Throughout the trilogy, the litany, list, or map of German cities would be repeated in various forms with increasing resonance, coming to represent the Holocaust as a scar that crossed and obliterated national and geographical boundaries.

After heated debate among the judges, *Images of a Relief* won the European Student Film Festival's first prize together with a special Channel 4 television award that guaranteed broadcasting in the United Kingdom. At home, it opened at the Delta Bio theater in Copenhagen, becoming the first Film School project to be shown commercially, and was broadcast on Danmarks TV (Stevenson, *Lars* 30). The film's controversial acclaim set the stage for Trier's first features, which were similarly groundbreaking, historically resonant, and surreal.

Hypnotic Virtuosity: The Europe Trilogy

Turning accepted history on its head and producing something like a recovered trauma memory, Trier's graduation project foreshadowed the Europe Trilogy in affect, tone, and central conceit. In *The Element of Crime*, a Cairo psychiatrist gazes down at the camera, addressing the protagonist who, under his suggestion, returns to a pestilential post-apocalyptic Europe to confront his past. In *Epidemic,* a young woman is hypnotized and returns to Europe of the plague years, becoming the hysterical medium for an epidemic in the present and a metaphor for the film. In *Europa,* hypnosis and cinema are equated: a narrator-hypnotist commands "you" to enter the film. In all three films, an internalized Europe is a site of trauma to which the protagonists return through hypnagogic trances in which the narratives partly or wholly take place.

In *Element,* an apocalyptic neo-noir thriller, a retired cop (Michael Elphick) suffers from crippling headaches and amnesia and hopes through hypnosis to recover memories of a job involving a series of murders of young girls selling lottery tickets. The most recent case is identical to four earlier murders attributed to one (supposedly dead) Harry Grey and solved by the protagonist's former mentor Osborne (Esmond Knight), author of a profiling method outlined in the tome "The Element of Crime." Working again with Elling and Gislason, and adding Niels Vørsel to the writing team, Trier took his fascination with melodramatic affect, monochromatic lighting, frame matching, and Tarkovskian mise-en-scène to a new level while blending American science fiction with European film noir. The geographical and temporal dislocation of *Nocturne* and *Images of a Relief* is shifted to a landscape two-thirds under water, with the protagonist aptly named Fisher. Long, fluid aerial pans expose a devastated terrain bathed in a degraded ochre light, an image of Europe "under the threat of nature" (Trier, qtd in Björkman, *Trier* 72). Skinhead gangs engage in bizarre bungee-jumping rituals from a bridge; other figures move sluggishly over mountains of rubble, through sewers, and in rooms standing in sludge.

The only geographical markers are small out-of-the way German cities such as Halberstadt, Friedingen, Oberdorf, Innenstadt, and Halle, and Fisher literally maps out the "geography of [this] crime" by drawing lines between the murder sites in the order in which they occur, revealing the letter "H," presumably the signature of Harry Grey. The evil designated as "Harry Grey" thus becomes a route on a map that Fisher generalizes as "Europe" but is unmistakably post-Holocaust Germany, as the theme song, "The Last Tourist in Europe," confirms. As in *Blade Runner* (1982), this vision of a ruined and haunted Europe takes place in a devastated near future. But in contrast to the conventional thriller, this is a surreal, slow-motion world in which guns rarely kill; instead they are fired randomly in darkness by Police Chief Kramer (Jerold Wells), Osborne, and Fisher in succession as expressions of stifled rage, paranoia, and futility against the engulfing disintegration. The titular "element" Trier explains in terms of "a locality that provides a sort of 'centre of infection' for crime, where, like a bacteria it can grow and spread at a certain temperature and in a certain element—moisture, for instance," the "element of crime" being a "force of nature that intrudes upon and somehow invades people's morals" (Björkman, *Trier* 70).

"Everything in the film has a history" that is patinated in layers of clutter and murk, Trier explained in the DVD commentary, and visuals draw on the Tarkovskian theme of the incursion of nature within a "world of decay" as perceived through the detritus of memory. Mise-en-scène is a representation of neither history nor memory, however, but of Fisher's unconscious, a highly subjective and possibly "infected" vision. An epidemic of hoof-and-mouth disease is in progress, and decaying animals float by, the stench palpable. A horse hitched to a cart—an anachronistic image associated with old Europe—falls off a bridge, and apples float away in what resonates equally as a visual joke about upset apple carts. Trier often lends the Tarkovskian motif of flooded interiors surreally funny twists as when Fisher somnambulantly makes coffee while slogging around in three feet of water.

Other scenes turn into bizarre visual puns. At Halberstadt, as prostitute/love-interest Kim (Me Me Lai) bends over the front of Fisher's car, moving in sync with the windshield wipers, an incredulous Fisher asks, "Do you believe me when I tell you I'm in the middle of Europe screwing a Volkswagen 1200?" In a later sequence, after a silence, the hypnotist inquires, "Where are you? Are you asleep?" "I wouldn't call it sleep," Fisher replies, leading into an elaborate visual pun: he is trudging in slow motion past a flock of sheep huddled in a tunnel as a man solemnly plays "Amazing Grace" on a flute. Later yet, Kim explains why she had to get out of Halberstadt: "It was always three o'clock in the morning. Do you know what I mean?" The dialogue matches the dreamlike visuals, its nonsensicality enhanced by the out-of-sync dubbing added as a deliberate effect. "Is it always as dark as this at this time of year?" Fisher asks Osborne's housekeeper, who answers, "There are no seasons any more. The last three summers haven't been summers.

The weather changes all the time. It never alters." Fisher's chant of "Harry me, marry me, bury me. Bind me" (from Joyce's *Finnegan's Wake*, the riddlelike product of its narrator's dreamwork [Björkman, *Trier* 79]) leads like everything else to the film's central "joke" and is resolved through an elaborate mathematical-linguistic puzzle into the meaningless term *Harry*.

Trier and Elling continued their experiments with illuminated darkness and monochrome lighting, filming at night with sodium lamps that, suppressing other colors, produced a yellow ochre, punctuating it with contrasting blue lamps and electronic screens. Because the color was not manipulated in postproduction, the trancelike mise-en-scène (enhanced by slow motion) was "a real 'happening'" enhanced by Wagner's music (*Parsifal, Tristan and Isolde*) playing throughout the shoots (Björkman, *Trier* 69). Other effects were achieved in postproduction. Osborne's account of Grey's death takes on visionary reality through a superimposed image of pounding rain and windshield wipers upon a picture of Grey's car on fire, which he claims is the only extant photograph of the man. As the flames catch, consuming what is already nonevidence of Grey's existence, the photograph morphs into a film-within-the film and finally blends with the image of a fire burning in a stove in Osborne's house (figure 2). Another shot zooms in on a child's toy car and is matched with a shot of Fisher getting in his Volkswagen, playing off the cinematic use of models and announcing that (as Trier once put it) "My films are very 'film'" (qtd. in Stevenson, *Lars* 39).

A precocious, hyperstylized art film, *Element* also represented the cutting edge of trends in American popular culture. It drew on the 1980s vogue of postapocalyptic neo-noir and anticipated the central trope in the "serial killer" subgenre of crime fiction in the 1990s, the "profiler" of films such as *The Silence of the Lambs* (1991) and *Se7en* (1996). Commenting in 1983, Trier said, "It's exciting to get your hands on a 'glossy plot' and then explore the genre to the limit—embellish it so that it will venture into places genre films don't generally venture" (Schwander 13). But as in the trilogy generally, Trier and Vørsel drew more heavily yet on classic noir, specifically Fritz Lang's *M* (1931), Carol Reed's *The Third Man* (1949), and Orson Welles's *Touch of Evil* (1958), which featured idealistic cops, officers, or informants undermined by the environment and the nature of their work to a point where the

Figure 2. *The Element of Crime.*
Michael Elphick and some trick photography.

line dividing the criminal and the "good man" is erased. In *The Third Man*, writer Holly Martins, seeking out his old friend Harry Lime in postwar Vienna, is sucked into the power struggles among occupying Allied forces, police, and black-market profiteers including Lime himself, whose trade in diluted penicillin has caused the deaths of children and soldiers. Playing off the name of that film's elusive culprit, *Element*'s Harry Grey, a signifier that turns up empty, indicates the collapse of morality and certainty.

Similarly, Fisher seeks out a mentor corrupted by the "element of crime" he purports to diagnose. As in *Touch of Evil*, where the cop Quinlan frames culprits to "prove" the rightness of his intuition, Osborne's zeal for tracking criminals detailed in his methodological treatise "The Element of Crime" has facilitated his corruption. In one scene, Fisher views a videotape of Osborne explaining his system as "a psychological identification" that enables a policeman to understand and imagine the crime. Challenged from the audience, Osborne replies that "We always run the risk of being corrupted. The morality of the police is no different from that of society." Later he comes to understand that his system was "naive, dangerous"—obsession or "fiction" rather than science: "The worst thing that can happen in the name of science is when the system becomes all-important." Yet for that reason the case requires Fisher, an "able man" versed in to the system to catch Grey, who may have been produced by the system itself. For Fisher, tailing Grey means becoming (retracing and reenacting) Grey, aided by the people who claim to have met him and now address Fisher as "Harry" along the way. When Kim (also Harry's former mistress) gives him Grey's headache medication, for example, he feels fine; it allows him (as it may have allowed Grey) to become Harry Grey without guilt or anxiety.

If what completes and "perfects" the so-called Lotto murder case is system itself, the film indicts professionalism, the perfectionist's devotion to science or art, and Trier himself. In the autopsy scene, a wild-haired coroner probes the latest victim and, pronouncing her "a beautiful corpse," points out that he and Fisher are professionals whose "admiration is for the criminal, not the victim. She's gone. He remains out there, leaving his little traces, his own little system. He cuts and leaves himself bare." "Where did you get your training?" Fisher asks. "Auschwitz?" By the conclusion, he will have joined the coroner and Osborne who in their pursuit and admiration of Harry Grey begin to leave their own "traces," completing the crime's "professional" design, and allowing the film to follow the motif to its logical conclusion in a postmodern conundrum. The solution is revealed ultimately in what Fisher calls "a recipe for producing" Harry Grey, as in the course of recovering Grey's signature, he repeats Grey's crime, a process visualized through Osborne's map, which forms a "geometric puzzle." The first four murder sites form the corners of a square that seemingly signifies that Grey's work is completed, but when an identical murder in a city in the bottom center of the square reopens the case, it resurrects "Harry" and Osborne's system, necessitating/predicting two more murders to form the letter "H." When Kim points out that Kramer can now wrap the case, Fisher cannot stop until he understands Harry Grey, claiming "I owe it to Osborne." When Kim replies, "You leave me behind, Harry," her slip is echoed by the therapist ("I'm afraid you leave me behind too, Harry") and forecasts the end of the film.

The redundant and arbitrary logic of this conundrum of a plot was reinforced by the rigidly parallel camera movements Trier, Elling, and Gislason had applied in *Nocturne* and *Images of a Relief.* Here they enhance our sense of being trapped in a subjective, self-contained universe inhabited by lottery numbers, signs, diagrams, visual puns, and rhymes with some sinister built-in—yet ultimately meaningless—logic. As Trier told Bo Green Jensen, he and Vørsel filled the screen with portentous but empty nonsymbols—piles of keys, chess pieces, curtains fluttering outside windows—using the phrase "Fucking mythological!" to describe the designated effect. An early scene in the whorehouse pans over Kim innocently reading Mother Goose's "The House that Jack Built" to her child: "This is the cow with the crumpled horn that tossed the dog that worried the cat that killed the rat," and so on. As the rhyme strings connections leading back to the "house that Jack built," the film leads inexorably to the vacuous Harry Grey. Does Grey exist? Is Fisher Grey? The strongest implication is simply that Fisher completed Osborne's work, which ended in the profiler's absorption of the killer's identity, a theme of *The Third Man, Touch of Evil, and Blade Runner.* Like Rick Deckard, who in hunting replicants becomes (or realizes he is) one, Fisher devolves into (rather than discovers) Grey, as Fisher's suffocation of a little girl in the service of catching Grey completes Harry's geographical signature. Like Osborne before him, Fisher has become a victim/perpetrator of the self-perpetuating system with its own perverse logic. This in turn is based on the concept of serial murder, which is mathematical and ritualistic to the extent that its compelling motivation may be seriality itself. The film is a circular tour de force; meaning collapses into the system that produces it (poststructural theorists would call this semiotics), and the film becomes almost completely self-referential. In the final frames, Fisher stumbles upon a sewer cover, and the camera peers down into the huge, depthless eyes of a loris, a small nocturnal primate. "I want to wake up now," he says, and when his plea goes unanswered we are left with him looking into an abyss that looks back at us.

Trier has acknowledged that the script was "theoretical," more "literary" than cinematic, so that "large parts of it" are interesting primarily for "locations and . . . atmosphere" (Björkman, *Trier* 80). The relentlessly manipulated viewing experience thus replicates Fisher's hypnotherapy, which leads him to a foregone conclusion, and the film is left open to an endless loop of resonating questions, to the point that Simons prefers to understand it merely as an elaborate game within a virtual world

(*Playing* 90–91). Trier nevertheless claims that *Element* introduces an ethical dilemma he would explore repeatedly: "Fisher represents the humanists who've often had central roles in my films. And everything keeps going wrong for them! He's working from the assumption that good and evil don't exist. But they're there all right, in strength. I can't really say whether they're represented by people or nature" (Björkman, *Trier* 81).

As the most hypnotic of Trier's films, *The Element of Crime* is a direct representation of Fisher's subjective reality that is, after all, a trance. The therapist appears only once, in the prologue set in Cairo, and his voice works like that of an interpreter; it periodically brings Fisher back to "reality," finally losing him in the abyss, while adding to the atmosphere of a film whose very stock appears damp, degenerated, and diseased. *Epidemic*, the second and pivotal film of the trilogy, would take *Element's* aesthetic to its logical conclusion, making infection its central theme and the fear of contamination its primary affect, equating the titular plague with the medium itself.

Trier's second feature continued Trier and Vørsel's shared obsession with the inheritance of the Holocaust. The most topical of the films, *Epidemic* was concocted for the decade when acquired immunodeficiency syndrome hysteria infused science fiction/horror blends such as *The Fly* (1986). About a director ("Lars") and scriptwriter ("Niels") who conceive a film about a plague, it was also Trier's first metafilm and drew on his phobias to spectacular effect, as the eponymous epidemic of the film-within-the-film erupts within the environment of the film-about-the-film, subsuming both in an apocalypse. *Epidemic* put spectators behind the scenes, demystifying the filmmaking process, yet ultimately lending it mystique. Finally, as a medical horror film made in pseudodocumentary style, featuring extreme situations and culminating in a spectacular female performance, it looked forward both to the television miniseries *The Kingdom* and to Trier's next phase.

A teasing hybrid of documentary and fiction culminating in a grotesque joke, *Epidemic* gave birth to the trickster and showman of Dogme95 and thereafter. Trier has a dual leading role as the framing film's director and, in the film-within-the-film, the fatally naive, portentously named epidemiologist Dr. Mesmer, who spreads the plague he travels across Europe to fight—and in *Epidemic*'s culminating moments the characters merge. Originating in a bet with Claes Kastholm Hansen, a Danish Film Institute consultant, that Trier could make a film for one million kroner (about US$150,000) and that Claes would appear in it himself,[3] the film was an unabashed do-it-yourself experiment in collaborative improvisation. Its cast included Trier, Vørsel, their wives Cæcilia Holbek Trier and Susanne Ottesen, and Udo Kier, with Hansen featured in the last sequence as the clueless witness to the show-stopping finale, a performance by a hypnotist and his subject. In the framing film, set primarily in Vørsel's apartment, the camera was unmanned or operated by the two filmmakers, who also provided props, costumes, and lighting. Interrupted by anecdotal digressions indistinguishable from the narrative proper, the film had the unscripted, half-edited quality of an amateur documentary (an impression enhanced by the professionalism of the film-within-the-film shot by Dreyer's cinematographer Henning Bendtsen). Hence an early sequence in which a cabbie (Michael Simpson) attempts to drive Lars to Niels's apartment and both break down in hysterical laughter was concocted from the fact that Simpson had never driven a car before and shot from opposing positions, breaking the restriction of the camera to a 180-degree axis and announcing a "punk" refusal of film-school standards.

Epidemic begins ominously on "Day One" (flashed onscreen), as the script for "The Cop and the Whore" (*The Element of Crime* in another life) has been erased by a computer virus (that seems to have afflicted the director and scriptwriter as well). As he addresses the task of writing a new script in five days, Lars wishes for something "more dynamic" than their previous idea, and at the moment of the film's conception, the trademark "EPIDEMIC" appears in lurid red capitals in the screen's lefthand corner. An indelible stain, it marks the site of infection and indicts both the medium and act of creation (while furnishing an early instance of Trier's genius for provocative titles). Then follows a slow pan over the ruins of a dinner party interrupted by some violent cataclysm—the floor strewn with broken china, a table with the cloth pulled halfway off, spilled wine, blood-spattered walls. This scene, a flash forward to the film's conclusion, is accompanied by the doleful voiceover remarking the "fateful coincidence" in which "during the course of five days, the manuscript of

Epidemic was created and written down in and around this apartment. That an actual epidemic was approaching [and] that its outbreak would coincide with the completion of the script was one of these."

The narrator's presence insists on the factuality of what we see while alerting us to the film's inherent fallacies. Is it a documentary? Mockumentary? Fiction? Some blend of the three? It poses as a "making of" documentary that includes footage from the eventual film. But the film-within-the-film is revealed as Lars's *fantasy* of the finished product. *Epidemic* thus looks forward not only to the deliberate amateurism of *The Idiots* but to artful hoaxes such as *The Blair Witch Project* (1999), whose theatrical release was presented as the fragmentary footage left by three missing filmmakers. Yet *Epidemic* documents its conception and "birth" not as a film but as a scripted event—a literal eruption into hysteria, boils, vomit, and blood that happily infects the audience. The typewriter is analogous to the camera—for example, in a crude superimposition of keys in motion over footage of Lars puttering followed by expository sequences in which the filmmakers research the plague. Shot in high-contrast chiaroscuro, the slow pans of library stacks and staircases at exaggerated angles recall Kafka by way of Welles's *The Trial* (1962).The librarian recalls how in 1348, Milan bricked up the homes of affected families and let them starve rather than allow the infection to spread. A harrowing descent into the basement reveals saltpeter noxiously oozing from the building's foundations.

The library's dank underside represents a repository of the "disease" of European history, thus connecting with the trilogy theme, a motif picked up even more explicitly on day three. Niels and Lars take an unexplained journey through the Ruhrgebiet, Germany's industrial center throughout the 1980s and the cauldron of both world wars, to Cologne, with Niels noting the vast polluted swaths that are "splotches on [Europe's] map." The excursion develops into an elaborate chronotope linking the bubonic plague, the Holocaust, the German occupation of Europe, and the Allied occupation of Germany with industrial dominion and pollution. One of the most flagrant digressions, a five-minute monologue in which Kier relates his dying mother's recollection of his birth during the Allied bombing of Cologne, links the Holocaust with the plague to come.

Travel, border crossing, and water are associated with contamination.

When Lars and Niels cross the bridge to Cologne, the narrator discloses that by day three the bacillus had permeated the soil and water, with the imagery implying that modern transportation had facilitated its spread. As in *The Element of Crime,* water is "everywhere and not a drop to drink," liquid a contaminating medium. At the end of day two as Niels and a wine connoisseur discuss vine rot plaguing the French industry, Lars retreats to the bathtub, drinks vodka, and envisions the iconic sequence in which Mesmer is lowered from a helicopter to the marshland below. The bathtub scene and the film-within-the-film are linked by a wry close-up of Lars's glass floating away and cuts to a matched image of Mesmer floating just above blowing marshland, sustained by the grand strains of *Tristan and Isolde,* his feet brushing grass as he grasps a rope flying a Red Cross flag (figure 3). Finally lowered to the ground, he kneels to drink water from his hands. Other scenes recall the besodden scenography of *Element*—as when Mesmer drags the remains of an artificial island through a stream, wading through waist-high water, visibly contaminating and contaminated by the elements.

One of the earliest instances in which Trier overtly exploited his phobias and obsessions—disease, hospitals, traveling, claustrophobia, hypnotism, filmmaking, and women in extremis—*Epidemic* was a source of countless subsequent ideas and techniques. But its "student film" look,

Figure 3. *Epidemic.* Trier as the idealistic Dr. Mesmer.

like the radical imperfection he would later cultivate, belies its historical and political astuteness and the fact that it is as rigorously conceptual as anything he has done. Speaking as "Lars," Trier introduces his trademark theme in which the idealist's quest produces the problem it seeks to solve—"without the idealist, there's no problem," Niels paraphrases. Insofar as we can see, Mesmer's "cure" (aspirin) produces the disease, as the two people he encounters, the nurse (Cæcelia Holbek Trier) and the priest (Michael Simpson), succumb during the course of his journey. The filmmakers' efforts, moreover, replicate Mesmer's: Their ideas induce headaches (Lars obsessively downs Alka-Seltzer), and the screenplay's completion produces an outbreak of hysteria and horror instead of a completed film. In the second act, Lars invokes the mantra "A film ought to be like a pebble in your shoe," meaning an irritant that provokes and inflames, and *Epidemic* literalizes the metaphor. The film swells into a boil that erupts into a medium of infection, and the filmmaker is the plague bearer or, as in Trier's later films, a provocateur.

The metaphor of film-as-boil is sustained in a series of digressive, self-referential episodes. On day two, Susanne begins preparing a multiple-course meal, a ceremonial setting for the completed screenplay's presentation to culminate in boiled goose. The food preparations complement the motif in which the filmmakers are "cooking up" the film. Tossing a cauliflower, Lars pronounces it a fine "boil," initiating an absurd discussion of how boils produce pus and blood in separate but equal secretions like striped toothpaste. This motif recurs when Lars and Niels solemnly dissect a tube of Signal to discover the mechanism that prevents the two colors from compounding. Niels, laughing, reads the label's promise of "prevention," and the parody-autopsy becomes a joke about the ineffectuality of modern purification rituals. This is followed on day four by Lars's attendance at a real autopsy in the bowels of Rigshospital, a scene that inspired the several graphic surgeries in *The Kingdom.*

As he would do in *Breaking the Waves* and *Dancer in the Dark,* Trier sets up opposing genres, aesthetics, and moods, with the framing film in monaural 16mm and the elaborately stylized film-within-the-film in exquisitely framed, lit, and filtered 35mm stereo. Drawing on German expressionism and film noir, with artful Tarkovskian touches and sweeping Wagnerian score, the film-within-the-film is as haunting and pretentious as the framing film is digressive and offhanded. The audience must work between the frame and the inner fantasy footage, the two producing a clash of codes, a typically Trieresque self-deconstruction and distanciation that is shockingly invaded in the climactic scene, which collapses distinctions between plagues past and present, imagined and real.

The filmmakers "invented an incurable disease, described its spread, based their words on the suffering of others. Their pages were filled," the narration tells us. But the twelve-page "screenplay" Lars hands Claes in the conclusion is more like a "skeleton," so that the film must be made in an "unconventional way." On one level, the film exposes itself as a strategy to obtain funds for another film. On another, it is an uproarious practical joke—on Danish film, Claes, and the audience. After presenting the script, Lars explains that the film ends when Mesmer, having survived the plague, emerges from a cave and falls on his knees, thanking God for his life. Clearly disappointed ("It's pathetic at best. I had expected a little more action."), Claes notes that in many films "people die onscreen," lamenting Danish cinema's having "less blood and fewer screams than there ought to be." "[Y]ou'd like a bloodbath," Lars volunteers and, smirking like the Hitchcockian showman in whose guise he would conclude each episode of *The Kingdom,* introduces some surprise guests.

Like the previous digressions, the thirteen-minute culminating sequence approximates real time. A hypnotist (Svend Ali Hamann) and a young woman (Gitte Lind), obviously nonactors, are awkwardly introduced and nervously sit down. The hypnotist commands the young woman to "enter the film." Relating a vision of people "scared of one another," of boil-covered and blackened bodies, then crying out at scenes of horror, she builds to a hysteria that becomes grotesquely physical: She keens controllably, throws herself about the room, and collapses against the wall (figure 4), exposing a mass of buboes below her ear. (Lind was actually hypnotized, periodically awakened for makeup, and placed back in trance, Trier explains in the DVD commentary.) The film ends in a "real" event that concludes the framing film and the film-within-the-film simultaneously, subsuming and transcending them in an apocalyptic moment. Niels sprouts virulent-looking blisters on his wrist as Susanne heaves and spews a great quantity of wine and blood on the wall. The camera then slowly pans over the catastrophe, repeating the flashback

Figure 4. *Epidemic*. Svend Ali Hamann and
Gitte Lind evoking the plague.

and leading to Lars who, slumped over, legs askew, raises his eyes in a
dying gesture. This cuts to a helicopter shot of the city's arteries trans-
porting dot-sized automobiles to the world, suggesting that the "plague"
of modernity is the appropriate inheritance of European history.

In such spectacular fashion, Claes gets the blood and screams he
asked for and, as Lars-the-filmmaker and the inner film's Mesmer, Trier
is doubly and retrospectively implicated as *Epidemic*'s real mesmerist
and plague bearer. In this fashion, Trier offers an effect to outdo previous effects, an ending in which the film transcends its own terms—to
which point the film proper has been leading. The culminating sequence
brings together three levels of reality and collapses them: (1) the epidemic within the (fantasy) film-within-the-film that (2) invades the film
proper to (3) contaminate the audience. In *Epidemic*, the film-we-are-
watching, the hypnotized Lind "enters" the historical and heretofore
imaginary art film-within-the-film "Epidemic" and literalizes it, brings
it to life, her performance transcending it and the documentary-style
frame, spilling over into the spectator's world to infect/affect us. Existing
nebulously between documentary and fiction, improvisation, horror, and
sideshow, in this moment *Epidemic* achieved the disturbing authenticity of a "snuff" film and had Cannes audiences wondering if Lind was
the best actress in the world or was really hypnotized. In such a tour

de force in which the truth was in between (she *was* hypnotized, the event staged), her performance would be topped perhaps only by Björk's hysterical nonacting in *Dancer in the Dark.*

The motif of hypnotism running throughout the trilogy led Trier to discover the performative on a radical new level that he would find inspiring as he conceived Dogme95 and the Gold Heart Trilogy. He had bracketed off a space within a film (one suffused in postmodern irony) for a "sincere" performance and created a contradiction in terms, a space within which real emotion is reached and communicated by the performer, disarming the audience's knee-jerk irony. This paradoxically real "effect," as he called it when describing the ending of *Images of a Relief,* would become a trademark when he sprang it with different and far more disturbing reverberations in settings from *Breaking the Waves* through *Antichrist.*

Epidemic introduced another trademark as well, the blurring of distinctions between documentary and fiction, reality and performance, exploitation and art, making attempts to categorize it futile except as metacinema. Flouting the limits of taste, joking at the industry's expense while posing as a recipe for a Trier film, it disassembled and exposed the filmmaking process and looked forward to Dogme and texts such as *The Idiots* and *The Five Obstructions* that are documentary-style workshops as well as films. Ultimately it provided Trier with an arsenal of strategies that would reappear in increasingly sophisticated contexts.

It was while making *Epidemic* that Trier and Vørsel came up with the idea for a "Europe Trilogy." "We thought it was a good name," Trier told Björkman, commenting that the trilogy should culminate in "a film called *Europa.*" The title and situation neatly reversed *Amerika,* Kafka's novel "about Europeans arriving in America. Here we have an American visiting Europe" (*Trier* 126). *Europa* is also the Italian word for *Europe,* which lent mythological and transnational overtones. *Europa* finally suggested the conflation of Europe with the film's German setting whether in the presentation of geographical space, nationality, ethnicity, or time.

In most respects, Trier's most mainstream and technically accomplished work to date, it relinquished the heavy Tarkovskian tone of the earlier films for a fast-paced, dazzlingly constructed, and stylized Hitchcockian thriller crossed with historical drama. Set in Germany year zero (winter 1945), depicted as the shadowy wasteland familiar from *The Third Man* and *The Trial,* it was the trilogy's most historically situated and political film and a culmination of its themes. *Europa* was nothing if not ambitious. Shot in black and white accented by bursts of color, it was intended as a masterpiece and for the Palme d'Or, although Trier had to settle for three less prestigious prizes: Best Artistic Contribution, the Technical Grand Prize, and the Jury Prize.

A truly international film—a rarity for its time—*Europa* was shot in Poland and Denmark in English and German with Swedish, French, and German actors and crew members. Produced by Nordisk under the newly redefined concept of Danish film, it epitomized a postmodern trend toward international genre pastiche. Like *Underground* (1995), *Cinema Paradiso* (1988), *Il Postino* (1994), and *Mediterraneo* (1991), all set retrospectively in World War II Europe, it signaled a new kind of transnational European film that emerged in the late 1980s and early 1990s to reflect the post-Wall era. The cast featured icons from Bergman, German Autorenkino, the American avant-garde, and the French New Wave: Max von Sydow (in voiceover); Fassbinder regular Udo Kier (Larry Hartmann), who had worked in Andy Warhol films; Barbara Sukowa (Katharina), who had starred in some of Fassbinder's best-known films; and Eddie Constantine (Colonel Harris), who had played Americans in countless European films including *Alphaville* (1965). The new face was Jean-Marc Barr as protagonist Leopold Kessler, a French-American actor just coming off the lead in Luc Besson's *The Big Blue* (1988).

As painstakingly crafted as *Epidemic* was not, *Europa* nevertheless continued that film's self-reflexive project of exploring the limits of— and demystifying—the medium, all the while pulling off a magnificent, shocking culminating effect. It also followed on that earlier film in references to German expressionism, film noir, and horror, using genre to explore specific national mythologies. Elaborately constructed, with up to seven layers in one frame, front and back projection, overhead shots, elaborate juxtapositions (of rich black and white photography [again by Dreyer photographer Bendtsen] with intense splotches of color) at moments of heightened emotion, the film disassembled itself and, with it, the classical Hollywood repertoire.

The trilogy's epitomizing film, *Europa* returned to earlier motifs. Like *Images of a Relief,* it empathized with Germany, targeting the opportunism and corruption of the Allied occupation, but Trier now treated the theme in a blackly humorous tone. In another link early in the film, the protagonist's shadow is outlined on a railway map of routed German cities. Like *The Element of Crime, Europa* takes the form of a hypnotic trance, but the address is different. Opening with the image of tracks shot from the bottom of a moving train and von Sydow's hypnotic voiceover, it addresses "you" as the subject of a trance that is equivalent to the film as it feeds rhythmically through the projector. "As you listen to my voice, you will go deeper and deeper into Europa," the hypnotist insists, equating the spatial experience of "Europa" with the temporal progress of the film, a journey into confusion, seduction, and death.

Rather than simply drawing us into the film, the voiceover is strangely self-reflexive, especially in the context of film noir, in which a voiceover would indicate a first-person confession. Thus it prevents complete suture (Galt 218–19), and the protagonist's two-dimensionality completes the alienation effect. Fresh-faced and handsome, Barr's Leopold [Leo] looks like a hero but instead of developing into one is revealed to be a fool and a cipher. With the vague mission of showing Germany "a little kindness," Leo becomes the screen for the sinister political, ideological, and psychosexual forces represented in the film. An American of German descent, he is offered a probationary position with the railroad firm Zentropa (owned by former war profiteer Max Hartmann [Jørgen Reenberg], now overseen by Allied forces) as a sleeping car conductor. In this absurdly soporific occupation, he hopes to help restore Germany's foundering economy and morale, for which the railroad is the central, ominous metaphor. After falling in love with Hartmann's daughter Katharina, who is a Nazi sympathizer or "Werewolf," he becomes trapped in the complications of postwar politics, manipulated and betrayed by Allies and Nazis alike. He is unknowingly used by the Allies to track suspected Werewolves, who use his rail access to facilitate an assassination, and he drowns in a fumbled assignment to blow up a bridge.

The sleeping car conductor has an important, even "mythological" task, Zentropa's chief inspector comments, but Leo proves a feckless Charon who conveys passengers, himself, and the audience "deeper and deeper" into the power struggle and paralysis of Europa. As a mode of transportation, the train (like hypnosis) takes over the subject's self-control, as the narrator warns Leo shortly after his marriage, "For the first time you experience the fear of being on a train with no possibility of getting off and no idea of where the journey may end." Through Katharina, the train is associated with Werewolves, a connection initially highlighted by the selective use of color. When the sleeping car is hauled out of retirement, Leo's reaction shot is in color in medium close-up with a disproportionately huge yellow moon looming behind him. Color highlights his first sight of Katharina in the Hartmann compartment, where she invites him to stay as the train approaches a tunnel, a classic sexual symbol. Later, taking him to the Hartmann mansion attic, she announces "I am Werewolf" as she unpins her cascading hair, adding "Or, rather, I was a Werewolf," as she lies down on her father's elaborate model train set, a miniature and double of the world of the film. With her elevated cheekbones, pointed nose, and long, elegant jawline, Sukowa's femme fatale (eventually Germany as monstrous-feminine threat) is seductively feral, especially when she poses in an enormous fur coat.

From the plot, whose multiple, noirish intrigues doom him from the beginning, to the mise-en-scène, the film puts blinders on its protagonist, quite literally "framing" him. In a heightening of film noir, *Europa* takes place exclusively at night, its world largely confined to the train interior so that little of the postwar context is verifiable by sight. As Galt notes, rather than depicting mountains of rubble as in the international *Trümmerfilm* (ruin film) of the 1940s, Trier portrays Germany as a construction of intertextual references (188–89) erected over a great black hole. In one episode, a Jewish man begs Leo to tell his wife that their home in Wöllstadt was spared from bombing; we later glimpse them standing in a darkened field of scattered trash and a bent sign. The frame is often matched with the perimeters of the train's interior, identifying it with the film, alerting us to the fact that vision is restricted and manipulated—or, worse, that Europa's haunted history cannot be imagined as an exterior, geography, or totality but only evoked as the nightmarish experience of riding on a train at night (Galt 178–91). Exterior train shots are usually imaginary—the "impossible" frontal shot of the train hurtling through the tunnel or the resonant composition in which the train moves across a darkened screen below an extreme close-up of Leo's eyes. At crucial points, the train moves in a strange loop that resembles a model train set, with the film taking on a Kafkaesque dream logic. Leo jumps off the train just before it reaches the Neuwied Bridge, changes his mind, chases it down, and disarms a bomb. Shortly thereafter (in some alternative universe?), the train again approaches Neuwied Bridge, where the bomb explodes, the car plunges into the river, and Leo drowns. Up to that point, Leo recalls the somnambulant millions who regardless of whatever strange loops they encountered went on performing their jobs under the Third Reich.

In many respects an extension of his "graduation film," *Europa* concerns among other issues the Allied (especially American) demilitarization and denazification of Germany. Many Germans had Nazi connections necessary for survival, and denazification became another kind of war profiteering, with Allies "whitewashing" Nazi sympathizers necessary to the occupation government infrastructure. Meanwhile, a more personal story of manipulation, national identity, ethnicity, and whitewashing occurred somewhat earlier, in April 1989, as the script was nearing completion, when a dying Inger Høst confessed to her son not only that he was not Ulf Trier's half-Jewish son but that his real father was really "more of a Nazi" than otherwise, with a German family that "went back two further generations" (Trier, qtd. in Nicodemus). "Before she died, my mother told me to be happy that I was the son of this other man," Trier told Katja Nicodemus. "She said my foster father had had no goals and no strength. But he was a loving man" (Nicodemus). The deception, together with the realization that he was the product of his mother's Mengele-like genetic engineering, resulted in feelings of betrayal and destabilized his already precarious sense of identity, ethnic and ideological as well as personal. No longer able to celebrate or mourn a Jewish heritage, he was traumatized by the loss of a shared history. Jewishness has "to do both with suffering and historical consciousness which I miss so much in modern art," he had said in 1984. "People have left their roots, their religion behind" (Stevenson, *Lars* 16). Speaking of his mother's revelation, he told Björkman, "I felt that I'd lost both my mother and my father at the same time" (*Trier* 13). Moreover his biological father, Fritz Michael Hartmann, then eighty-one and the well-to-do retired chief of a disability claims court, refused to acknowledge his son, blaming Inger's failure to use proper birth control, threatening a lawsuit if Trier insisted on further contact. Trier kept the secret until Hartmann's death in 2000, whereupon the story became tabloid fodder (Stevenson, *Lars* 64).

But he wrote the secret into *Europa,* whose intrigues provided a geopolitical context for exploring his personal crisis—especially in Max Hartmann, whose surname is shared with the biological father who refused to acknowledge his son's existence. Trier plays the role of a Jew bribed by the colonel to "whitewash" Hartmann for his collaboration with the Nazis in a scene that initiates one of the film's major crises. A slouching, bespectacled Trier, his long, sharp nose accentuated by the camera angle, scowls over the doctored papers (figure 5), stands, embraces Hartmann and says, "Max Hartmann is my friend. He hid me in his cellar and gave me food." Looking repulsed and disgraced by this charade (in which he is thanked for doing essentially what his namesake refused to do), Hartmann barely returns the embrace and retreats to the bathroom where, as Katharina seduces Leopold in the attic overhead, he commits suicide. As Katharina explains at the film's climax, "transport was a sacred word" for her father, who saw Germany as his "model railway," repressing knowledge that his trains conveyed Jews to camps and "American officers first class afterwards." Hartmann is no simple villain. As Stevenson suggests, he feels shame of recognition that he has served as a tool in Nazi Germany and is now "playing the game again under very different rules . . ." (*Lars* 67). In the ambiguous Max Hartmann, Trier portrays Fritz Michael Hartmann as a weak man torn between guilt and pride, who, because of professional and family allegiances, refused to acknowledge his child (Stevenson, *Lars* 67). Trier's performance as the Jew is equally complex and self-reflexive; he

Figure 5. *Europa.* Trier as the whitewashing Jew, with Jean-Marc Barr, Erik Mørk, and Udo Kier.

spits on the doorstep as he exits and shouts that he will never play this role again, a declaration he continues to honor.

Moving beyond these intertwined personal, ethnic, and ideological issues, the film explores contrasting (yet equally conflicted and suspect) German and American mentalities. In Uncle Kessler (Ernst-Hugo Järegård), Giralt points out, Trier caricatures Nazi Germany's punctilious and dehumanizing obsession with order. This is contrasted with the Werewolves' hysterical nationalism that is like religious fervor on the one hand and feral savagery on the other. Hartmann is the tragic victim of both, as his shame and suicide demonstrate. On the whole, however (with the possible exception of Uncle Kessler), the Germans represent a complicated range of ideological and ethical positions: Ziggy, a Werewolf who thinks nothing of using children as assassins; Katharina, a Werewolf at night who loves Leo by day; Hartmann, a whitewashed war profiteer who cannot live with his guilt; and his son Larry, a cynical homosexual who, identifying with no side, becomes the mouthpiece for the film's critique of ideology. Ultimately Germany is up for grabs; even the Scandinavians (who have demanded the heaters on the trains as war reparations, forcing passengers to resort to blankets) take advantage.

Barr's Leo together with Constantine's Harris draw on the Hollywood image of Americans as confident, casually optimistic, and good at heart—or something close to caricature—anticipating *Dogville*'s Grace Mulligan and Tom Edison, whose idealism disguises ulterior motives even from themselves. When Björkman notes the film illustrates "how economic power allies itself to military and religious power," Trier comments that it takes place in the American zone and if political at all, adopts "an almost anti-American attitude" (*Trier* 130). Thus if Colonel Harris chides German culture for its dehumanizing nationalism, Leo exemplifies the American do-gooder who tries to "liberate" Germany from guilt and grief, leading to self-destruction (Giralt). More importantly, both embody American historical amnesia—a lack of or indifference to history and culture that Europe is seen to possess and value. Leo is duped because he lacks a situated understanding of European culture, a lack indicated in his blankness and malleability, which allow him to be used. The complexity of Europe's recent history bewilders him; when Katharina explains that people he sees every day "have all murdered hundreds of times" to survive, Leo can see only a monstrous crime embodied in the Werewolf. Yet Katharina claims to have loved him as only Werewolves can—during the day, when she wanted to forget "the nightmare" of Germany's history.

A foil to Leo, Colonel Harris embodies the darker side of the American character: opportunism and pragmatism disguised as extroverted affability. Presenting himself as a friend concerned for Hartmann's well-being, he blackmails the former war profiteer to further the American occupation's goals. In the film's climactic sequence, Leo discovers he has facilitated Harris's plan to trap Nazi sympathizers while securing American control over German transportation. When Leo confesses that the Werewolves used him in their assassination of the mayor, Harris discloses his real views: "Germans killing Germans—that doesn't break my heart!" The film explores the Allied capitalist collaboration with and exploitation of the Germans before, during, and after the war to suggest the occupation was part of one vast, primarily economic game in which Americans were often the oppressors. Blasting is heard in the distance as Americans blow up German chemical plants, having stolen the formulas beforehand. The crowd gathered for Hartmann's funeral, conducted in secret because Germans are not allowed to assemble, is dispersed with American gunfire.

Yet if the film has an ideological or moral position, it is stated first by the priest, who asserts that God is on all sides and blames those who, with no belief, "are doomed to eternal wandering." Katharina restates the point when, revealing that she drove her father to suicide, she says to the stalwartly, fatally neutral Leo, "In my view it is only you who have committed a crime." While expressing a dark irony about the politics of the postwar era, Katharina's position strangely anticipates the aesthetic philosophy of Dogme and *The Five Obstructions* in which rules, beliefs, and boundaries, however arbitrary, are necessary. In fact, Leo is an early—and notably male—variation on Grace in *Dogville* and *Manderlay*, the American liberal humanist, a nominal pacifist who wants to show a downtrodden, impoverished people "a little kindness" and offer "a small contribution to making the world a better place." As Trier explained to Björkman, "Yes, God supports those who believe in their actions, regardless of which side they're on. He's a democratic God, you could say. But Leo can't really understand that" (*Trier* 130), adding that while he feels "sympathy towards humanists" and their humiliations, "[t]he idea that people will take the trouble to co-operate and work for the good of their fellow man is deeply naïve" (*Trier* 143).

Like the Germany-haunted Europe of *The Element of Crime*, *Europa* entrances, seduces, and submerges the protagonist in a whirlpool of subterfuge, ending in what Ebert describes as "an incredibly evocative sequence on what it must be like to drown" ("*Zentropa*"). In contrast to the grand mal seizures in which *Epidemic* finishes itself off, it is eerily invasive. The hypnotist informs "you" that at the count of ten you will be dead, concluding when "in the morning, the sleeper has found rest on the bottom of the river": "Above your body, people are still alive. Follow the river as days go by. Head for the ocean that mirrors the sky. You want to wake up to free yourself of the image of Europa. But it is not possible."

Like *The Element of Crime* and *Epidemic*, *Europa* draws on German expressionism, postwar film noir, and the horror film. If the "darker" genres are obvious dominants, Trier juxtaposes genres and tones as much as film stocks and colors, and *Europa* is also satire—of a sort that would become a signature. The humor, ranging from deadpan to Kafkaesque black comedy to slapstick, is insinuated into what otherwise would be dramatic or action sequences. In the final thirty minutes, for instance, as Ziggy demands that Leo detonate a time bomb, Kafkaesque officials arrive unannounced to administer his conductor's examination. Bounced between Werewolves and examiners, he struggles to pass both tests, treating them with equally profound seriousness. Speaking in reactive monosyllables, pushed and shoved by Uncle Kessler, Katherina, Harris, Ziggy, and an irate man demanding to have his shoes polished, Leo descends from stone-faced silent-film comedians Charlie Chaplin, Harold Lloyd, and Buster Keaton.

Leo's comic blankness is enhanced by the multilayered technique that renders him, a "flat" character already, into a two-dimensional figure framed by surrounding images, as in the early scenes when, poked and prodded by doctors or measured by Uncle Kessler and a tailor (on either side), he is represented solely by his mirrored image, suggesting his reflexive and "framed" situation, or in his final-act race against time, which positions him against the image of a massive stopwatch out of *Safety Last* (1923), and/or *Metropolis* (1927). In the most arresting sequence, "WEREWOLF" flashes in huge uppercase letters across the screen, miniaturizing him in a fetal position in the left-hand corner facing an enormous, screen-filling image of the lower two-thirds of Katharina's sleeping face (figure 6). Such sequences render him a cartoon to suggest that he is "out of his depth" in this fragmented, surreally fluid world of political, economic, and sexual intrigue. Back projections further emphasize his stoogelike reflexivity. When, after her father's death, a needy Katharina proposes marriage to Leo (to strains from Hitchcock's *Vertigo* theme), the romantic couple is posed against a back-projected and slightly distorted image of a river. The music swells, and before he can answer, the backdrop is replaced by a cathedral altar and a priest who finalizes their marriage. This is followed by a shot in which they literally float down the aisle of St. Christopher's Cathedral where Ziggy's face, in color, looms out of the crowd. *Europa* presents Leo as a puppet behind whom scenes are easily, instantly changed, treating him as a function of the plot. Only at the film's conclusion does his dim bulb light up as he declaims ingenuously to the screen: "I've gotten this rotten feeling that everyone's been screwin' me since I got here. And it makes me mad!"

The comedy extends to a near-parody of classical Hollywood style with specific evocations of themes and scenography of film noir. Lighting is *never* natural, with the film insisting on its status as neo-noir construct, yet emotional moments call for isolated images to glow suddenly with color. Whereas *Epidemic* had reduced film to its common denominator, demystifying the filmmaking process in a film about making a cheap film,

Figure 6. *Europa*. Jean-Marc Barr and Barbara Sukowa.

Europa does something similar from within; it produces a clash of codes in the Barthesian sense, a deconstruction of Hollywood techniques and effects, as the techniques and "seams" invisible in classical Hollywood film themselves become spectacle (Galt 222–23). The film's bricolage resembles an exotic pop-up book of enfolded cutouts; thus Trier exposes and transcends the limits of a medium he proclaims archaic.

Problematizing the image to produce intellectual and aesthetic distance (Galt 222), these techniques also implode distinctions between image and frame, producing a powerful or shocking effect. The assassination of Mayor Ravenstein resembles three-dimensional animation. An image that seemed contained in two dimensions suddenly breaks through to another previously invisible layer, threatening the spectator. Facing the audience and invisible to the mayor, the boy assassin, in extreme close-up/low angle, drops a bullet that looms disproportionately large at the bottom frame. As he shoots, an enormous image of Ravenstein's face abruptly fills and falls back off the screen at a grotesque angle as great splotches of red (shot separately in color and superimposed) spatter the window. Size and perspective, like color, fail to conform to the laws of nature or realism, instead indicating dramatic intensity and narrative significance. If color triggers emotion, it simultaneously announces that it is doing this, creating an estrangement effect that anticipates the Brechtian detachment of *Dogville* and *Manderlay*.

In another distancing device, Trier constructs impossibly complicated takes in which the camera takes center stage, "topping" Welles and Hitchcock. In the Hartmann attic, Katharina and Leo make love among the model trains as the camera cranes down through the floor to reveal Hartman's suicidal bath, his blood spurting red against the black and white background (figure 7). An overhead shot follows the bloody water flowing under the bathroom door. Then, zooming out to expose the backdrops, walls, beams, and seams, the camera shrinks the set back to model size, putting the audience on a level high above it, with the filmmaker. Moving from one level to another in this way, such shots threaten to break through the limits of the frame.

In exposing this simulacrum so meticulously constructed from archaic materials, foregrounding its director's virtuosity, *Europa* shared the postmodern sensibility of many films of the era. Beyond this, it registered his own personal sense of dislocation after his mother's deathbed revela-

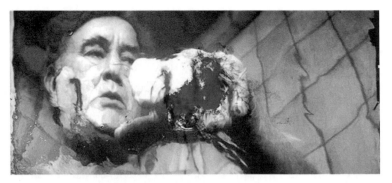

Figure 7. *Europa*. Jørgen Reenberg
in Max Hartmann's suicidal bath.

tion. Finally, as his films would increasingly do, *Europa* simultaneously registered the shock of the present—the opening and fall of the Berlin Wall and the dislocation and exhilaration of the New Europe taking shape. In late 1989 through early 1990, as the crew shot in Poland, traveling back and forth with equipment and props, they found themselves, like Leo, "hostage" to events (Björkman, *Trier* 143). Thus as Galt notes, *Europa*'s multilayered aesthetic and pastiche of genres and tones reflect both the no-man's-land that Germany was just before partition and the filmmakers' awareness of an unimaginable new Europe, one including the collapse of the Soviet Union and the looming prospect of a reunited Germany (226). Projecting the image of a fragmented, demoralized Germany as a trauma from which the West can neither fully recall nor completely awaken (as the history that haunts us is also unrecoverable), *Europa* is a palimpsest in which the fracturing present of the late 1980s, a map still being drawn, lightly overlays the fractured past of 1945, to comment on another "year zero."

Equally important, however, is the extent to which the film strains to transcend the medium, to turn it into something more than or other than film. In its collagelike foregrounding of its construction and materials, *Europa* has more in common with Eisensteinian intellectual montage than the Bazinian realism with which Trier is often associated. Or, as Simons fruitfully suggests, it is assembled out of discontinuous bits of information in a manner that is analogous to digital compositing (as opposed to an analog mode in which information is relayed in a continuous stream) (*Playing* 97–103). Aesthetically, then, *Europa* anticipates Trier's more recent composing, shooting, and editing practices in which contexts are staged as intellectualized constructs and sequences assembled from images linked by jump cuts. In the meantime, however, Trier had to find a way to give up the Hitchcockian control that *Europa* had required, a way that would eventually necessitate liberating his actors— and himself—from the frame.

Subverting the Kingdom: Television

The needed change was provided by television in the late 1980s, beginning with several distinctive commercials Trier made for the pop band Laid Back ("Bakerman") and the tabloid *Ekstra Bladet* (notably "Sauna" [1986], featuring male and female nudity, a peephole, and an erection). At the other end of the spectrum was the "alternative television" experiment *Medea* (1988), a liberal fifty-seven-minute "interpretation" of a Dreyer script adaptation of Euripides' tragedy of a scorned woman who wreaks revenge, a sorceress who helps Jason get the golden fleece, marries him, and has his children, and, when he leaves her for a politically advantageous marriage, murders them in revenge. More Tarkovskian than Dreyeresque, *Medea* initially polarized critics (Stevenson, *Lars* 54), but when released on DVD in 2003, it was deemed a revelation: bleak, stark, almost silent except for natural and animal sounds, with characters awash in a landscape of shimmering, windswept marshlands. It was shot in three-quarter-inch videotape and transferred to 35mm to fade the color and degrade and flatten the image, producing something rawly primitive and archaic. The gender war and suffering woman at the center anticipated the melodramas to come, and the sadistic intensity and bottomless grief of Kirsten Olesen's Medea would resonate especially in Gainsbourg's archetypal "She" in *Antichrist*. Unlike Dreyer's heroine, who poisons her children, Trier's Medea hangs them to make the death more truthful and "consequential," lending the film "more edge" (Trier, qtd. in Björkman, *Trier* 118).

That "edge" would be equally evident in his next effort at alternative television, although after this the comparison fails. *The Kingdom*, his 1994 television miniseries shot inside Rigshospital, Copenhagen's largest, provided him with a completely new way of working. With its handheld cinematography, natural (yet unnaturally intense) acting style, and wild genre and tonal contrasts, it differed from anything yet seen in the Danish media and made him a household name. Written by Trier and Vørsel in three parts, part I was broadcast in Denmark, Germany, Italy, and Sweden and screened at film festivals as a four-and-one-half-hour film, becoming an international hit. Now regarded as cinema, ranked by critics such as David Bordwell with Trier's best work ("Cinema") and revered among horror/science fiction/fantasy fans and film buffs, it resides in that eminent paracinematic space shared by shock video, cult movies, and the avant-garde.

Much as *Alfred Hitchcock Presents* inspired *Psycho* (1960), *The Kingdom* made possible the "reinvented" Lars von Trier, inspiring key aspects of Dogme95 and the Gold Heart Trilogy, which ushered in the New Danish cinema of the 1990s. One inspiration was Lynch's *Twin Peaks* (1990–91), which Trier found a brilliant piece of "left-handed" work from an auteur liberated from expectations of feature filmmaking (Anderson 94). From Lynch, he adopted a soap-operatic structure with interwoven narrative strands while introducing serious themes and a diverse range of characters (Creeber 389), a form that forced him to work intimately with a large cast of distinguished actors. With fifty hours to shoot five hours of on-location fiction (Stevenson, *Lars* 77), working on the fly, they had to collaborate and improvise. Adopting a visual and editing style from *Homicide: Life on the Street* (1993–99), Trier used handheld 16mm cameras for in-the-moment realism and disregarded "the unwritten rules governing direction . . ." (Trier, qtd. in Björkman, *Trier* 146). Seizing chance opportunities, he asked actors to change motivations and positions for each take, later editing in "psychological leaps" (*Trier* 155) to produce the staccato jump cuts and emotional shifts with which he would become associated. Such constraints stimulated creativity, and some three months after the series aired, he and Thomas Vinterberg would unfurl the similarly constraining and liberating Dogme Manifesto.

As in *Epidemic,* Trier took advantage of a "found" location complete with props, costumes, and hot-button issues, and as the national symbol of rational collusion (of science, technology, and the welfare state), Rigshospital was the ideal space for staging an eruption. In *Epidemic's* film-within-the-film, the state is subsumed by a board of grotesque-looking physicians assembled in a Gothic underground chamber, and when young

Mesmer proposes ministering to the sick, they exile him to a foredoomed fate. In a comparable conceit, *The Kingdom* is a microcosm of the state; administrators and senior physicians belong to the Freemason-like Sons of the Kingdom and conspire to advance their careers.

The miniseries offered a canvas for Trier's phobias and his parents' taboos against emotion, the supernatural, and kitsch. Encompassing medical soap opera, ghost story, mystery, splatter film, and dark comedy, it exploited the low genres and most hackneyed horror clichés—the fog-enshrouded building, the restless spirit, and the failure of science in the presence of the irrational. Veering from horror to black humor and melodrama within minutes, it was replete with malpractice victims, séances, exorcisms, and monstrous births. The first episode introduces the rich cast of characters: the arrogant Dane-hating neurosurgeon Stig Helmer (*Europa*'s Järegård) exported from Sweden with a dubious professional reputation; the cluelessly cheerful staff chief Moesgaard (Holger Juul Hansen), author of "Operation Morning Breeze," a morale-building campaign; junior registrar Krogshøj (Søren Pilmark), who cunningly "recycles" medical equipment and pharmaceutical cocaine from his basement apartment; Dr. Judith Petersen (Birgette Raaberg), whose unnaturally accelerated pregnancy makes *Rosemary's Baby* "seem like a blessed event" (Avinger); and the "malingering" career patient and supernatural sleuth Mrs. Drusse (Kirsten Rolffes), who, assisted by her bumbling son Bulder (Jens Okking), a hospital porter, makes contact with the spirit of a little girl, Mary (Annevig Schelde Ebbe), in the lift. The illegitimate daughter and murder victim of hospital founder Aage Krüger (Udo Kier) a century ago, Mary has her modern counterpart in Mona (Laura Christensen), the brain-damaged victim of Helmer's malpractice.

Apropos of Trier's perennial theme, an epidemic of hilariously misdirected idealism has infected *The Kingdom.* Operation Morning Breeze's parody of the Danish group ethic enhanced by positive-think pop psychology is an example. Senior physicians use reason and cutting-edge technology to pursue increasingly absurd goals as they ignore, condescend toward, harm, or kill their patients—or themselves. (Pathologist Bondo [Baard Owe], whose specialty is a rare form of liver cancer, sacrifices his healthy liver to obtain, through transplantation into his own body, the only such hepatosarcoma in Denmark, nourishing it until it grows to record size.) With the spiritualist detective Drusse, Trier offered a feminine (if not quite feminist) twist, a trend Trier would follow through the Gold Heart and USA trilogies, as she uncovers the evil root of the present reign of malpractice. In part II, however, she leaves the portal to the spirit world open too long, unleashing the chaos with which the series (minus part III) is left hanging.

As a microcosm, *The Kingdom* suggests that postenlightenment medical authority under the modern welfare state has lost touch with its mission: working for the common good. The central conflict, as Tangherlini observes, is between competing discourses: of globalized modern medicine, founded in the assumption, as per Foucault, that opening the body and bringing the unseen to light produces knowledge, and "the marginalized discourse of folk belief," which fears and respects the invisible (*Birth* 4)—between Drusse's spiritualism and Helmer's contemptuous rationalism, regulation, and surveillance. Dedicated less to healing than to the expansion of medical knowledge through the dissection of the bodies at its disposal, the hospital hierarchy and building that houses it correspond with the "map" of the body vis-à-vis the classification of diseases and treatments. Upper levels are dedicated to the rationally designed main hospital and contrast with the irrational, murky lower realm (Creeber 392–95). At the top is neurosurgery, where, as Drusse explains, "it is very difficult to get a place." The lower levels house the kitchen, where a chorus of two dishwashers with Down syndrome (Vita Jensen and Morten Rotne Jeffers) comment in uncanny epigrams on the events above their head, and the basement, near the archives, which Krogshøj has converted into a recycling center for hospital surplus. Thus the Kingdom is also envisioned as a haunted Freudian/Jungian subject with a collective unconscious represented in the archives and the marshlands below with their folkloric/pagan past (Creeber 394–95).

Like the Europe Trilogy, part I concerns a repressed history of traumas and misdeeds while reflecting the present situation: Danish culture threatened by the economic difficulties, absorption into the European Union, and globalization, with Helmer epitomizing a materialist worldview opposed to the ethics of the Danish welfare state. Each episode finds him racing to the hospital's roof and, peering through binoculars across the strait, spots Sweden. "Thank you, Swedish watchtowers," he addresses the twin nuclear reactors at Barsebäck, a source of friction between the two countries, adding "Your plutonium will bring the Danes to their knees." Comforting himself with a liturgy of Swedish brand names, he concludes with the rant/refrain, hurled at the heavens: "Danish scum!" Underlying all is a critique of a medical profession organized like the clergy and invested with similar powers (Foucault, *Birth* 31) in which rational empiricism and clinical surveillance have replaced older forms of authority (religion, ritual, and myth). Thus the Sons of the Kingdom swear "eternal enmity to the occult" and have the attributes of a religious cult including ludicrous rituals, gestures, titles, and terminology. As in *The Element of Crime,* the institutions and authorities most bound to reason and empirical "truth" are systemically infected.

Reinventing *Element*'s degraded sepia, the series was shot on 16mm, transferred to video to create grain and again to 35mm. The prologue depicts a similar atmosphere and theme, the incursion of nature and the repressed past: As the narrator intones, "the cold and the damp" that enshrouded the ancient marshland on which the hospital was built has returned, and "the portal to the Kingdom is opening once again." In a nod to the elevator sequence in Kubrick's *The Shining* (1979), a wall cracks open under a floodtide of blood. The impenetrable fog of the prologue is replaced by that of the film stock itself, Glen Creeber suggests, provoking viewers to penetrate the murk while implicating televisual and surveillance technology in the confusion. In episode 1's opening sequence, a blurred CCTV image of an ambulance appears and vanishes. Throughout, ghostly computed tomography scans, magnetic resonance images, and X-rays appear, foregrounding the clinical-technological gaze while revealing a vast subterranean unknown (Creeber 392), as when an audiometer voices Mary's plaint, "Why do I have to die?" Identified with Drusse, the camera moves through corridors, around corners and up and down the lift, insinuating into the Kingdom's secret recesses as she accesses technology for antirational purposes. Co-opting medical technology to destabilize reality, the camera is used finally to diagnose the body of the state, turning the gaze on itself (Creeber 388).

Exploiting the televisual medium to explore the range of the liminal and the carnivalesque, Trier jumps wildly from character to character, breaking through to the collective unconscious, unleashing a profusion of voices, visions, and modalities—in stark contrast to *Europa*'s omniscient, controlled, "hypnotic" point of view. In episode 3, Judith appears transparent, and Krogshøj concludes that she is a ghost, her transparency indicating her liminal (border-crossing, uncanny) status (she is pregnant with a spirit's offspring). In episode 2 when, over Helmer's objections, Hamann (from *Epidemic*) hypnotizes a surgical patient sensitive to anesthetics, the trance is visited by Mary's spirit, whose superimposed image rebukes the clinical gaze. As Helmer operates, the patient utters a protracted moan, transgressing the rule in which bodies are silent while confessing the pain hidden within the archives. This protest, like Mary's aural communications including a "death bell" (that Helmer cannot hear), may refer to a preclinical era when doctors listened as patients confessed their symptoms.

The polyphony increases tenfold in *The Kingdom II* (1997). Shot just after *Breaking the Waves,* it enacts a carnivalesque inversion and travesty of all norms—especially those set in part I. Satire diffuses into universally distributed subversion as specific content gives way to affect—not, however, without social and political implications. The repressed spiritual world, given voice in part I to expose *The Kingdom*'s occult infrastructure, spews forth monsters, displacing its relatively restrained effect with a glossolalia of voices, spirits, and practices—materialized demons, Haitian-style zombification, Satanic rituals, cannibalistic/"psychic" surgery, and the grotesque realism of Mary's "Little Brother," Aage Krüger's and Judith's gargantuan offspring. Underscoring the change is the "evil eye," a striated green screen that represents the chaos-inducing gaze of Satan himself. As characters are possessed, they undergo destabilizing reversals and mutations of their former selves.

Exposed and/or demoralized, the Kingdom's Sons turn to the occult. After Operation Morning Breeze's failure, Mosegaard promotes Helmer to chief-of-staff and takes up regressive therapy in the basement, where a renegade psychotherapist has set up shop. Cowed by a malpractice deposition, Helmer turns to voodoo, converting his nemesis Krogshøj into a zombie with infelicitous results. When Bulder divulges to him that doctors can become ill, Helmer becomes scatologically obsessed. His comeuppance is underlined by part II's variation on his "Danish scum!" refrain after taking to heart Mosegaard's suggestion that he monitor his bowel movements. Now shot from the bottom of the toilet, he peers anxiously down at its contents, ruminating in despair.

In the most dramatic reversal, Mary's ghost is replaced by her abject counterparts, Mona and Little Brother, producing a tonal shift: from the uncanny, with its mystery and hints of the sublime, to the grotesque, which Thomson defines as inspiring laughter, revulsion and/or fear (12–19). Idiot savant dishwashers preside as pagan rites are restored, death and life are continuous, normally hidden functions and fluids invade public space, and the underclass rules. A mystery until his birth at the conclusion of part I, Little Brother is part II's central spectacle. A monstrously growing infant, he is also a fully articulate man, growing literally into death and articulating the death inherent in natural process (the theme of *Antichrist*). Yet his deformity enables his gargantuan capacity for joy, as he escapes suffering by imagining a future he will never have. In spite or because of its over-the-top outrageousness, the "Little Brother" narrative insists on an ambivalent mixture of extreme emotions: disgust, laughter, pain, fear, pathos, and embarrassment tinged with shame.

But Trier also refers to an older version of the grotesque, the medieval/folkloric view in which monsters are sacred and a soul's moral character is expressed in bodily characteristics. And if abject bodies often betray demonic origins, grotesques are just as often blessed with special insight, with prophets, martyrs, monsters, and idiots sharing liminality. As Kristeva observes, "the abject is edged with the sublime" (11). Derived from the Latin *monstrum* (omen) and *monēre* (to warn), *monster* refers to a divine sign in positive as well as negative senses. Obsessed with the castoff and disabled, Trier makes the monstrous/tormented/possessed body the source of the sublime, as in the dishwashers' predictions and parables. In episode 7, Dishwasher 1 finds an object that "doesn't fit" the rack. "Like the baby that is too big," Dishwasher 2 adds: "If it is not a jug, or a vase, it is nothing, and you needn't wash it up, because it can't get dirty. Put it aside and keep it close to your heart." Mary's hump becomes a sign, like Little Brother's gigantism, of her role as suffering mediator. Mona's mental disability, the product of Helmer's malpractice, turns her into a seer in episode 8, as she spells out "I know something" and "Helmer" in blocks. An infant suffering from a bizarre form of gigantism, Little Brother is the dishwashers' inverse twin. Both are unclassifiable either as precocious children or adults and speak in cryptic parables in strange keening tones, and both have cinematic ancestry in Johannes from Dreyer's *Ordet,* who prophesies (accurately) in similarly strange keening tones. Begotten so that Aage Krüger can reclaim The Kingdom for Satan, he has a gargantuan capacity for good; struggling against his "evil" half, which he "confesses" somatically in accelerated growth, he dies on the cross of his own body.

If Gargantua as Christ figure were not enough, in a variation on the Golden Heart theme, Trier insists on the sanctity of the mother-son relationship. In episode 6, he lends the sepia a rosy hue, creating a "golden" moment in close-up as Judith nurses her infant. The scene is played straight, down to a stray drop of milk on her breast, until the pan out reveals the "child's" shockingly spindly legs spilling over the bed. In such moments, which replicate and/or travesty the juxtaposition of poignancy with strangeness in *Breaking the Waves,* Trier attempts to convert grotesque realism into sublime expressionism. As he had drawn out and sexualized Bess's suffering and would put us through Selma's death-row agony, Trier makes the audience feel every second of Little Brother's bizarre "passion": Moving from flagrant sentimentality to revulsion and horror—with the impulse to laugh never far away—he nevertheless insists on sincerity, down to the moment when Judith releases her son from his scaffold/cross/body as it collapses limb-by-limb upon itself.

Performative Politics: Dogme95 and *The Idiots*

Made with what Vørsel described as a "punk-like energy" (Trier and Vørsel), *The Kingdom II* provided a dress rehearsal for *The Idiots,* Trier's outrageous Dogme film about the carnivalesque performance of disability and excess as access to the sublime. A similar cheek sparked the politics of the movement itself. As for its famously prohibitive "rules," Dogme95 simply enforced many of the same situational limitations that had made television a liberating experience. Composed legendarily by Trier and Thomas Vinterberg in less than forty-five minutes, the manifesto opened with a hectoring pastiche of Marx, the Surrealists, and the major documents of the 1960s new waves, announcing, "Today a technological storm is raging, the result of which will be the ultimate democratization of the cinema. For the first time, anyone can make movies." Releasing filmmakers from a studio or state-controlled aesthetic, Dogme sought to restore the creative anarchy of early filmmaking.[4] Situating itself in relation to Soviet revolutionary cinema, Italian neo-realism, and the nouvelle vague—Trieresque in flaunting its many heritages—it claimed (via Truffaut) to be a "rescue action" aimed at "certain tendencies" in current cinema. Originality was not its goal. Instead, context and situation were new, making this particular staging the issue. Denouncing the Hollywood blockbuster mentality, while disowning the "bourgeois romanticism" of the nouvelle vague, the manifesto's revolutionary rhetoric issued a grassroots and collectivist—situated *and* international—challenge to the status quo.

Switching to high-church rhetoric, the ten-rule "Vow of Chastity" followed, climaxing in a volley of pledges to "refrain from personal taste," "regard the instant" over the whole, and force "truth" out of characters and settings "at the cost of any good taste and any aesthetic considerations." Dogme exposed and subverted the Hollywood "formula" by prohibiting its unwritten rules, with the prohibitions composing a set of guidelines with their own aesthetic. Rules 1 through 4 forbade sets and imported props, requiring on-location shooting in color in natural light (no filters or post-production manipulation allowed), and direct sound (no extradiegetic music). Rule 2 required handheld cameras. The "temporal and geographical alienation" Trier usually employed was expressly forbidden—a Dogme film had to be made in "the here and now" to capture a sense of real time, space, and emotion. Genre films involving "superficial action" (weapons and murders) were off-limits. The film had to be calibrated to old-fashioned, almost square 35mm academy format. The director could *not* be credited in the final rule that, however laughable coming from Trier, underscored an underlying counterhegemonic goal of decentering the filmmaking process all around.

Born out of Trier's creative needs, Dogme differed from most manifesto-led movements in being confined to aesthetics. The rules circumscribed film *production* in a very literal way, saying nothing about *content*. More important than the rules themselves, however, as Simons argues, was the redefinition of filmmaking as a "rule-bound practice" or *game*. In a game, rules prevent players from performing tasks in a conventional or convenient way, forcing them "to develop skills and strategies"; thus Dogme limitations were not prohibitive but productive ("Von" 1). As the Web site's FAQ section explains, the director is forced as in a game "to come up with creative solutions" to problems posed by limitations. Yet in spite or because of its personal and aesthetic focus, the movement had political repercussions, with the manifesto associating technique with revolutionary ideology, medium with message. "[C]reating even a small rupture," as Barthes and Benjamin, among others, have shown (and Tim Walters notes), "can throw the entire system up for analysis, precisely by challenging its status as 'nature.'" Thus implicated in a performative politics, Dogme marked the point at which Trier began consciously to situate his personal crisis within a global postmodern context. Meanwhile, his crazy publicity stunt reverberated around the world.

At their Cannes premiere in 1998, Dogme #1, Vinterberg's *The Celebration,* took the Jury's Special Prize, and Dogme #2, Trier's *The Idiots,* the most coveted ticket, provoked controversy. Shot and edited on video (transferred to 35mm), the first two films proved the digital revolution underway and contested cinematic practice for the first time since the 1960s, with *The Celebration* convincing skeptics that the digital camera had specific aesthetic advantages. Their challenge was followed by #3, Søren Kragh-Jacobsen's *Mifune* (1999), acclaimed for "humanizing" the movement, where #4, Kristian Levring's fierce, visually arresting *The King Is Alive* (2000), shot in the Namibian desert, demonstrated the digital medium's artistic range. Dogme became international with #5, Jean-Marc Barr's *Lovers* (France, 1999), and coincided with a burst of premillennial energy from American independents including Jim Jarmusch, P. T. Anderson, and Harmony Korine. Sharing the American indies' stance of punk disaffection, it also energized the DIY rebellion of the late 1990s led by Robert Rodriguez, Kevin Smith, and Quentin Tarantino. The success of *The Blair Witch Project* validated the Dogme aesthetic, which in turn offered the indies a coherent anti-Hollywood stance, European edge, and technique. The connection became official when the collective invited Korine to make the first American film, arguably its most experimental, *julien donkey-boy* (1999).

Dogme also removed technological barriers among filmmakers, actors, and setting. Where celebrity culture and CGI technology had turned acting into little more than image lending, the limitations required actors to improvise costumes, makeup, movements, and even lines. Unencumbered by a large crew and uninterrupted by setups, allowing actors to interact naturally and sustain momentum, Trier often shot forty-five minutes at a time, editing down to two or three (Björkman, *Trier* 153). Shooting *The Idiots* (with celebrated ineptness and with boom occasionally in view) Trier developed his method of "pointing" the camera (a Sony VX-1000 Digital Handycam) at the action rather than framing a scene, a documentary-style practice that has since become a signature. Pointing meant shaping the film around what actors brought to the scene as it developed, while experimenting with different takes. Filmmaking recovered something of the experimentalism and freedom of early cinema, and younger viewers brought up on MTV-style jump-cuts found the result both familiar and a revelation.

A stunt or performance to begin with, one that Trier described as "set up like a theatre-school game" (Björkman, *Trier* 155), Dogme was inherently theatrical, the films initially perceived as dramatic and interpersonal rather than political. Child abuse and racism provoked conflict and epiphanies in *The Celebration* and *The King Is Alive,* as did disability, sexuality, and discrimination in *The Idiots,* but issues were rendered peripheral or metaphorical, in service to some melodramatically revealed, intuitive "truth." Yet in imposing minimalist austerity upon explosive situations, Dogme exploited a form of psychodrama that, widely perceived as "Scandinavian," had international cachet and was subversively different from McMovie. Aimed well below the Hollywood radar, Dogme came to be understood in quite political terms by European and American indie filmmakers.[5]

Beyond the manifesto's precepts, the foundational Dogme films, which the filmmakers planned in a series of meetings before any shooting started, shared at least three formal and thematic elements that drew on Trier's latest enthusiasms: collectives, "holy fools," and metacinema.

Self-defined as a collective, Dogme practiced a playfully collaborative approach to filmmaking that its Marxist ethic (opposed to individual and marketplace values) and the manifesto's emphasis on location, situation, and actors made natural. The films themselves often featured ensembles and family/alternative family melodramas (Badley, 85–86; Bordwell, "Risk")—for example, Lone Scherfig's "blockbuster" *Italian for Beginners* (Dogme #12, 2000) or Jonathan Demme's post-Dogme *Rachael Getting Married* (2008). Concerned with interplay within and among groups, they offered a "sectional view of life" against Hollywood's emphasis on an individual hero with an obvious goal (Schepelern and Björkman).

Another source was the Scandinavian communal ethic, a product of Jante's "law" against exceptionalism and Denmark's reputation as a provident, homogenous welfare state that denied the existence of hierarchies or outsiders (Stevenson, *Lars* 128–31)—a myth *The Kingdom* had hilariously exposed and *The Idiots* proceeded to explode. Dogme both reflected and tested the group ethic within volatile familial and social relationships, exposing repressed issues and bringing factions into open conflict. Outing the abusive Danish father, *The Celebration* replaces the hierarchical extended family with a nontraditional one including the daughter's African-American partner and the son's housemaid lover. In *Mifune, The King Is Alive,* and especially *The Idiots,* the group forms an alternative family and redemptive experience for purposeless individuals. A commune of young urban professionals led by Trier surrogate Stoffer (Jens Albinus) use his uncle's mansion as a platform for a series of situationist-style attacks on middle-class values. Well off, with respectable family connections and jobs (a doctor on research leave, an art professor, an advertising sales executive)—they are insiders who identify with outsiders partly to protest against bourgeois hypocrisy, partly to find a presocialized subjectivity but finally for a wide variety of psychosocial and quasipolitical reasons.

The collective emphasis facilitated Dogme's reverence for the "instant"—the moment of emotional truth—over plot or the whole. Of the four films, however, only *The Idiots* discarded Hollywood-style dramaturgy. For most of the film, whose screenplay Trier claims to have written in four days, we follow a series of absurdist/situationist parodies of everyday life united tenuously by the idiots' group dynamics and collective and individual purposes, which are confused at best, and it is impossible to pick out a protagonist until the last fifteen minutes, when Karen (Bodil Jorgensen) a soft-spoken, middle-aged housewife, emerges to create the moment that is the film's raison d'être.

Trier's most Danish and personal film up to that time, *The Idiots* also represented a half-serious return to his youthful "cultural radicalism." About a leftist social experiment, *The Idiots* was intended along with Dogme to *be* a leftist social experiment reminiscent of groups and movements of the 1960s and 1970s. Cultivating the ebullience of the French New Wave and Swinging London—thinking of Beatles films "where they ran through London carrying a giant iron bedstead" (Trier, qtd. in Knudsen 118) on the one hand, the film also tested Trier's former communist ideals. Dogme shared with eccentric socialists such as Oscar Wilde, John Ruskin, and George Bernard Shaw the view that true art can flourish only in a social democracy, and Trier had hoped for the actors to live together as communards in character—as his audio diary explains, to "feel something for the props and the house"—a plan that *partly* succeeded (*Humiliated*).

The film reflected conflicts inherent in the situation. Jesper Jargil's "making-of" documentary *The Humiliated* (1998) portrays a Trier desperate to transcend his position of power and achieve meaningful connection with others. Like Stoffer, he alternates between gentle, patient coaching and hissing sarcasm, hubristic ecstasy and dejection, and his mixed signals combined with his intense involvement with the actors echo the tensions and conflicts explored in the film—and vice versa. A sequence in which he operates the camera while wearing only a t-shirt says it all; he undermines his authority, to say the least, and (childishly) commands the spotlight while making a "statement" about his vulnerability—or is this a commercial for stripped-down filmmaking? At a low point, he confesses, "I become a little child when I realize it is a game. . . . there is no reality. We are 190% alone in our tiny, ridiculous, humiliating worlds." Thus his aim of making the film coincide with the experience/experiment of making the film—a film after all about testing the extreme limits of socially and politically "safe" behavior—succeeded.

Trier aimed at more than a glorified form of group therapy, however, and to take on Hollywood without the latter's high-tech arsenal, Dogme needed powerful medicine. On the local front, it aimed to rout a tradition of Danish "modesty" or, as Dogme filmmaker Lone Scherfig calls it, a "fear of being over-expressive" (Kelly 130) to which urban postmodern culture had added a layer of irony. To breach this and to achieve "authentic" emotion, the original Dogme films (and many thereafter) featured the performance of a "holy fool," often a literally disabled person, but as often a dramatization or metaphor of disability reinforced by a conspicuously stripped or "disabled" film technique. On one level, a refinement of the "sacral grotesque" in which *The Kingdom II* had resoundingly ended, the holy fool had a long and respectable Scandinavian heritage. Derived from Gnostic mystical traditions and associated with Russian culture through Dostoevsky's *The Idiot* (1868), it had regional roots in Calvinism, existentialism, and the works of Søren Kierkegaard. It most obviously capitalized on the art film tradition of perverse, spiritually obsessed psychodramas of Dreyer, with their persecuted witches and visionary saints, and Bergman, in whose films Nordic repression was pitted against itself to produce moments of naturalistic transcendence. Less obvious but equally effective was a sentimental theme from Danish kitsch, a picture book (*Guld Hjerte*) Trier had loved as a child about a little girl so good that she gave away all her food and clothing (Thomsen 109).

Maudlin emotionalism, holy idiocy, mental illness, hysteria (real or performed) as truth serum became a strategic Dogme trope. In *Mifune,* an urban careerist returns to the family farm upon his father's death to reclaim the emotional vitality of his mentally disabled brother. In *The King Is Alive,* an incompatible group of tourists stranded in a Namibian ghost town undergo extreme physical and psychological disorientation. *Julien donkey-boy* is based on Korine's schizophrenic Uncle Eddie, and the all-but-Dogme *The Anniversary Party* (2001) follows an Ecstasy-induced orgy of truth-telling at an all-night Hollywood "family" gathering. The idiots in *The Idiots* "perform" mental impairment, referred to as "spassing" (the Danish equivalent of *spazzing*), in public places. On one level, these performances are part of the ongoing gesture represented by their "drop-out" lifestyle. Traveling around in their van, they invade bourgeois spaces—a restaurant, a Rockwool insulation factory, a public swimming pool, a mansion driveway in Sollerød—and create chaos. Shedding physical dignity with their clothes (figure 8), they drool, urinate, and violate the personal space of appalled citizens.

Spazzing is also an absurdist quest for psychic authenticity; as Stoffer explains to Karen, its goal is to break through to some pure emotional truth, the "inner idiot" lost beneath the urban professional façade. Eshelman finds this "retrograde self-fashioning" profoundly "sacral" in that at its center is a "context-disrupting act of sacrifice" that threatens to destroy the subject. Or, as Trier said in his audio diary, the film is an inquiry into the value of "borderline areas" beyond socialized identity— the psychology and spirituality of the liminal and grotesque explored it in *The Kingdom* and *Breaking the Waves* (*Humiliated*). The idiots' performances therefore function on at least two levels. As a carnivalesque reversal of bourgeois norms, they address issues of concern with personal resonance for Trier, who had grown up in Sollerød, and his mother's work involved locating homes for the mentally disabled. On the psychological level, however, their performances challenge socialization itself. In both senses it was what Trier called a "more political film" than his others:

Figure 8. *The Idiots.*

"On the surface, it's about our attitudes to the mentally handicapped. . . . At a deeper level it must appear to be in defense of abnormality" (Knudsen 118). This brings us to the paradox at the heart of the Dogme project, which creates artificial norms in the absence of Patriarchal Law in order to achieve the opposite: an affect that transgresses the notion of normalcy or law altogether, making *The Idiots* (as Trier admits) "dangerous" (Knudsen 118).

The "idiot technique," as he has called it, equating it with the "Dogme technique" of relinquishing technical control (Knudsen 123–24), attempts to break through aesthetic and social artifice to recover something authentic. The idiot's presence—for instance in *The Kingdom's* Down syndrome chorus or *Breaking the Waves's* Bess—creates moments of grotesque awkwardness and "political incorrectness," evoking (as in *The Kingdom*) a profusion of emotions, provoking confusion and trauma. The film's technical regression to spastic amateurism had a complementary aim: to seize on the naked emotion of the moment—the more awkward or disturbing the better.

Together with the idiot technique, the certificate opening the film, "confessions" signed by the first six filmmakers, and the hype surrounding the movement worked something like the Marxist apparatus with which Brecht created his *Verfremdungseffekt*. They created a metacinematic space in which the conflict between the film's performativity and its (self-advertised) search for authenticity became highlighted. Also, the absence of what usually constituted a film (e.g., nondiegetic music) caused audiences to attend more closely to what was left, to focus on technique and message. The early Dogme films played to this expectation through overt theatricalism that extended to a minimalist, hyperrealistic play-within-the play. If *The Celebration*'s protagonist performed madness to catch the conscience of the incestuous patriarch, *The King Is Alive* spoke directly about performance as the stranded tourists are persuaded by a former actor to perform *King Lear* as a collaborative diversion and via this endgame, undergo a "purification" like Dogma's purification of cinema, losing themselves in their performances to find something authentic.

The Idiots, which Trier once called "the truest and most genuine thing [he had] made" (Schepelern, "Film"), is the testamentary Dogme film. About acting and role-playing, one of whose themes is "the relation between playing a role and being a person," as Ove Christensen observes ("Spastic"), it is an essay on the uses and abuses of the performative. Posing as a documentary, yet using technique to call attention to itself as a film, it is ultimately about its own making and a self-referential performance of the Dogme principles. The idiots, like the Dogme brethren, are a bohemian, "truth seeking" collective whose performances are followed by group analysis sessions and subsequent variations on those performances. Punctuated by a series of interviews voiced by Trier, the film's visible surrogate is Stoffer, the idiots' demanding and tantrum-prone agent provocateur and "stage director" (who sheds his clothes in moments of duress). Jargil's *The Humiliated,* filmed simultaneously with the feature and with narration from Trier's audio diary, adds another layer of self-reference and specious authenticity. The result is a film he calls "much less calculating than *Breaking the Waves* and yet much more calculating" (*Humiliated*): "a more complex, far weirder film, [one] you ought to be amused and moved by, but also a bit disturbed by" (Knudsen 118).

The Idiots creates an impression of historical and physical presence and projects a documentary mode of address (Bainbridge, *Cinema* 96), as when Susanne (Anne Louise Hassing) uses subjective past tense to say to the screen, "it was I who was . . . with Karen on the last day." With ancestry in Direct Cinema, an American documentary movement whose Vertov-inspired manifesto proposed on-location minimalism, handheld cameras, and fealty to "truth," Dogme inspired Trier's documentary initiative *Dogumentary*, which required the film to include an opening statement that outlines the director's "goals and ideas" (Christensen, "Documentary" 187). Thus, Trier has it both ways: Dogme's documentary "elements" may enhance the "realism" of fictional films, but Trier's audible presence in *The Idiots* has the opposite effect of calling attention to the illusion in which the film appears factual and unscripted. Revealing that the film is his fiction or game (as Dogme is a Trier-authored game), his intrusions turn pseudodocumentary into metafiction. This oscillation between "reality effect" and metafilmic artifice, as Christensen observes, turns *The Idiots* into an "investigation into the status" and "grammar" of film ("Spastic"). Destabilizing the audience's understanding of what is "real," it prevents passive looking; it requires that we engage with it in order to recover meaning, a process that itself produces authenticity.

Where fictional cinema manipulates through scopophilia and empathy, a documentary addresses spectators as active and critical agents, inviting judgment. By mixing the two modes, Trier plunges us into a productive, intellectual-emotional confusion, especially where the idiots' "politics" is involved. Their stunts may confront and satirize bourgeois hypocrisy, yet their performances are often, as Trier notes "disastrously silly: malicious, foolish, and meaningless" (Knudsen 118), and spazzing condescends toward the people whose rights the idiots profess to defend, as Karen says, by "making fun" of the less fortunate. Thus the film creates a discomforting uncertainty about the ethical and ontological status of what we are watching, as Anne Jerslev elucidates (55–62), starting with the scene in which we observe the idiots for the first time in an exclusive restaurant. Sympathizing with Karen against a condescending waiter, we transfer sympathy to Stoffer when, assisted by Susanne, he refuses food, wanders to the next table and starts to cause a scene as Henrik (Troels Lyby) begins to cry, and the waiter discreetly tells them to leave. When Stoffer clasps Karen's hand and won't let go, she (and we) willingly go with the group, identifying with the outsiders. When Stoffer, Henrik, and Susanne break into hysterical giggles, the joke is on us as much as Karen.

The next target is the Rockwool foreman (Claus Strandberg), who is so spontaneously uncomfortable as to make it impossible to know if he is acting. Later, Stoffer (playing "normal") leaves Jeppe (Nikolaj Lie Kaas) in a bar with a group of menacing bikers. When he panics and attempts to wander off, they unexpectedly show compassion, decide he "wants a piss" and even aim his penis into the urinal as he desperately tries to perform in character. At this point, the physical signs of Jeppe's—and possibly Kaas's— "real" discomfort are indistinguishable from his spazzing/acting. This confusion of reality with fiction reaches yet another level, as mentioned in the DVD commentary, when audiences think the bikers (bouncers hired for the scene) are real Hells Angels and the scene improvised (it was scripted) (Trier and Albinus). In the final subversion, the scene intensifies our empathy with *both* the idiots and their target audience (the bikers) who, as Trier observes, are "the only ones who treat the retards decently" because they too are regarded as freaks (*Humiliated*). Moreover, it is Stoffer's treatment of Jeppe that is sadistic.

Scrambling expectations in such ways, *The Idiots* is deliberately offensive, transgressing boundaries public and private, fake and real, arranging confrontations that allow audiences no safe—personal or political—space, particularly in a scene in which the collective is visited by a group of authentically disabled people, plunging the pretending idiots *and* the actors playing them into depression and disarray. With this exception, the truly disturbing thing about *The Idiots,* as Jerslev explains, is that authenticity is not derived from a simple contrast between "real" and performed, or from an insistence on the reality of the performative. It lies in these moments in which all such distinctions collapse—when we cannot tell whether characters are performing or have broken through to their inner feelings—or whether the actors have blurred with their characters (56). As the collective begins to disintegrate, the confusion—and our discomfort—increases proportionally. When Sollerød City Councilman tries to bribe Stoffer to move his "home for the disabled" to a suburban ghetto, he becomes enraged and then hysterical, going (whether voluntarily or involuntarily) into spasm as he chases the councilman's car down the road. Tearing off his clothes, he runs naked in the streets screaming "Sollerød fascists" until tackled and subdued by the group. Stoffer's politically inspired performance, if it can be called such, degenerates into real, near psychotic, frenzy.

If the "idea of able-bodied individuals voluntarily mimicking the involuntary behaviors of the disabled is intentionally distasteful," Hjort comments, it becomes more so when Trier emphasizes nudity and sexuality ("*Globalisation*" 149) in scenes that show indisputable evidence of desire (Jerslev 59). Stoffer, playing an idiot at the swimming pool, accompanies Susanne into the women's dressing room and "performs" a real erection. Next, a spontaneous "birthday party" degenerates into an orgy that Nana (Trine Michelsen), who specializes in public disrobing, calls the "healthiest" idea Stoffer has ever had, a line echoed by Trier's assertion in the DVD commentary that sex brings about connections between people. In spastic group sex, viewed as a carnivalesque disruption of public versus private borders, nobody remains on top. Even this was not enough, though, as Trier wanted to show "disabled" sexuality authentically, and brought in porn actors to supply penetration, zooming in for a tight "meat" shot—making *The Idiots* the first mainstream film to include unsimulated sex. Rather than provoke spectator desire, however, such *signs* of "real" sex confront spectators with their own voyeurism, providing an element of "danger that makes it impossible to dissociate oneself from it," Trier dictated in his diary: "That is disturbing—someone playing idiots and having real sex at the same time" (Jerslev 56).[6]

The provocation of this moment is reversed by the delicacy of the next, to produce another level of disturbance. Away from the action, the camera finds Josephine (Louise Mieritz) approached by Jeppe; spazzing, they embrace and achieve a spontaneous connection for the first time. Immersing us in their emotional experience rather than positioning us as voyeurs (in a lapse from the predominant "documentary" mode), the moment is marked as private or unseen, suggesting that cinematic intimacy can be conjured only through fictional affect (figure 9). Its authenticity is heightened, moreover, when Josephine's father arrives, reveals that she should be taking psychotropic medication, and (embodying the Law of the Father) denies the validity of what we have witnessed. Together, these sequences return to the ongoing question of the group's—and the film's—definition of *idiocy,* much less its ethics, and personal and political aims. (Over Josephine's sobbing protests that as an idiot she has been happy, Stoffer refuses to take real risks, admitting that "we can't cure anybody here.")

As the group disintegrates, an increasingly belligerent Stoffer ups the ante; fake spazzing yields to real hysteria and becomes threatening. When the idiots are unable to pass his ultimate (Trieresque) test, which

Figure 9. *The Idiots*. Nikolaj Lie Kaas
and Louise Mieritz.

demands that they spazz in their workplaces and homes, the group
disperses and their experiment fails. Their failure seems to expose the
limitations of performance which, like Carnival, is primarily an escape
valve for elements and impulses repressed by the dominant culture.
Exposing the film's (and Dogme's) *lack* of authenticity, *The Idiots* seems
able only to force a negative version of the "truth" from its characters—
until the devastating final scene that allows the "idiot technique" and
the film to succeed. Here the film enters a completely different world,
shifting to a fictive, melodramatic mode as Karen, having accepted Stoffer's challenge and accompanied by Susanne, returns home to a bleak
flat, pausing to touch a small picture of an infant. (Her sister reveals that
she disappeared just before the child's funeral.) The family assembles in
frigid silence for coffee, the reserve palpable. Her husband Anders sits
down heavily. Against the decorous clinks of forks against china, cake
begins to ooze from her mouth and down her chin as, throwing her head
about in oblivious abandon, she reverts into the child she has lost (figure
10). Suddenly he strikes her, with the camera anticipating the move and
her recoil from the blow, intensifying the aftershock as she weeps and

Figure 10. *The Idiots.* Bodil Jørgensen
and Hans Henrik Clemensen.

trembles silently like a rebuked child. "That's enough, Karen," Susanne
says gravely. "Shall we go?" As they walk out, the screen goes black. "It's
a real Nora moment," Trier sighs (in reference to Ibsen's *A Doll's House*)
on the DVD commentary.

The point, Trier has said, is that "you can practice the technique—
the Dogma technique or the idiot technique—from now to kingdom
come without anything coming out of it unless you have a profound,
passionate desire and the need to do so. Karen discovers that she needs
the technique, and therefore it changes her life" (Knudsen 123–24). But
the scene resonates beyond any such "moral." Written before the rest of
the film, it was the film's raison d'être, and as Jens Albinus explains, the
group "had to propel the rest of the film toward it" (Trier and Albinus).
Its authenticity was to stand in relief against the pseudodocumentary
mode of the film as a whole, which provided the performative context
of self-reflexive postmodern irony. Although a performance itself (a diegetic staging of a role, in the fictive and melodramatic mode), it creates
a portal into pure preverbal emotionality. Or as Jerslev observes, the
end of the film replaces "ideologically motivated provocation" with the

"existential necessity" of Karen's performance. It is perfect because it expresses her being; her spazzing "transgresses the symbolic order" and "her inarticulate bodily behavior symbolizes this other place" (62).

Far from advocating an ontological realism, a faithful transcription of "reality," *The Idiots* and Dogme reverse the documentary notion of "truth," positing it as a connection between film and audience in which subjectivity is breached. When Karen exits, the spectator is left with her, in a blank space outside boundaries hitherto established, with no safe entry back in. That lack, however, is disturbing, provocative, reflexive. The film's unresolved dialectic between performing and "being," acting and therapy, documentary and fiction ultimately forces the audience, like the idiots, to reflect on the ethical implications and responsibilities of spectatorship, as Bainbridge also suggests, and therein lies the film's and Dogme's politics (*Cinema* 95–97).

This foregrounding of the performative is characteristic of many subsequent Dogme films including *Camera* (2000), *Fuckland* (2000), and derivations such as *Full Frontal* (2002), *Monsoon Wedding* (2001), and *Shortbus* (2006). Through provocation and insistent self-referentiality, Dogme stirred up what Hjort has discussed as a metaculture, a context in which films were perceived as theorizations put into practice, requiring "political" analysis and debate (Hjort, "Dogma 95"; "Globalisation"). Thus Dogme became an international public forum whose very existence presented an alternative to Hollywood's hegemony. *The Idiots* together with *The Kingdom* created controversy locally over its treatment of disability and the Sollerød community, and internationally over nudity and foreign censorship—which led to the discussion of cinema, professionalism or its lack, and Dogme rules observed and broken. Demystifying itself and the filmmaking process, Dogme was also a global workshop and, as Hjort has argued, a small nation's response to globalization, with the Vow of Chastity framed to challenge "the ever-narrowing conception of what constitutes viable or legitimate film-making . . ." (Hjort, "Dogme" 39). As Trier has said, it is "fantastic—that people in countries like Estonia or wherever can. . . . look at Dogme and think, 'If *that's* a film, then we can make films too.' Instead of just thinking, 'Oh, if it doesn't look like *Star Wars,* then we can't make a film'" (Kelly 146).

Dogme was also pivotal for Trier's trilogy about excessively "good" women. *The Idiots* overlapped *Breaking the Waves,* which Trier began in 1991 and filmed a few months after issuing the manifesto in March 1995, and the future movement's objectives and rules forecast the film's naturalistic style and affective simplicity. Bess McNeill's female variation on the holy fool is repeated in *The Idiots'* central character. The single authentic idiot who opens and closes the film, its emblematic "Gold Heart," Karen serves as the audience's surrogate, asking our questions and eulogizing each member as the group disperses. Throughout, the camera makes her an exception, holding her face in extreme close-ups (reminiscent of Dreyer's *Passion* and *Breaking the Waves*), and in a penultimate scene inspired by *Persona,* she and Susanne share a moment of silent empathy. At the film's conclusion, which is radically open to interpretation, she simply exits, but what is clear is that she has broken free of her family's patriarchal order. Karen's initiation, education, and final performance thus provide the centerpiece in a kind of workshop in how to achieve a "Real" act (as Slavoj Žižek calls it) of absolute freedom that produces a rift in the symbolic order, disrupting the phallic economy and the psychic apparatus of (masculine) reality ("Why?"). In Trier's oeuvre, this kind of "transcendence" is something only women (Bess, *Dancer's* Selma) and "wise children" (Little Brother, Jeppe) achieve—with Stoffer providing the most dramatic examples of how *not* to go about it.

Performing the Feminine: *Breaking the Waves* and *Dancer in the Dark*

Where gender is concerned, Dogme95 represents a fascinating paradox. A "brotherhood," it advocated an aesthetic Puritanism and "military" discipline likened to male celibacy. Yet its purpose was to elicit an "authenticity" associated with "borderline areas" to which the feminine is relegated. *The Idiots* revels in non-normative intersubjective experience and ends as a woman's melodrama performed with inimitable compression and rawness. Dogme was therefore pivotal to Trier's shift from a "masculine" to a "feminine" mode: from the Euro thriller to a relinquishment of genre, from ("male") ironic distance to ("female") immersion and emotion. Eventually it lent an aesthetic and performative politics to the exploration of the feminine that began as early as 1992, with the development of *Breaking the Waves* (1996), or even earlier, with *Medea* (1988).

This gender shift was announced in Trier's manifestos over the years (Bainbridge, "Making" 353–55). Equating "politically correct" filmmaking with castration, the Europe Trilogy manifestos proclaimed a masculinist, individualist (autoerotic) aesthetic. "Manifesto 1" (for *The Element of Crime*) called for "heterosexual films, made for, about and by men" and the third (for *Europa*), ended with the "confession": "LARS VON TRIER, THE TRUE ONANIST OF THE SILVER SCREEN." By "Selma's Manifesto" accompanying *Dancer in the Dark*, however, Trier was openly projecting himself onto female characters as if to "perform" and explore "the feminine." Many if not most feminists would regard this as a pernicious form of displacement. As Tania Modleski explains it, the male represses and reprojects "feminine" (masochistic) aspects of himself on a woman who suffers for both of them (13), thereby reinstating stereotypes of female victimization and male dominance.

When asked the (loaded) question of why he makes women suffer in (and for) his films, Trier's answer is disarmingly straightforward: "Those characters are not women. They are self-portraits" (Thomas), and his films are psychodramas in which gender roles are metaphorical projections in a role-playing project whose core is an urgent identity politics. Vibeke Windeløv, Trier's producer from 1996 through 2006, offers this spin: "In society, women are allowed to express more, emotionally, verbally. Think how rare it is for a male in a movie to say and do all the things women say and do in Lars' films" (*Tranceformer*). Portraying himself as the victim of a kind of male repression, Trier claims to be repossessing aspects of himself that his parents had discouraged—emotions, religious yearning, *Guld Hjerte* itself—and that the melodramatic Gold Heart Trilogy, being "feminine," was therapeutic. As he insisted to Gavin Smith, all his films involve "a clash between an ideal and reality," and his females are stronger than his men. They "take the ideal all the way." "My mother was strong. I think maybe that's why," he adds. "But let's not talk in terms of men and women. I feel kind of female, myself, to some degree" (25). Trier of course *does* talk in terms of men and women, especially in his role as a moralist whose ethics, Bainbridge claims, are framed by gender "as a component of human nature" (*Cinema* 45). The performance of gender is thus central to his explorations of extremes of sadism and masochism in self, culture, and politics.

This, his most dramatic career move may be approached as a shift from the distanced, cold, and "masculine" to the intimate, florid, and "feminine," and from protagonists who are failures to protagonists who are successful—if in a seriously qualified sense. While all Trier's protagonists follow a "failed idealist" trajectory, those in the Europe Trilogy become lost in labyrinthine networks of power and end up harming those they sought to help. They are victims of their own logic, limited to the discourses of power that constitute "Europe" or the symbolic order, and each film ends in a figurative or literal abyss. In contrast, the Gold Heart heroines adopt an oppositional "feminine" logic and "transcend" the symbolic in exemplary acts of self-martyrdom, affecting witnesses and shocking audiences. In contrast to Trier's male failures—who simply fail *at* power relations—his excessively "good" women oppose power, often (as Bainbridge argues), through a Christian humanist ethic based in love ("Making Waves"; *Cinema* 135–38). If, from the perspective of power relations and material conditions, the "Gold Hearts" reenact the victimization and failure of women throughout history, they have the dubious consolation of transcendence.

With *Breaking the Waves* and Emily Watson's astonishing performance as Bess, the transformation of Trier's directorial style was recognized worldwide. Summarized as "a simple love story, something I would never have considered a few years ago" for audiences wanting "human emotions from identifiable people made of flesh and blood" (Trier, qtd. in "A Story" 15), the film was anything but simple in evolution and execution. After the cold brilliance of *Europa,* persuading backers that he could make a US$9-million romance was difficult, and the project languished until *The Kingdom* revealed his ability to direct actors and enabled Jensen in tandem with Vibeke Windeløv to strike deals with investors from all over Europe (Stevenson, *Lars* 93–94).[7] Opening to widespread acclaim, the film demonstrated a visceral power and emotional range no one had suspected Trier capable of, catapulting him into the inner circle of European auteurs. But as critics registered their views, controversy emerged. "High-wire filmmaking, without a net of irony," David Ansen described it. "There are few movies around that take such huge risks."

Stylistically the film was unlike anything Trier, or anyone, had attempted: an international art film in the dramatic tradition of Dreyer and Bergman with disorienting jump cuts and deliberate amateurism more typical of Godard. "[R]endered with a conventional technique," the story would have been intolerable, "far too suffocating," Trier explains. "What we've done is to take a style and put it over the story like a filter" (Björkman, "Naked" 12). Shot primarily on location in natural light with a 35mm Panavision handheld by cinematographer Robby Müller, the film was transferred to video and back, producing a washed out, granulated image. When its success ushered in *The Celebration* and *The Idiots*, it became regarded as proto-Dogme.

Filmed during summer and fall of 1995 off Scotland's northeast coasts and the Isle of Skye, it takes place in an early 1970s community ruled by a repressive, "Scandinavianized" representation of the Presbyterian Free Church. Bess McNeill has established a direct line of communication with God, with whom she has passionate dialogues, playing both parts—one in a deep patriarchal voice and the other in a plaintively submissive one. The nature of Bess's "specialness" is unclear. In a moment's anger, her best friend and sister-in-law Dodo (Katrin Cartlidge) calls her "not right in the head," and we are unnerved by her openness and volatility, unsure of whether she is extremely high strung, mentally disabled, some kind of saint, or all three until Trier converts the mystery of her condition into the aesthetic and emotional equivalent of a medieval miracle.

The film begins as Bess throws herself into marriage with carnal joy, but when her oil-rigger husband Jan (Stellan Skarsgård) returns to work, she becomes wild with despair. Her prayers for his return are answered in a grimly parabolic twist when, injured in an accident, he is paralyzed from the neck down. Realizing he will never make love to her again, Jan asks her to perform sexual acts with other men and tell him about them. Believing these acts are God's way of saving Jan, yet driven into increasingly depraved and dangerous situations, she is tortured by a sadistic sailor and dies. When the church consigns her to hell, Jan, suddenly recovered, organizes a secret nighttime burial at sea. The next morning a pair of huge brass bells, suspended from the heavens, ring out in joyful recognition of the "goodness" of her life and death.

At once tawdry, sentimental, prurient, and possibly sacrilegious, the film provoked Terrence Rafferty to remark that Trier had given "the highbrow audience precisely what it lusted for in the boom years of the fifties and early sixties—nudity plus theology." No wonder. Trier had conceived the project as early as August 1991 as a variation on the Marquis de Sade's *Justine* (1787, 1791). Schepelern's examination of script drafts reveal that it evolved from an "erotic melodrama" with pornographic highlights to a more commercial (yet more fundamentally disturbing) "religious melodrama with erotic overtones." Where early drafts show the heroine relishing her assignments and asking for more, Trier now underscored her revulsion (Stevenson, *Lars* 90–93) to the point that the conflict between purity and sensuality she is forced to embody leads to her martyrdom. Thus what began as a flirtation with pornography shifted to a philosophical and aesthetic experiment in which female sensuality and unfettered emotion were conflated with divine transcendence.

Many viewers assumed the supernatural ending, which overinsists Bess's "goodness," was ironic. But Christian journalists have often taken the film at its word, extolling Bess as a modern Christ figure (Heath; Wall; van De Walle). Victoria Nelson finds that to dismiss the ending as ironic misses the point: By "going backward" into convention and cliché, Trier discovers "an emotionally richer aesthetic vocabulary" (229). But the morality tale–like simplicity also masks the film's conceptual complexity. An intellectual as well as emotionally draining experience, it was provocative to a degree Trier had never before achieved. The "kitschy" ending alternately moved and taunted audiences with its postmodern insufficiency, leaving them transported, troubled, forced to rethink the film.

In the "Director's Note" (subtitled "—This Film is about 'Good'") prefacing the published screenplay, Trier explains that he wanted "to conceive a film in which all driving forces are 'good,'" but because "good" is so rare, when encountered it is often "misunderstood or confused with something else," and conflicts arise.

> Bess is good in a spiritual sense . . . living mostly in the world of her imagination. . . . a strong person taking full responsibility for her life even though others might think that she is not capable. . . . master[ing] rebellion against the strict suppressing rules of the little community. . . .
>
> Jan is 'good' in a much more difficult way—because he consciously aims to do 'good'. He inhabits the real world, where doing 'good' is of course much harder. (20)

Jan's request for Bess to take a lover begins in "good," selfless motives; he pushes Bess away so she can find love he can no longer give. In fact, it is "painful" for him to hear her stories ("Director's Note" 21). Associating goodness with wanting the best for the person one loves, Trier explores the contradictions in Judeo-Christian ethics: "By doing 'good,' he loses her" and by "trying to save him" she is cast out by the world she loved. "But the 'good' will always be recognized . . . somewhere!" ("Director's Note" 22).

In *Breaking the Waves,* Trier also vented his desire for spiritual faith. In 1996, speaking as a recent Catholic convert, he described faith as a performative act comparable to miracles: "I don't believe in them but I hope for them to occur. . . . I'm standing at a crossroads where the child who creates rituals in order to control the world meets the adult who creates a faith," adding that religion was "a quest for a childhood I never had" (Thomsen 109). Positioned between childhood ritual and adult creation, *Breaking the Waves* attempted to produce an aesthetic/emotional experience of transcendence. Yet its subtexts and stylistic contrasts spoke of the impossibility of adult faith in a postmodern world, and the quest for childhood and religion are conflated within an exploration of the "feminine" partly inspired by Carl Th. Dreyer.

Seven years earlier, on a television airing of *Gertrud* for the hundredth anniversary of Dreyer's birth, Trier, kneeling at the director's grave, proposed a "little experiment" to awaken his spirit "through our childhood faith, the way it happens in *Ordet*. I believe that if we all make an effort, we can raise that love of film, which I today trace in very few places, so that we can all enjoy it again" (Schepelern, "Making" 111). In *Ordet,* set in rural Denmark, two families with opposing religious beliefs—one rigid, the other life-affirming—are brought together by a marriage, a death, and a resurrection. In the film's climactic moment, Johannes, the film's "holy fool" who believes he is Christ incarnate and, strengthened by a child's faith, raises his sister-in-law Inger from death, confirming that faith can indeed produce miracles in the modern world. *Breaking the Waves* similarly contrasts two belief systems, one represented by the church (where music is prohibited and women may not speak), and the other by Bess's intuitive, humanistic faith that includes rock music and her husband's snores among the gifts of God. Bess's prayers result in two miracles: Jan, restored to health, literally gets up and walks, and heavenly bells affirm the virtue inherent in Bess's actions.

If Dreyer's aesthetic and philosophical interest in religion was the obvious connection, another was his focus on female sacrifice in increasingly spare, theatrical, and parabolic films. *The Passion of Joan of Arc,* pared down to Joan's trial and execution at the hands of a patriarchal religious authority and shot almost entirely in close-ups, immersing spectators in her suffering, was a major influence. Having studied Falconetti's performance, Watson similarly looks up to heaven when talking to God. The film opens with one of several interrogation scenes in which a grotesquely condescending church father is shot (as in Dreyer) from below looking down on her, asking her catechistically, "Bess McNeill, do you even know what matrimony is?" and, after a deep pause, she replies, "When two people are joined in God." Similarly the elders are never in the frame with her, suggesting their representation of radically opposed concepts of "goodness."

A critique of Judeo-Christian culture, the film entered territory cinema rarely explored—of Mary Daly (*Beyond God the Father*) and Louise Kaplan (*Female Perversions*), for instance, who unearthed the patriarchal and misogynistic assumptions of Western religious institutions. Yet as a morality tale of masochistic female virtue that required the heroine's death, *Breaking the Waves* seemed misogynistic. The ending roused critical and academic debate among theologians, philosophers, and feminists in particular. A patently tacked on, supernatural "event" in an otherwise naturalistic film, it seemed to answer the film's central question while associating Trier with the misogynistic god Bess believes requires her death. A film whose "treatise on 'goodness' . . . not only requires the woman's demise but articulates her power," it "appears to defy any appropriation by feminism," Suzy Gordon writes (206). But what becomes clearest is its power to provoke controversy, especially among feminists, who have found it so affecting as to deserve censure (Faber) or, more often, like Heath, Gordon, Bainbridge ("Making"; *Cinema* 102–38), and Makarushka, who *attempt* to "appropriate" it for feminism, or both.

Breaking the Waves was the first of Trier's films to be disparaged for his now-signature use (or abuse) of women to perform an extreme stereotype (of martyred femininity) in order to produce a preternaturally intense affect. While sustaining the elite tradition of Scandinavian existential melodrama, it also drew on the classical era "woman's picture" or "weepie" epitomized and ironized in the films of Douglas Sirk. At one time nearly alone among Hollywood films in articulating women as active subjects (rather than objects of what Laura Mulvey has described as a fetishistic or voyeuristic-sadistic "male gaze"), this subgenre as Molly Haskell first noted, put a woman "at the center of the universe" (155). The catch debated by feminists (Doane and Williams) was its inherently masochistic theme (sacrifice for love) and the "wet, wasted afternoons" that it produced (Haskell 154). Trier represents the alternatives while pulling out all stops, celebrating a woman's sacrifice for her husband (*Breaking the Waves*), adoptive family (*The Idiots*), and male child (*Dancer in the Dark*). As Haskell sees it, the woman's picture was intrinsically manipulative, based on a conservative, pseudo-Aristotelian aesthetic "whereby women spectators are moved, not by pity and fear but by self-pity and tears, to accept, rather than reject, their lot" (154–55).

Psychoanalytic approaches took this a step further. Lacking enabling "masculine" distance (the male gaze's defense/displacement mechanisms), the female spectator is vulnerable, positioned to "over-identify" with the suffering heroine and succumb to deliciously passive melancholy (Doane 137). Nicole Kidman's 2008 *Entertainment Weekly* article might seem a case in point. After seeing the film, she canceled a dinner appointment, "went home, got into bed, curled up in a ball, and cried," adding "I don't know why I had such a profound, deep reaction. . . . It disturbed my spirit" (34). Yet rather than simply "wasting" an afternoon, the film moved her to write about her distress twelve years later and provoked her to work with Trier on *Dogville*. Unlike the typical tear fest, the experience of *Breaking the Waves* went beyond pleasurable emotion, provoking deep ethical and intellectual discomfort and the sort of boundary transgressing stimulation that Žižek, among others, calls *jouissance*.

Žižek finds the key to its effect in the tension between its melodramatic narrative and naturalistic style ("Death" 215), causing audiences to experience the film in all its excess as "real." In contrast to the visual arena projected by the typical camera "gaze," the spectator's relation to the image is haptic, reflexive-kinesthetic or, to use Per Kirkeby's term, "tropistic" (12). Plunging us into a succession of one- or two-person close-ups, invading spectators' space to the point of inducing nausea, the film insists on proximity, restricting us within Bess's emotional space. Images are always fragmented; faces never fill the screen, an effect enhanced by the widescreen CinemaScope format. Constant panning and harsh edits break up the already washed out, dissolving image, with the visual disorientation projecting her increasing delirium. Immersing us in her unprotected emotionalism, the film forces audiences regardless of gender to experience the brunt and range of her desire, pleasure, and suffering. Thus converted into an unsettlingly vital experience of the world, Bess eludes fetishization.

Refusing to "capture" her essence onscreen, Trier's camera allows her to elude the frame. Or, rather, something of her is constantly moving outside it, suggesting as Žižek puts it "a mysterious *jouissance* beyond Phallus about which nothing can be said" ("Death" 214).

Complementing this is the self-reflexive gesture in which she looks directly at the camera, breaking the frame and creating complicity with the audience (figure 11). As Watson has said, "For an actor to look into the camera" is a "great privilege," like looking "into the heart of the film" (Fuller). Thus *Breaking the Waves* embodies a paradox. If it forces women into a "feminized" proximity to the image without refuge from the masochism of Bess's position, it also demonstrates the image's ability to gaze *back,* asserting its/her autonomy and control.

Figure 11. *Breaking the Waves.*
Emily Watson smiling at the camera.

One issue often taken for granted in feminist responses is the *male* spectator who, considering Trier's inspiration in Sade's *Justine,* is important. A related issue is Trier's conception of the trilogy as a relinquishment of "masculine" distanciation in an attempt to recover the "feminine" in himself. The period setting reflects an era of sexual discovery and conflict between the "sexual revolution" and the nascent feminist movement of which Trier was acutely aware. While playing off pornographic clichés, the scenes before Jan's illness insist on a female perspective, emphasizing Bess's mixed curiosity, pleasure, pain, and wonder as she initiates her own "deflowering." In their hotel room, Jan performs a strip tease; she, still clothed in bridal white, looks over his body, digs her fingers into his pubic hair and experimentally touches his penis. When Jan calls from the rig she delights in porn cliché transgressions ("It's sooooo huge!") and pronounces words like "prick" with a blend of childlike and sensual relish. Bess experiences the penis not as the Phallus, the emblem of patriarchal law/word, but as a transgression of its Puritan power, or simply as Jan's body and a living, responsive expression of their connection. To the extent that it is a medium for her discovery of desire and pleasure enabling her to become a fuller, more expressive version of herself, Jan's body takes on a traditionally feminine role.

After his accident, which renders him impotent and suicidal, Jan's requests for male masturbatory fantasies underscore his abject and "feminized" state while also allegorizing the "male gaze" as sadomasochism by proxy and a defense mechanism against castration, calling attention to the *issue* of voyeurism in a profoundly disturbing way. It is easy to position Trier and the hypothesized male spectator with Jan as an unbalanced man manipulating Bess to "feed his sick fantasies," as Dodo puts it, speaking for feminists in the audience. Elsewhere, the gaze is foregrounded and caricatured, as in the bar lined with bestial-looking, stuporous sailors or on the ship, where Udo Kier plays a leering sadist. What is potentially the most voyeuristic scene, in which Kier tells Bess to "do it with the sailor while I watch," is overstated then abruptly truncated as she fights her way out, providing information about her final "sacrifice" while keeping it off-screen. Conversely, Trier highlights the image of the sexualized woman in order to disallow or skew it. Only Bess's first, comically fumbled sexual exploits are shown; later intimacies are cut to reflect the "spiritual connection" she claims with Jan. Attempting to seduce Dr. Richardson, she lies stiffly on the bed like a medical patient, his rejection excruciating. The naturalistic awkwardness of her performance as a "tart" (with borrowed clothes and makeup) is highlighted to evoke empathy. Audiences regardless of gender are forced to endure her final abjection *with* her and the group of empathetic characters who helplessly watch over her.

Sabotaging what Mulvey calls (male, Hollywood) "visual pleasure," the film offers aesthetic and ethical discomfort in spades. Given the personal, social, and political aims of Trier's subsequent deployment of naturalism with unprotected emotionalism (in *The Idiots* and *Dancer in the Dark*), it seems designed to dispossess the male—or, rather, the masculinized—spectator who, regardless of gender, is trained in classical Hollywood-style expectations. Thus, along with *Dancer in the Dark*, *Breaking the Waves* might be called a "male weepie" of a self-conscious, therapeutic sort, a film designed to break through "masculine" distance, to make men (and women) uncomfortable, to break men (in the spectatorial sense) down into transgendered beings—in short, to make the "male gaze" including Trier as hypothetical spectator and auteur of the coldly cynical Europe Trilogy, cry. Detecting this, critics have called Trier on "emotional pornography" (Stevenson "Lars"), a label he no doubt welcomes. Soon, in reference to *Dancer in the Dark,* he would speak openly of trying to manipulate audiences beyond their comfort levels.

This effect extends to the film's treatment of space, which harnesses Scandinavian naturalism to expressionism. Confining spectators to Bess's hamlet and Jan's oil-rig "island," Trier limits landscapes to a bleak and claustrophobic palette. As the church fathers gather to consign sinners to hell, the seaside cemetery setting's harshness reflects the church's uncompromising edicts (figure 12). In others—Bess howling and flailing like a wounded animal as waves crash upon the shore—nature signifies unleashed passion. The camera's sweeping pans cut off by brutal and incessant edits echo the windswept landscapes bordered by breaking waves as the film's title speaks of an opposition between passionate, limitless movement and its truncation, of "breaking through" and "making waves"—referring to Bess and the film itself.

The indoor scenes are comparably dingy and claustrophobic, and the film proper refuses the picturesque landscapes we would expect in a sweeping romantic epic, confining us within the narrow limits of

Figure 12. *Breaking the Waves.*
Against an unforgiving landscape, the
church fathers consign Bess to hell.

Bess's world—for instance, Bess's cramped childhood bedroom after Jan returns from the hospital. The film also deprives us of music, limiting it primarily to the congregation's unaccompanied hymns while making us aware of the deprivation. In the prologue, when the elders ask Bess what of value the outsiders have brought, she replies, "Their music," which she listens to (soundlessly) on the radio in Jan's absence. "Our church has no bells," the chairman explains to the expectant Terry after the wedding.

This absence of "real" music makes the final "miracle" of the bells (shot from above, literally pealing from heaven) the more powerful, aligning it with eight chapter interludes that break the narrative with blasts of 1970s rock music. Computer-generated sequences, imperceptibly moving picture-postcard landscapes, their lushly textured surfaces (with visible brush strokes and oversaturated colors) express what is drained out of the film proper. Inspired by J. M. W. Turner's romantic, "soul moving" paintings in which "the skies and the mass move about in an 'inner' way," as designer Per Kirkeby puts it (12–13), they have a pulse beat and register subtle changes in light. Fusing movement with stillness, the sublime with the banal, the "soul" of art with kitschy "mechanical reproduction," each is a dialectical construct like the film as a whole (figure 13).

Both visually and aurally the interludes express a sensual aesthetic that Bess is not allowed. In expressing her inner landscape, her vision of the world as it should be, they function like the musical numbers in *Dancer*

Figure 13. *Breaking the Waves.* |

in the Dark. Yet they also suggest omniscience, and the production notes call them a "God's eye view of the landscape in which this story is unfolding, as if he is watching over the characters," subtly foreshadowing the performative gesture that ends the film in a miracle in which Bess's and God's eyes are conflated. For spectators, however, they provide a space for a detachment the film otherwise disallows. The first interlude, "Bess Gets Married," is a self-reflexive variation on (otherwise missing) establishing shots: A tiny helicopter emerges from the clouds as Mott the Hoople blasts out "All the Way from Memphis," and we cut to Bess pacing at the airport before for Jan's late arrival. Anticipating the chapter titles of *Dogville* and *Manderlay,* they foreground the film's allegory while offering obvious (*almost* ironic) spoilers: "Life with Jan," "Life Alone," "Jan's Illness," "Doubt," "Faith," "Bess's Sacrifice." Yet where the visuals suggest universality, the songs are like David Bowie's "Young Americans" at the end of *Dogville,* blasts from the real world. In this role they historicize the narrative, making space for cultural critique.

The misogynistic logic informing the film can be better understood through a return to sources, beginning with the fairy tale *Guld Hjerte* and Sade's *Justine,* which tells an "adult" version of the same story. As Trier remembers the former, a little girl goes into the woods "and on her way she gives away both her food and her clothes. And when the rabbit or the squirrel tells her that now she doesn't have a skirt on, her answer is the same every time: 'I'll be all right'" (Thomsen 109). Attempting to lead a pure life in France just before the Revolution, Justine, as Trier puts it, is "exploited, raped, or whipped by everyone she meets" (Thomsen

110)—including representatives of the church, the aristocracy, and the law—while unshaken in her faith in God's "goodness." Justine's devotion to institutionally defined "virtue" leads her into greater degradation until, in the abrupt conclusion, lightning "entered her right breast, found the heart, and after having consumed her chest and face, burst out through her belly" (742) followed by the lines: "May you be convinced . . . that true happiness is to be found nowhere but in Virtue's womb, and that if, in keeping with designs it is not for us to fathom, God permits that it be persecuted on Earth, it is so that Virtue may be compensated by Heaven's most dazzling rewards" (743).

Bess lacks Justine's "self-righteousness," Trier explains (Thomsen 110), but *Breaking the Waves* otherwise follows Sade. At the wedding reception, Dodo claims Bess will "do anything for anybody" down to giving Dodo's bicycle to a stranger. Caught up in the absurd idealism of female submission in the name of love's "mighty power," Bess takes on Jan's perverse request as a challenge to her faith, her victimization inevitable, with Trier lacing it all with Sadeian irony as her prayers (for Jan's return, his life, and his restoration to health) are granted with a cruel literalism. In place of Sade's cynical deus ex machina, however, he ushers in the final-act miracle of the bells, deferring the expected irony.

Breaking the Waves thus has the contours of a perverse fable that stops just short of satire—an effect enhanced by the plot's rigid binaries (echoing *Justine*'s): insiders and outsiders, "Faith" and "Doubt," strength and weakness, goodness and "going to Hell," the Word (also the Law), and the (silenced) woman. *Breaking the Waves* similarly demonstrates the contradictions inherent in culturally coded expectations for women under the church, medical science, and the law. The difference is that Trier does not stop there. He asks what it all might mean within a context cognizant of the cultural shifts of the late twentieth century, highlighting the conflict between institutionalized religion and feminism. His use of Sade might even be viewed as fulfilling Angela Carter's call in *The Sadeian Woman* (1978) for a "moral pornographer," a savage satirist whose texts, representing "a critique of current relations between the sexes," might "penetrate to the heart of the contempt for women that distorts our culture" (19–20).

Making Bess's struggle to be a "good girl" central, Irena Makarushka observes, Trier focuses not simply on whether Bess is "good" or "bad" but on prevailing perceptions of "goodness" in regard to women. Bess embodies the conflict between "two radically different ways of being 'good' in the world." One, associated with Old Testament Law and the Word, is the church's demand that women be submissive and silent. The other is based in Bess's personal faith in/practice of love. Choosing to be "good" on her own terms, creating a flexible, dynamic ethics based on her relationship with Jan, she is cast out of her community. Trier thus highlights the issue of moral relativity, as Makarushka explains. After marrying Jan, Bess must negotiate between her community's ethics and her changed understanding, and her "goodness" becomes defined in increasingly disparate ways. Where the church values her faith, and many speak of her generous heart, which Jan appreciates as openness and unaffected sensuality, Dr. Richardson values her ability to feel pain as intensely as joy and refuses to pathologize it. Bess demonstrates such a plenitude of "goodness" that it transgresses the brittle logic sustaining the church, medical science, and rationality itself.

Outside the Law/Word, Bess invents her own space, both inside and beyond the church, where she speaks for "God the Father" to herself. Filtering the church's values through her faith in love, she "performs" the Word as a condescendingly patriarchal presence who commands her to do mysteriously (absurdly?) contradictory things: She must endure her loneliness, but she must not love Jan too much. She must obey her husband, but she must not commit adultery when he tells her to for his sake. When she requests forgiveness for her "sin" on the bus, the heavenly "Father" explains that Mary Magdalene, who also "sinned," is among his "dearly beloved"—answering her prayer while sticking to the book in which she occupies the stereotypical space of the "sinful-woman-who-is-forgiven."

Bess's struggle to be a "good girl" *and* a full subject is shown to be impossible within the symbolic order. "I'm sorry I could not be good," her last words to her mother, must therefore take the negative logic of church dogma. Her struggle can succeed only in what Žižek understands as the ultimate performance of femininity in an act of self-annihilation that embodies "absolute freedom," interrupts the phallic economy, and hints at a range of meaning beyond the symbolic. At the inquest, the coroner repeats Dr. Richardson's testimony describing "the deceased as 'an immature, unstable person. . . . who gave way . . . to an exaggerated, perverse form of sexuality.'" Wishing to amend the statement, the doctor explains that "instead of 'neurotic' or 'psychotic,' my diagnosis might quite simply be 'good.'" The incredulous coroner's response, "You wish the records to state that . . . the deceased was suffering from being 'good'? That this is the psychological defect that led to her death?" states the crux of the film's dilemma in which real "goodness" is incompatible with reality.

In the final third of a film without a single direct reference to the New Testament, Bess's struggle takes on a load of Christian symbolism. In her darkest hours, she experiences the agony of God's silence, crying "Dear Father, where are you?" and undergoes her Way of the Cross as schoolboys pelt her with stones. Like Christ, Bess dies alone in sorrow until the miracle of the bells, witnessed by Jan and Terry, provides a performative space for her "gospel" of love. Bess in red vinyl hot pants, fishnet stockings, and wobbly high heels is a bedraggled, impossibly sexualized Christ who professes that in turning tricks she can save Jan's life. In her logic, these acts are sacralized into a kind of transubstantiation. Or else, in offering up her body as a medium, she literally "makes love" out of sex, performing the role of sacred prostitute from pagan ritual. From the beginning, Bess's sensuality, associated with nature and outsiders, is transgressive, but it is here that it gets really dangerous. In turning Sade's Justine into a type of Christ, Trier simultaneously exploits and exposes the misogyny that consigns Bess (and all women who attempt self-authorization) to hell.

For creating an aesthetic experience that simulates a premodern religious sensibility, Trier is regarded by many, such as Jonathan Rosenbaum, as a shameless manipulator, although Richard Corliss, like many others, finds that the film's "pagan fervor" achieves a "religious experience" in its own right. Whatever the case, Breaking the Waves is Justine done up in a way Dreyer would have approved, as a film that can make grown men cry. In its aesthetic as well as its themes it follows Dreyer's fusions of faith and sensuality, and Trier echoed Passion in his use of close-ups of Watson's unadorned and emotionally open face. In Ordet, the "insane" idealist and Christ figure (Johannes) who reconciles the two churches and faiths, one austere and one life-affirming, is ascetic, male, and safely separated from the feminine (embodied separately in Inger, the loving young wife and mother he resurrects). As Inger's husband

Mikkel says just before the miracle, "I loved her body too." *Breaking the Waves* replaces the ascetic Johannes with a sexualized variation on Inger, conflating Christ with Mary Magdalene and Justine. Trier's twist on *Ordet* (*The Word*) is best suggested in the scene in which the exhausted, assaulted, taunted Bess enters the sanctuary as the elders are sermonizing about their "unconditional love for the Word" and speaks "in service" for the first and last time: "How can you love a word?" she demands. "You cannot love words. You cannot be in love with a word. You can love another human being. That's perfection." "No woman speaks here," the minister responds, casting her out.

Johannes's insane "leap of faith" in *Ordet,* dismissed as the product of reading too much Kierkegaard, recalls the latter's resolution of Abraham's dilemma in *Fear and Trembling* when, in a test of his faith, God asks him to sacrifice his son's life. In sacrificing herself through a transgressive sexual act identified with Christ's martyrdom, Bess takes risks far greater than Johannes or, in the context of 1996, possibly even Abraham. Whether viewed from a Christian or feminist perspective, the film is rigged to offend on multiple levels. Read as a risk-taking "remake" of *Ordet* by way of *Justine, Breaking the Waves* challenges Western religions' disassociation of (male) spirit and (female) flesh and also challenges feminism with its conflation of ethics and female masochism to expose what Žižek calls "the inherent deadlocks of Goodness" (212).

Like many, Žižek reads the miraculous bells as a "postmodern appendix to an otherwise tragic modernist existential drama of Faith" that allows audiences to experience a miracle as an aesthetic spectacle without "really believing it" but also without ironic distance (219). The reaction to the film, however, suggests that Trier had issued his first widely heard provocation. By returning to the stereotype in which, as Francine du Plessy Gray puts it in reference to Princess Diana, "the 'good' woman is the dead woman who can be safely mourned when she can no longer disrupt the 'natural' order of things" (Makarushka), he leaves the audience with a "disturbed spirit." The problem of Bess's failed quest for "goodness" within the world is thus thrust on us.

Shifting from sexual ethics to global politics in *Dogville* and *Manderlay,* Trier would continue to explore "deadlocks of Goodness" found in the misadventures of Justine and in the process reconceive the character of the "good" woman. But the film's celebration of martyred female moral superiority was, for many, inexcusable for condoning real women's material subjugation. Žižek's and Bainbridge's Lacanian arguments, being based on an economy of desire, are equally indifferent to the material conditions of things. With *Dancer in the Dark*, we see a distinct shift that begins in the last fifteen minutes of *The Idiots*, as Karen's performance is defined within the context of the patriarchal lower-middle class. From this point on (until *Antichrist*), Trier's heroines' self-sacrificial acts become meaningful or not within specific social and political contexts.

Dancer in the Dark was also designed to make men (and women) cry but, in contrast to *Breaking the Waves*, generated one of the more polarized critical responses in film history. This began at Cannes, where it won the Palme d'Or and Best Actress awards to applause mixed with boos, becoming a cineaste's barometer. *Entertainment Weekly* called it "a triumph of form, content and artistic integrity" (Schwarzbaum); *Variety* condemned it as "artistically bankrupt on every level" (Elley). Strained Cannes press conferences fueled the fire already inflamed by publicity surrounding the shoot. Playing up conflicts between Trier and his star/composer Björk Guðmundsdóttir, it alleged that she frequently left the set and once "ate" her costume in a fit of rage, and enhanced Trier's reputation as a misogynist who enjoyed making actresses suffer—this time, to the point of foaming hysteria. For some, this view was confirmed by the final sequences on death row in which Björk appeared to be (and reportedly was) in real torment.

More controversial yet, the film was a strange amalgam, a mostly handheld Dogme-style musical in which Trier, as in *The Idiots*, had operated the camera much of the time. This suggested to some pundits who assumed that Trier had taken the Vow of Chastity for life that he was guilty of breaking his own rules. The alleged infractions called attention to the film's truer eccentricities. It attempted a quintessential Hollywood genre, the musical, breaking rule #8, albeit ineptly, and was set in 1960s America, thus made neither in "the here and now" (#7) nor on location—it was filmed primarily in Denmark and Sweden, violating rule #1. The musical sequences were filmed with as many as one hundred randomly fixed cameras and had postproduction-enhanced color and lighting (breaking rules #3, #4, and #5) yet looked muddy and ragged nevertheless. It was obviously dubbed (breaking rule #2), and the pivotal murder scene violated rule #6 prohibiting weapons and "superficial action"). It credited the director as *Breaking the Waves* had, in a font ten times that of the film's title. As a "Dogmatic" musical it had to critique the genre and Hollywood illusionism generally, yet raised issues Trier could know only secondhand: American poverty, immigration, capital punishment, and capitalism itself.

Trier has emphasized the similarity of the first and last Gold Heart films, calling *Dancer in the Dark* "sentimentality number two" (*In Lars*). A Czechoslovakian immigrant and single mother going blind from a hereditary disease, Selma Jezkova (Björk) works overtime in a metal press factory to afford her young son Gene (Vladica Kostic) an operation to save him from the same fate. But she is betrayed by her friend and landlord Bill Houston (David Morse), a debt-ridden policeman who steals her savings and, in suicidal despair, drives her to kill him to recover the money to save her son. Refusing to betray Bill's trust or defend her actions, she is tried, found guilty, and executed for murder. As her life grows literally dark, Selma turns to daydreamed musicals in which "Nothing dreadful ever happens." "I've got a little game I play when it goes really hard," she confides to Bill. "When I'm working in the factory and the machines, they make all these rhythms. And I just start dreaming and it all becomes music." Bess's love for Jan becomes Selma's all-consuming love for her son, and Bess's conversations with God are replaced by Selma's fantasies of living a musical. As she is increasingly isolated in her blindness and her purpose, her "musicals" (like Bess's faith) offering her only refuge, Selma's ideals clash with reality, ending in her death.

But in important ways, this was a very different film. Where Bess was inordinately attached to Jan, Selma is stubbornly self-sufficient, insisting she has no use for a man. And if Bess sentimentally embodied Trier's reaction against his communist, atheist upbringing, Selma sentimentally *reflects* that upbringing, specifically the period when he and his mother legendarily threw bricks at the American embassy in Copenhagen. *Breaking the Waves* explored a range of religious experience his parents had kept off limits. *Dancer in the Dark* is grounded in the material; repression and social alienation are among the deepest emotions expressed, and in place of philosophical allegory it offered cultural and political critique.

Dancer is more obviously constructed than the earlier film, and Trier admits that the task was interesting to him as an exercise in "manipulation" (Filmmaker commentary). Wearing its genres and intentions on its sleeve, it challenges audiences to take it seriously. On one level it is a concoction of melodramatic clichés that (as Ebert suggests) might have been expected in a 1912 silent film starring Lillian Gish (*"Dancer"*). It deploys the most hackneyed of "woman's picture" tropes, the mother consumed by sacrificial maternal zeal (the theme of *All That Heaven Allows* [1955]) and *To Each His Own* [1946]), embellished with the maudlin theme of the woman going blind (*Dark Victory,* 1939). Selma's love for Gene is instinctual (blind). (Asked why she bore a child destined to inherit her disease, she answers, "I just wanted to hold a little baby in my arms.") Uninterested in sex, she sublimates desire into relentless work and refuses her dogged suitor Jeff (Peter Stormare). Like the 1940s woman's melodrama, the film ends in her resignation to her lot as she is hanged for a murder she has been forced to commit.

Where love of music is an aspect of Bess's faith, music *is* Selma's religion. "Why do I love it so much?" she sings "In the Musicals," answering that the transcendent experience of music "will always be there to catch me when I fall." Where Bess embraces the outsiders' rock music, associated with America and 1960s–70s British pop, a similar connection plays a much deeper and more complicated role in *Dancer.* In an unabashed bid for mainstream attention, the film alluded to the musical genre from its Hollywood heyday in the 1940s and the 1950s to its decline in the 1960s and the 1970s to the present, in which MTV had more or less subsumed it. It featured the Icelandic star Björk, an international cult phenomenon for her ethereal experimental compositions and videos, the iconic French actress Catherine Deneuve, star of Jacques Demy's musicals *The Umbrellas of Cherbourg* (1964) and *The Young Girls of Rouchefort* (1967), and Joel Grey, the sardonic Master of Ceremonies in *Cabaret* (1972).

Several elements, however—including a four-minute "Overture" and the integration of musical numbers into the narrative, lending emotional continuity—indicate that Trier intended to something more like European opera than a musical (in the sense of an upbeat narrative interrupted by song-and-dance numbers). Trier was fond of melodrama at the time, he told Gavin Smith, so why not try to effect "the emotion of an opera?

That is, melodrama with music," adding that in musicals "you can't really go all the way with the feelings" (25). In a statement on the film's Web site, he explains that people actually cried at operas, whereas the musicals he saw as a child were "never really dangerous" ("Lars"). As a fusion of the arts, film has been called the opera of the twentieth century, and *Dancer in the Dark*'s experimental synthesis suggests he had in mind an approximation of Wagner's concept of *Gesamtkunstwerk*, an ideal synthesis of ideas, visual arts, poetry, and music. If so, he seems to have succeeded. In 2001, the composer's grandson commissioned him to direct the 2006 *Ring des Nibelungen* for the Bayreuth Fespielhaus (Rockwell, "Von"), and in 2007, the Royal Danish Opera commissioned composer Poul Ruders to create an opera based on the film. Calling *Dancer* "the most emotive and evocative film I ever recall seeing," Ruders describes "stagger[ing] out of the cinema [knowing] this was the ultimate blueprint for a new opera—universal, timeless and engaging" (Schweitzer).

Trier's films are perhaps most operatic in what John Rockwell calls their ability "to mine the emotion of film as a replacement for the emotion of music" and describes the soaring intensity he obtains from actresses as "a new kind of hyper-emotional artistic experience." Like the Gold Heart Trilogy, Wagner's sources, the *Edda* and the *Nibelungenlied*, are adult fairy tales with suffering and saving women at their centers. Wagner viewed ideas and words as masculine and music and emotion as feminine, and in Trier's work, "feminine" emotion is concentrated "by 'masculine' Eurointellectual conceits and multilayered film techniques and references" (Rockwell, "Von"). This hardly makes his films more palatable for feminists, supporting the view expressed by Björk that he uses women as surrogates to "provide his work soul"—the emotion he is unable to feel himself—and "envies and hates them for it" (Sweet).

In fact, for many fans, the real opera was the struggle between director and star. The controversial Björk was Trier's "pop equivalent" and the union of the two "insurgents" provoked strong reactions (Powers). The battle over Selma became *Dancer*'s popular hyper/subtext, enriching the gender and identity politics now inseparable from the film as well as Björk's performance. The Icelandic diva used to running her own show now "found herself at ground zero in the 'world of Lars von Trier.' *Danish Imperialism—The Sequel*," as Stevenson puts it, with Iceland's history as a Danish colony for 500-plus years lending their struggle historical dimensions (*Lars* 153). As an outsider and hireling on his largest production yet, her role was unhappily similar to Selma's.

Trier had invited her to compose after he saw the music video for "It's Oh So Quiet," from her 1995 album *Post*. Set in a used tire shop, it featured Björk turning the industrial setting's noise into a big band Broadway-style routine. Having worked in fish packing and Coke bottling plants and, in a widely publicized incident, assaulted a journalist who had approached her ten-year-old son, she identified intensely with Selma. As composer, she cocreated the role, developing a view of the character as a strong single mother like herself (Trier viewed her as more vulnerable). Paradoxically, the battle for Selma began in a space in which the two artists found common ground including an aesthetic of "found" music and imperfection that coincided with the director's latest phase (as suggested in the Trier-penned "Selma's Manifesto"). Moreover, Selma seems to have tapped some of the darkest elements in them both including a visceral fear of death, an abhorrence of capital punishment, and an intensely personal investment in their work. But where the film was primary to Trier, Selma's music was everything to Björk. As she admitted to Greg Tate, the conflict was less between Lars and herself than between Selma and Björk-the-composer, who fought when her music was changed to fit the film.

In many senses, Björk won the battle for Selma. Once, when told that several bars of a song had been cut, she disappeared for days, meanwhile issuing a manifesto asserting her right to final cut on her songs and complete control over the soundtrack CD, which, consisting of remixes, would be issued as *Selmasongs* (2000). Although Björk and Trier cowrote lyrics with Icelandic poet Sjón (notably the Academy Award–nominated "I've Seen It All"), "New World," which played over the end credits as a hopeful continuation of "Next to Last Song," was her idea, and she had the last word on the film's coda, overall "meaning," and tone (Lumholdt, "There" 165). Thus Trier admits *Dancer in the Dark* is "very much Björk's film" (Filmmaker commentary). Certainly for Björk fans such as Lucas Hilderbrand, it is hers more than Trier's: "Björk doesn't shed her 'musician' persona, but rather complicates her own mythology with this character's tragic circumstances. Because Björk wrote the songs, they sound like Björk's other work. So the film reads

. . . as if Björk is experiencing Selma's plight. In a meta-narrative way, the viewer cares about Selma not simply because of the character as written but because the viewer cares about Björk." In the same way, Trier fans may read the film as Lars's psychodrama.

As hostilities settled, Björk reluctantly expressed pride in the film, stating that "Lars and I had so much trust we never wrote anything down." Asked if she had to sacrifice spontaneity, she replied that "it was all improvised" and that, unable to memorize Selma's lines, she reacted instinctively to situations. For the music scenes, shot with multiple cameras fixed at different positions, "you'd just do your thing from camera to camera." After "talking to a lot of actors since, I realized it was probably the most spontaneous film ever shot" (Tate). As the conflicted body of evidence suggests, *Dancer in the Dark* is like Dogme and *The Idiots,* one of Trier's difficult, deliberately imperfect experiments in simultaneously achieving and losing control—and one that reflexively subverts any simple understanding of the auteur theory. Certainly if an ensemble film such as *The Idiots* encouraged collaboration and improvisation, this "Dogme-style" musical starring a composer accustomed to complete control over her own productions and directed in part by Vincent Paterson (choreographer of Madonna's and Michael Jackson's then-current videos) in many ways demanded more.

As *Moulin Rouge* (2001) director Baz Luhrmann has said, Trier likes to create unachievable goals for himself and to make art of the process of attempting to realize them (Rockwell, *Idiots* 75). His aim, to sum up the previous discussion, seems to have been to create an "operatic," European, socialist materialist, collaborative, and international—at the very least "trans-Hollywood"—musical. Nevertheless, the classical Hollywood musical was the original reason for setting the film in America. As Trier explains in the production notes, he returned to a childhood fascination with Gene Kelly musicals and tried to "recreate some of that feeling." As usual, his aims had personal roots; his communist parents thought all musicals were "American rubbish." But fusing the denigrated *Guld Hjerte* with the equally denigrated musical, he could make operatic "art" out of "rubbish," constructing the greatest possible challenge to his (dead) parents, his postmodern audience, and himself.

As if to announce these intentions, the film is bookended with renditions of "My Favorite Things" from Rogers and Hammerstein's *The*

Sound of Music, the Broadway musical (1959) and film (1965) about the singing von Trapp family. The opening sequence in which Cathy and Selma rehearse the song for a community theater production draws on the self-reflexive convention in which characters are singers and dancers (as in *42nd Street* [1933], excerpted twice). Such self-reflexivity is rarely subversive, as Jane Feuer has observed; its purpose is to naturalize the song-and-dance sequences while valorizing the genre, whose raison d'être is pleasure (x). Hence, musicals render rehearsals and the work that goes into production not as labor but as flawless entertainment (12). In *Dancer,* however, *The Sound of Music* is nothing *but* labor: We never witness a completed number, and rehearsals are amateurish, possibly miscast (a stubby Maria wears coke-bottle glasses), and tediously repetitive (McMillan). More telling yet is the discrepancy between Selma's private musicals and a reality that grows literally and figuratively dark. In foregrounding the work of production and the illusions produced, Trier refuses simple Hollywood-style pleasure.

Through plotting, sequencing, and jolting contrasts in lighting, color, and cinematography, Trier also heightens tensions between narrative and musical elements that American musicals usually understate. For the narrative, as in *Breaking the Waves,* Trier used a handheld digital camera limited to a small field, jostling between actors to suggest Selma's narrowing range of options. In the scenes in her trailer, for instance, it lurches between Bill and Selma in a tight close-up that evokes her cramped financial straits and failing vision. In contrast, the musical sequences—the first occurring some forty-five minutes into the film—are signaled by a vibrant rush of color (enhanced by transferring the video to a high quality film stock), a shift from monaural to stereophonic sound, and from subjective camera to an omniscient visual field created by one hundred cameras placed in various positions—in "Smith & Wesson/Scatterheart," from the treetops to the frame of Gene's bicycle. Positioned to catch Selma at different ranges and angles, creating a plenitude of images edited later into compositions, Trier's "100 Eyes" (Forbert) attempted to turn the experience of music into a transcendence of subjectivity. Selma, immersed in a totalizing experience of song, movement, and limitless expansion, "becomes" music (figure 14).

In what becomes an increasingly difficult narrative to watch, Selma's songs provide moments of poignancy, if not relief. Tortured plotting,

Figure 14. *Dancer in the Dark.* "I've Seen It All":
Björk "becomes" music.

made grotesque through inelegant blocking, awkward jump cuts, and overstated acting (alternating with Björk's "nonacting") heightens the contrast between reality and the visionary world of music. Bill's death feels like the most clumsily choreographed homicide in film history. Improvised around Björk's real anguish, the sequence is devastating because of its bizarre messiness (a policeman wrestles a sobbing, screaming blind woman into shooting him in order to get her life's savings back; unable to finish him off, she bludgeons him to death with a safety deposit box). But it is followed by "Smith & Wesson/Scatterheart," a song of denial and wish fulfillment focused on Bill's resurrection and forgiveness choreographed with delicate naturalness, as Selma blames herself, Linda sings for her to "Run for your boy," and Gene's clear boy soprano offers the refrain "You just did what you had to do."

In setting off contrasts between their idealized "New World" and the real inequities of capitalism, the musical sequences eventually shift *Dancer in the Dark* toward explicit social and political critique. This is a land of Technicolor dreams and almost no social security, where good, middle-class people are seduced into a spendthrift lifestyle until debt drives them to desperation. A factory worker must save all her money to afford one operation. Immigrants are treated with a superficial generosity that masks condescension and xenophobia, and the film ends in a devastating critique of the death penalty, an issue around which anti-Americanism had taken shape throughout Europe. In contrast, in the future Selma envisions for Gene, America and the musical are conflated into a harmonious, utopian "land of opportunity," lending support to

Ken Woodgate's suggestion that Hollywoodized illusions are partly to blame for her death. Selma's musical "daydreams" arguably provoke or signal the downward-spiraling narrative (395–96). Her lapse into "Cvalda" causes her to break a machine and lose her job, and her music becomes devastatingly and increasingly at odds with the narrative. "In the Musicals" imagines Samuel and Oldrich Novy as dancer-lovers who catch her when she falls; in reality, Samuel calls the police, and Novy denies knowing her. In "Next to Last Song," she drops to her death in the middle of a line. Many discussions have therefore assumed that Dogme's founder had made a satirical, anti-illusionist, anti-Hollywood, and rabidly anti-American film.

Brian McMillan therefore observes that Trier plays upon the familiar "association of Hollywood with artificiality versus the independent and real," confining music within the domain of the "unreal." Yet things are not so simple. While breaking with Dogme prohibitions against dubbed sound, filters, and color enhancements, the musical numbers nevertheless ground "transcendental" moments in graphically "real" situations and imperfections. Thus to keep edges sufficiently rough, Paterson limited dancers to two or three rehearsals, and in "In the Musicals," they leap from the frame in irregular succession, scrambling courtroom order. *Dancer in the Dark* may not "look like a conventional musical," Trier explains, but "it's a musical to me"—"it's not like I'm trying to change anything" (Kaufman 156)—and distinguishes his intentions from the parody of Dennis Potter's *Pennies from Heaven* (Lumholdt, "There" 163–64). We should therefore take *Dancer in the Dark* as a musical in the sense that Martin Sutton describes it: A genre concerned with "the romantic/rogue imagination and its daily battle with a restraining, 'realistic,' social order" expressed in a tension between story and spectacle (191).

Rather than "anti-" *or* Hollywood, the film was insistently international in its actual locations, frame of reference, and cast that, with only five Americans, included Icelandic, French, French-Canadian, Swedish, English, Danish, and German actors. The result was an obviously "foreign" and fabricated pastiche, as Smith puts it (24). Or as Adrian Martin suggests, *Dancer* "denaturalizes the American provenance of the musical genre" (106). If Selma's fantasies often work variations on the American Dream, they lean, as Trier has commented, "much more toward the European traditions," resembling *The Umbrellas of Cherbourg* in ideas and social themes (Lumholdt, "There" 163). Czechoslovakia was chosen "as a contrast and counterweight to the USA," he said, adding, "It's all a bit *Joe Hill*" (Björkman, *Trier* 225). The reference is to the 1971 film about the Swedish-American socialist labor activist and songwriter executed for murder after a trial in which his activism cinched the verdict.

Noting the film's socialist-realist ambience (relentless, dehumanizing work, drab, hopeless people, callous authority figures), Hoberman finds: "Björk's character lives in an imaginary America that, despite its *Twin Peaks* patina, is far closer to the invented USA of Soviet propaganda films like *Silver Dust*." One of Selma's cherished fantasies is that her father is Oldrich Novy, a Czech musical star during the communist era. Selma's communist background is fleshed out further in two sequences staged much like the USSR musicals of the late 1930s and 1940s. Film historian Maya Turovskaya explains that the Soviet musical, adapting a type of Hollywood escapist entertainment to communist goals, produced an oxymoron. Its theme, like its model's, was happiness, but found in work rather than in the pursuit of romance or individual goals. Soviet musicals therefore turned physical labor into choreographed collective pleasure (*East Side Story*). *Tractor Drivers* (1939) and *Cossacks of the Kuban River* (1946) were shot in fields where masses of strapping young people sang about production quotas and collective farming. In the Cinderella story *The Shining Path* (1940), a simple farm girl goes to the city, excels as a factory worker, and saves the day (and the state) in a crisis.

When in *Dancer* simple Czechoslovakian single mother Selma goes to America and works double shifts with a dream of saving her son's sight, the socialist realist fairy tale fuses with the capitalist American Dream. "Cvalda" (aka "The Clatter Song" and "The Factory Dance"), a duet between Selma and Cathy in babushkas and accompanied by dancers in proletarian attire, has a chorus of "Clatter, crash, clack/Racket, bang, thump!" about machines that "greet you" with rhythms that "sweep you away." It cites simultaneously Björk's "It's Oh So Quiet" and a Soviet musical cliché that celebrates the mechanical: Dancers mount and perform the functions of a metal press machine, putting a positive spin on the theme of the mechanized worker in *Metropolis* and *Modern Times* (1936) (figure 15).

Unlike Hollywood musicals, which mask the labor involved in the

Figure 15. *Dancer in the Dark.*
"Cvalda": celebrating the mechanical.

production of entertainment, Selma's song-and-dance sequences are often *about* work and expose their apparatus—the rough cuts, arbitrary shots, and visible editing of consumer-level digital cameras—in what finally resembles montage. "Cvalda" alludes to Eisenstein who wrote in 1924 of "revealing the machine's soul" and introducing "creative joy" into mechanical labor (42) as Selma envisions a humanized, intersubjective workspace, a factory that dances and sings. Selma's fantasies ultimately merge communist kitsch and Eisensteinian didactic aesthetics with land-scapes and icons associated with the American Dream. The showpiece "I've Seen It All" expresses Selma's resignation to blindness and refusal of desire. This proletarian utopia, in which laborers march with tools of their trades on flatbed railway cars as rural couples dance balletically over rolling hills, recalls American Depression-era films and 1950s–60s musicals like *Seven Brides for Seven Brothers* (1954) but draws equally on Soviet-era farm musicals. While the musical sequences take on a saturated faux-Technicolor hue, they also sustain the un-Hollywood earth colors of the film as a whole. Even the color enhancement remains embedded in social reality. In contrast to Hollywood dreams of individual fulfillment and romantic love, Selma sings of common pleasures and the "new world" future generations will see.

Selma's music reflects her geopolitical situation, her songs envision-ing what the American Dream would be were it more forgiving, just, provident—more "socialist" in an idealized sense. In "I've Seen It All," this is a subjectless proletarian heaven Selma chooses over the nuclear family Jeff offers. In "107 Steps," Selma lies down with inmates on death row, breaking down racial, territorial, and legal borders, releasing them from bondage. "I used to be a communist," Trier reminds us on the DVD commentary: "I think it is beautiful to dance around the machines. That is what we were taught," adding a half-joking aside that he and Peter Aalbæk understood the importance of "control over the apparatus of production" (connecting the scene with Dogme's Vertov-quoting manifesto and anti-Hollywood aesthetic). As a blend of European with Hollywood traditions, Selma's "musical" within the diegesis is both an idealized multicultural space and a challenge to the view of Hollywood genres as definitive or, considering her idolization of Oldrich Novy, who was in the first musical she ever saw, "original." The film lends Selma's fantasies European resonance to demonstrate that alternatives to the Hollywood tradition—and utopias other than the American Dream—did and still exist. And if one wants to find a critique of Hollywood's entertainment hegemony whose other side plays a dark vision of capitalism, one may.

Trier observes that the film is "about musicals in the sense that [the musical] comes out of the film"—much as *The Idiots* is about the performance it exemplifies (Filmmaker commentary). Similarly Selma's fantasies have a performative function. She "us[es] these fantasies to change perspective," to view "her own reality" in an enhanced form (Trier, qtd. in Kehr). As Trier's films are controlled environments that enable him to survive, Selma's enhanced perspectives enable her—to complete the night shift, to get the money to the hospital, to endure the trial, to make all 107 steps to her death. Finally the film echoes Joe Hill, whose final words urge his supporters not to "waste time in mourning" but to "organize" (Zinn 335); Selma sings defiantly of a present that continues in its impact on her audience.

Two of Selma's last three songs, sung without orchestration in the presence of a diegetic audience, can be identified neither strictly as fantasy nor reality but somewhere in between. In the first, as she awaits a stay of execution, an empathetic guard (Siobhan Fallon) finds her cue in sounds from a vent, enabling her to sing "My Favorite Things" as the room becomes bathed in color, signaling her changed perspective—in two senses. She is now completely blind, living in her visual imaginary, but the shift into heightened reality culminates in her temporary stay of execution. And in her (final) "Next to Last Song" (in reference to her ritual of leaving before the finale so that the music never ends), even the sound cues she uses to generate music/fantasy are absent. When, at her execution, Cathy hands her Gene's glasses, the sign that he no longer needs them and her vision has come to fruition in his sight, she finds the song completely within herself. She sings, faltering, then gathering strength: "this isn't the last song—there're no violins," it can't be the last song as "no one takes a spin" (figure 16). When the song and her life are truncated, the film simultaneously contradicts and supports her assertion. It is indeed her last song but she has escaped before its end, and the film's final performative gesture, "New World," which Björk sings over the end credits, vindicates it with an ecstatic evocation of "a new world to see."

"New World" notwithstanding, the truly unnerving thing about the hanging scene is that for a moment Selma's musical utopia and the real world have coincided. Its witnesses, her diegetic audience, give out distressingly mixed signals. What do they see and hear? Is she actually singing? If so, this is her only song (other than "My Favorite Things") with a "real" audience, making us aware of our role throughout as willing (or unwilling) observers. Adding to the impact, Selma cannot be distinguished from Björk, as the scene has been described by cast and crew members as "real" trauma and judged both as award-worthy acting and as completely unprofessional. Was it even a performance? As in the most disturbing scenes in *The Idiots,* the borders between real-

Figure 16. *Dancer in the Dark.* Björk, "Next to Last Song."

ity and simulation, performance and being, masochistic empathy and sadistic voyeurism collapse. We become witless witnesses of *someone's* real trauma, and the film ends in agonizing rupture.

From a twenty-first century audience's perspective, Nicholas Rombes asks how "a musical about the death penalty by a Danish director who is, to say the least, ambivalent about the Hollywood tradition, [can] be considered anything other than ironic?" Irony, as Rombes reminds us, is produced within a context that includes not only the director and the actor but an audience's expectations, and for an audience educated in the poetics of irony, deconstruction, and self-referentiality, *Dancer in the Dark* cannot be read in any other way. Yet what is oddly powerful is the film's "refusal to acknowledge this," offering up Selma and her fantasies with a completely straight face ("Sincerity and Irony" 84–85). Like Eshelman's claims about "performative" cinema, Rombes's emphasize the way "new punk" films encourage audiences to identify with their protagonists within a context that acknowledges the risks of such identification. This context does not interfere with identification and even lends it a kind of necessity, a "relaxing of critique" that Rombes considers new punk cinema's "signatory gesture" ("Sincerity and Irony" 85).

As before, Trier manipulated audiences into feeling the cruelty of a senseless death as a way of provoking ethical discussion, relaxing critique to produce a traumatic effect that provoked outrage, confusion, and debate. But this time he went further, venturing into international politics. Vincent Paterson recalls how the Cannes critics' morning preview was severely polarized, with many Americans protesting a distorted representation of the U.S. justice system, where the open evening screening elicited weeping throughout the film's last third until Selma's body thudded through the trap, followed by silence until the credit sequence rolled, followed by a standing ovation and a heated discussion of the death penalty (Choreographer commentary). Intended or not, the emotional provocation made *Dancer in the Dark* a politically charged film.

The polarized response reflected American outrage at Trier's presumption in making a film set in United States without having visited it. Unlike other foreign filmmakers (Wenders, Herzog) who shot their "American" films on location and in an authentic cinematic "idiom," as Nataša Durovičová puts it, Trier presumed to address the United

States "from another environment" (Durovičová and Rosenbaum 144). Worse, like the communist sympathizer the prosecutor makes Selma out to be, he was an ungrateful "foreigner" profiting from the American Dream that he disparaged. Attempting "an idiom acceptable to a broader audience"—the American musical, familiar character types, and larger-than-life stars—Trier had delivered a sermon about the brutality of the death penalty (Durovičová and Rosenbaum 144). And if Jack Stevenson, summarizing the critical reactions, is correct, he failed. What offended most was Trier's indifference to realism or accuracy. *Breaking the Waves*'s Scottish setting seemed visually and linguistically authentic, whereas *Dancer in the Dark* was "riddled with a hodgepodge of inappropriate accents" and unconvincing settings (Stevenson, "Wave"). Yet as we have seen, Trier was less interested in producing an "authentic" representation than in creating an openly hybrid and transnational film, an imperfect fusion of genres (melodrama, musical, opera), aesthetic visions (his, Björk's, and Paterson's) and even gender identities—in "performing the feminine" through Björk. I would argue further that the film followed logically on the cultural politics of Dogme95, as his subsequent trilogy makes obvious. It represented a crucial stage in his effort to add a consciously European or "accented" perspective to the United States's presumption of monolingualism in an increasingly multilingual world, one that takes false umbrage under Hollywood's hegemony. Durovičová is spot on when she calls it

> an attempt to send a letter to America in its own language, to say something like "this is how you look to us from where we stand" . . . in an entertainment idiom. . . . what it had to say and how it was saying it can give us an insider's insight into a particular outsider's view of the US. That if one wanted to put up with its "broken Hollywood English," as it were, one could hear a kind of early warning, even one possible proleptic answer to that key post-9/11 question, "Why do they hate us so?" (Durovičová and Rosenbaum 144)

What Stevenson disparages as a "hodgepodge" of accents actually speaks volumes. In *Dogville*'s production notes, three years after the polarized response to *Dancer in the Dark,* Trier announced his intention of making a trilogy about America whose "broken Hollywood English" would be precisely the point.

(Up)staging the American Dream:
The USA Trilogy (Minus One)

As a recent Palme d'Or winner at a peak of international visibility that co-incided with the Bush years just before and after 9/11, Trier moved from the defensive to the offensive. Yet his replies to journalists' questions about the new trilogy were predictably paradoxical. Asked by Emma Bell if *Dogville* and *Manderlay* were "straightforwardly anti-American," he explained the films' "deeper conflicts" as personal, *Dogville* especially: "Being an immigrant or a refugee was very important in my family. My father and my mother both escaped to Sweden during the Second World War." As he also explained, the film reflected his response to the Danish 2001 elections in which a populist right-wing anti-immigrant party won 24 percent of the popular vote and forced compromise on the more tolerant center (Elsaesser 123). Then there was his repeated claim to be "60% American"—or 80 or 90 percent—making *Dogville* personal in another, highly politicized sense. "We are under the influence" of America, "a very bad influence," he added, the American entertainment industry having "standardized our culture in a most moronic fashion. Entering a country with troops is small change compared to the way we have allowed ourselves to be occupied" (Koster, May 23). Claiming to "know more about America from various media than the Americans did about Morocco when they made *Casablanca*" (Björkman, *Trier* 245), his desire to make a film set in the legendary territory of Rocky Mountains, gangsters, Elm Street, and Tom Sawyer should seem completely natural. At the same time, he slyly added, "Americans may benefit from [the film]. It'll give them an idea of how they're regarded from without" (Koster, May 23).

Like Kafka's blackly humorous *Amerika* and Brecht's early "American" dramas, the USA Trilogy was a strategic play in Trier's ongoing game of identity/cultural politics. "My mother was crazy for Brecht and dragged me to the theater to see his plays," he explained (Merin), and the "great revenge motif" in Brecht's "Pirate Jenny" (from *The Threepenny Opera,* 1928), had inspired the idea of "build[ing] up everything leading to the act of vengeance" (Björkman, *Trier* 144). Trier often refers to the period in which American influence dominated German popular music, fashion, and manners (Ruland 372) and the fledgling Marxist wrote five plays about America (before going there in 1941), exploiting in *The Rise and Fall of the City of Mahagonny* (1927–29) a ready-made Hollywoodized mythology of urban jungles, gangsters, and prostitutes. After reading Marx and Lenin, Brecht reflected America back to itself in increasingly conceptual and political plays such as *St. Joan of the Stockyards* (1927–29) and *The Seven Deadly Sins* (1933). Accused, as Trier would be, of ignorance of the country he was obsessed with yet had never visited, Brecht responded with the poem "Understanding," which ends with the assertion that "You understand me very well when I talk about America," the "best thing" about America being "That we understand it" ("The Impact of the Cities 1915–1928," 156). Similarly, in that "we" in the twenty-first century are all compulsory Americans, and much as he earlier used postwar Germany to comment on Europe in the late 1980s, Trier used the Depression-era United States as a "common language" for provoking dialogue about liberal democracy, capitalism, immigration, race, nation building, and globalization.

The (American) taboo against foreign criticism of America, remarked as early as volume II of Alexis de Tocqueville's *Democracy in America* (1: 275–77), was a special enticement. *Dogville* would be a European indictment of the self-righteousness that characterized the post-9/11 Bush administration's War on Terror against an "Axis of Evil." Exploding at Cannes in May 2003, two months after the U.S. invasion of Iraq, the controversy over *Dogville*'s alleged anti-Americanism anticipated a cycle of primarily American-made films that were sharply critical of U.S. foreign policy—with the uproar preceding Michael Moore's box-office-record-breaking documentary *Fahrenheit 9/11* by a year. Similarly in 2005, as even negative critics admitted, *Manderlay* brought issues to the surface that no mainstream American filmmaker had dared touch.

Dogville lacked the manifestos for which Trier had become notorious, instead unfolding from a perspective of Brechtian *Verfremdung* in which far-away period settings enabled audiences to analyze characters and issues dispassionately as part of a Marxist dialectic. The snarky title constituted fair warning of a shift from a "dogmatic" aesthetic to satire. With characters out of Steinbeck, Twain, and Anderson, the film's anachronistic/archetypal setting (a former Colorado mining town), Brecht-meets-*Our Town* stage design, condescendingly urbane narrator (John Hurt), captioned chapter divisions, and conspicuous deployment of music (from the somber strains of Pergolesi's *Stabat Mater* to the end-credit sequence featuring David Bowie's deliriously irreverent "Young Americans" over a montage of "sacred" Depression-era Farm Security Administration photographs, *Dogville* was its own manifesto. In contrast to the "patinated" style of the holocaust-haunted Europe Trilogy, the visual field was drastically simplified, projecting a lucid, two-dimensional surface. In this alienated cinema of transparency (developed with photographer Anthony Dod Mantle), the USA Trilogy effected the antithesis of Trier's earlier trilogies' goals of hypnosis and immersion.

Dogville's depthlessness also reflected a uniquely American shallowness, the composite result of its pragmatism, parochialism, and historical amnesia. As a nostalgic, sepia-toned representation of the Depression era, the mise-en-scène designated not the United States so much as a replica of the American imaginary constructed by the mass media. In such fashion, Knox Peden suggests, Trier announces his real subject as the globalization of American fantasy images of itself based in a mythical past and sustained by Hollywood. For Trier and anyone else in the Western hemisphere, reality is governed by a constellation of genre conventions, an understanding of which, as opposed to physical encounter with the world, is necessary for comprehending it, as Fredric Jameson has demonstrated (91). Eliminating distractions such as props and locations, Trier thus forces the audience to operate in an abstract realm of generic conventions and ideological critique. There he defamiliarizes and exposes the material foundations of American liberal democracy (Peden 119).

Dogville opens with an impossibly high overhead shot, literalizing Brechtian distanciation. A grid of lights and fixed digital cameras supplemented by a crane-mounted high-definition Sony CineAlta reveals a cavernous 240-by-75-foot soundstage on which the town is laid out like a chalk map. The shot projects an omniscient space; a godlike gaze penetrates invisible walls and roofs, serving several purposes. Like many of Trier's films, but in starkly conceptual terms, it presents identity as the subject's relation to a community, exposing the claustrophobia, petty jealousies, and hypocrisies of small-town life (figure 17). Further, as A. O. Scott comments, "everyone lives in a fundamental state of isolation, but no one is ever alone," and the citizens sustain a "repressive, willed innocence" that speaks of Foucauldian regulation.

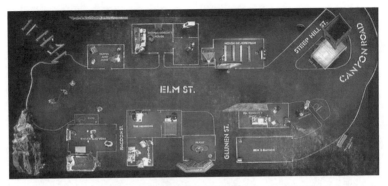

Figure 17. *Dogville.* |

The lack of cinematic verisimilitude makes active viewing, or reading, necessary, turning cinema into a "literary" experience. After twenty minutes, this lack intensifies engagement with the characters, as Brechtian distanciation is counterpointed by the contrasting principle of Dogme-style immersion, and the erratic shooting and editing keeps the audience off guard. With an HDW-F900 CineAlta mounted on his shoulders via a custom-made Steadicam rig, Trier was able to sustain the intimacy and emotional intensity of the Gold Heart films, with the occasional uncanny zoom out to reveal the town without walls that is perhaps the film's principle character.

While developing *Dogville*'s Brechtian mise-en-scène, Trier was simultaneously at work on epic theater's antithesis, the production of Wagner's *Ring* for which he had proposed another minimalist principle of stage design with a drastically reduced visual field, a variation on "theatre noir" he called "enriched darkness." With an elaborate system of spotlights that would selectively limit vision (as in cinema) and "control the way the set and the world grew and evolved in the minds of the audience" (Trier, "Deed"), it resembled *Dogville*'s restriction of attention by filming in extreme close-ups against a nearly blank set.[8] The black floor was a counterstatement to The *Lord of the Rings* (2001), which had shown that "we can now present any fantasy on computers," he explained: "I thought there must be another way of doing this—because I truly believe a dragon is more frightening if you don't see it. Which is why most horror films are made in darkness, right?" (Merin). So as often as not *Dogville* employed Brecht's anti-illusionist techniques for *anti*-Brechtian purposes. Imposed on provocative material performed at close range, they created a profoundly claustrophobic effect, repressing emotion and building tension to a point at which they served, as Robert Sinnerbrink notes, to release precisely the sort of affect Brecht forbade, and produce a whopping Götterdämmerung of an ending.

Like *Dancer in the Dark* only more so, *Dogville* was a calculated extension/reversal of techniques, characters, and themes from Trier's previous career including unabashed theatrical and literary derivations. The influence of filmed theater, especially Trevor Nunn's production of *Nicholas Nickleby* and Kubrick's *Barry Lyndon,* adapted from classic Victorian novels by Charles Dickens and William Makepeace Thackeray, respectively, made *Dogville* the most literary and theatrical of his films so far, with defenders arguing that as in Thornton Wilder's *Our Town,* the lack of sets lent allegorical resonance. But the most dramatic move was the gameboard-like mise-en-scène. Calling its visual world something between film, theater, and video game, Mantle recalls how during the writing process he played Lars's Game Boy and "it was *Silent Hill,* which incidentally has a[n] Elm Street in the middle of the game" (Ogden). At a Cannes 2003 press conference, Trier described *Dogville's* narrative principle as "the same as you see in electronic games. Everything means something to the story even if you don't see it at once" ("Meeting").

It is then damningly self-reflexive when, early in chapter 2, when the town's self-appointed "philosopher"/author Tom Edison, Jr. (Paul Bettany), proposes that Grace offer something "quid pro quo" in exchange for the town's hospitality and she observes, "You make it sound like we're playing a game." "It is. We are," he replies. Edison is a negative representation of the "godlike" gamer's perspective who is manipulating or "playing" Grace, and she is his avatar in two senses, the character representing the player and an embodiment of a philosophical principle (the gift from God, Christian grace-as-infinite compassion). In another closely related metaphor, the perspective created by the opening crane shot suggests a giant petri dish (Peden 119), and *Dogville* is another Trier film that doubles as a social experiment. We are reminded that America was born as an experiment that Edison, named for the prototypical American scientist, inventor, and pragmatist, embodies. This Edison's experiment/game/novel, however, is loaded with risks—social, economic, and personal—that underlie a host/guest, gift/recipient relationship, and the film becomes a lesson in the economy of desire and the sadomasochistic relations of power.

The socioeconomic meaning of Grace's presence is underscored in the beginning. Foregrounded by Tom's overseer's role, the narrative ("As told in nine chapters and a prologue") assumes a repetitive, dialectical inevitability. Title cards foretell events and underline their import. In chapter 1, "In which Tom hears gunfire and meets Grace" fleeing from gangsters, he finds the specimen/catalyst/"illustration" for what turns out to be an ethical test of the town, whose problem he conceives as "acceptance." Convincing them to give Grace two weeks to prove her worth, he proposes a reciprocal relationship in which she will offer services—from physical labor to caregiving to companionship—in exchange for sanctuary. For these downtrodden people, Grace is a risk, a burden, and a redundancy. Her services are luxuries—things (Tom explains) "that you'd like done, but that you don't think necessary" such as weeding Ma Ginger's (Lauren Bacall's) wild gooseberry bushes and cleaning house for the black "cleaning lady" Olivia (Cleo King) who works for better-off people in the next town, or teaching Vera's homeschooled children—but once provided are expected. Grace's acceptance into the community at the film's midpoint, marked by the Fourth of July celebration in which she is honored (via "America the Beautiful" as the "grace" of God "shed" on the community), is the film's turning point, whence the narrative inverts into a Marxist parable that might have been derived from part III of *Capital,* volume I.

On the most obvious level, Grace is a refugee whose host exploits and ostracizes her while making her increasingly dependent. As the luxuries she offers become necessities, the class gap is widened, especially in chapter 5 after "Wanted" signs appear proclaiming Grace's illegal status and doubling the ante. As reimbursement for her employers' "risk," she is required to work twice as long with lower wages. When her "unnecessary" work becomes indispensable, she develops into a correspondingly greater liability. The surplus of services and "goods" overstimulates Dogville's subsistence economy and is devalued into an infinitely exploitable commodity. "[P]eople are the same all over, greedy as animals," Chuck grumbles in what proves to be a spot-on prediction: "Feed 'em enough, and they'll eat till their bellies burst." Rather than mitigating hunger, Grace's "gift" stimulates greed, lust, and systematized rape and leads to a violent end.

In a closely related subtext, she appears as the proverbial "gift from God"—a stranger whose generosity evokes the town's better instincts—and devolves into a walking illustration of the poisonous nature of gift giving. Playing off German for *gift* (which means poison), Jacques Derrida concludes that the very structure and possibility of the gift annuls it: A gift is a gift only when there is no recognition of it as such on either side (12).[9] Gifting is especially problematic in capitalist economies founded on self-interest, competition, and payback as Trier illustrates when Christian "grace" is reconciled with the logic of commodity exchange. Dogville's generosity as host is loaded with clauses; Grace's compassion is even more so in being based in privilege and moral superiority, and her ideology of bestowing and forgiving especially disrupts the town's customary relations of power, creating a sadomasochistic and potentially explosive dynamic.

Dogville refers not merely to a system of domination but, as Sinnerbrink observes, to "an underlying economy of desire" sustaining capitalist democracy's inequality and exploitation, concealing its violence "under the masks of nature and morality." At midpoint, this theme is subtly introduced when Tom confesses a feeling for Grace he can define only in terms of its difference from his physical attraction to Liz Henson (Chloë Sevigny). When coerced by power from outside (the lawmen in collusion with the gangsters), Tom's and Dogville's desire degenerates into lust that increases with the town's sense of its power over Grace. Encouraged by her attention to his apple orchard, Chuck (Stellan Skarsgård) makes a pass, roaring, "I want you to respect me" as he threatens blackmail, and Grace responds, "You've been alone for so long up here. . . . I should ask you for forgiveness." This moment teeters on the edge of absurdity, as John Hulsey comments: Grace's empathy seems to have "pushed her toward total self-abnegation," "shout[ing] that Grace will become the town's scapegoat."

Thus in chapter 6 ("In which Dogville bares its teeth"), the narrator almost salivates as he informs that Grace "dangled from her frail stalk like . . . an [Edenic] apple so swollen that the juice almost ran." Grace's "punishment" officially begins in her dealings with the representative family headed by Chuck and Vera (Patricia Clarkson). The sadomasochistically precocious twelve-year-old Jason (Miles Purinton, another Lars surrogate) is the first to take advantage, blackmailing Grace into spanking him over her lap (and breaking Vera's ban on corporal punishment). Chuck, threatening to alert the police, rapes her as the camera zooms out in a shot that frames Skarsgård's thrusting buttocks as in the foreground the townspeople go about their business behind invisible walls. In omitting walls, Trier has stripped away the institutional and domestic facades that conceal the violence of the underlying political economy while evoking an image of Foucauldian surveillance, inverting the image of small-town hospitality into a vision of regulation and repression in which sexuality is converted into increasingly sadomasochistic forms.

Capitalizing on Tom's plan to smuggle her out of town, and as reparation for his "risk," Ben (Zeljko Ivanek) rapes Grace in the bed of his truck (with a transparent canvas cover simultaneously revealing/concealing the act) and returns the runaway to Dogville where—in a grotesque, medieval-looking arrangement—she is attached by an iron collar and a bell to a flywheel she drags from house to house as she performs her chores. By chapter 8, she is raped routinely in her bed by Dogville's male citizens, her status as "gift" devolving to exploited laborer to slave to slave whore, as the town's women look away or demand compensations of their own. The increasing sadomasochism is rationalized by the citizens through an elaborate and didactically reiterated system of reparations that go back to the "game" of quid pro quo. (In chapter 7, in retaliation for Jason's spanking, Chuck's "seduction," and fabricated damage to her seven children, Vera smashes the seven Hummel figurines to which Grace has devoted her wages.)

On a more obviously political level, Grace's fate exposes the sadomasochistic logic of the Ideological State Apparatus, enhanced through hegemonic discipline and staged in the oppressive, panoptical transparency of the mise-en-scène in which everyone is visible to everyone else (Goss 156). The carceral state is represented by the police (Goss 155–6) and ultimately by the gangsters, who pressure the police to exact reparations from Dogville's citizens, who in turn exact reparations from Grace. References to the noise of a prison under construction nearby refer to a trend beginning in the 1930s in which the prison industry exploited a ready workforce in impoverished areas (Goss 156) and reinforce an image of Dogville/America as prison and/or as criminal. Otherwise the state as civic body has fused with the church; the "mission house" is the center of civic life, having been converted into a town hall where Tom, posing as intellectually and morally superior overseer, catechizes the assembly on ethics, democracy, and political economy, suggesting the assimilation of the state's governing functions under a hegemonic moral imperative (figure 18). Along similar lines, the film's heavy religious allegory masks (and sardonically marks) Dogville's *lack* of religious institutions separate from the state. Christianity is omnipresent, "mingle[d] with all the habits of the nation and all the feelings of patriotism, whence it derives a peculiar force," as Tocqueville once put the issue, becoming an "established and irresistible fact" accepted "without inquiry" within the pragmatics of the American way of life (1: 5–6). Thus, it is hardly a coincidence that at five o'clock in the afternoon, as so often remarked by Jack McKay (Ben Gazzara), the mission house spire points its shadow at "the 'O' for 'Open' in the sign in the window" of Ma Ginger's store (which, as Tom notes, is "expensive" and "exploit[s] the fact that nobody leaves town").

Tocqueville hoped Christianity would check the self-interest inherent in American democracy, but Grace's Christian selflessness stimulates unregulated exploitation. In Brecht's *St. Joan of the Stockyards* (1928), another probable source, a young Salvation Army lieutenant's campaign to bring Christian values to a Depression-era Chicago meatpacking plant results in her conversion into the corrupt boss's tool and mouthpiece. Grace's practice of "grace" is similarly incompatible (or too

Figure 18. *Dogville*. Paul Bettany catechizing
Dogville's citizens.

compatible) with capitalism; she contributes to a culture of hypocrisy and *ressentiment,* Nietzsche's term in *Genealogy of Morals* (1887) and *The Antichrist* (1895) for the pious arrogance inherent (and repressed) in the practice of Christian submission—and whose other side is vengeance in the name of justice. In fact, the selflessness Grace brings to her father's understanding of justice makes it more destructive than his openly self-interested pragmatism, as the film's conclusion, containing the full force of her ressentiment, reveals.

After an exhausting 150 minutes, the audience shares Dogville's nervous anticipation of the action promised by the gangsters' "long-awaited visit"—or at the very least a go-for-broke performance by Kidman. What they/we desire (as IMDb user comments reveal) is payback—poetic justice violently played out. What they/we get initially is more Brechtian discourse: a protracted (ten-minute) yet witty and riveting philosophical argument between Grace and the mob boss (James Caan), revealed as her father, and resumed mid-sentence after her abrupt departure a year ago. Asserting via Nietzsche that (Christian) forgiveness reeks of condescension (arrogance), he challenges his daughter to judge and enforce by assuming the power that is her due—in short, to make Dogville accountable for its actions according to the same standards she holds for herself. And when her unconditional mercy reverts to an equally unconditional "justice" based on Old Testament moral absolutes, the "new" Grace's idealism is more rigorous than ever. Deeming Dogville "not good enough" to salvage, she has its citizens gunned down and the town burned to the ground. Evoking, tongue-in-cheek, an aura of genocidal wrath and biblical inevitability, the scene pretends to be no less than Armageddon, a blood bath amid the flames of hell. It is an equally biblical moment when the dog Moses, spared by Grace, materializes and charges from his chalk outline, snapping in savage fury at the screen as Mosaic Law made flesh.

Moses's alarming incarnation announced a new Trier: a new heroine, a new trilogy, and a newly cynical and politicized perspective. As he told Ole Koster at Cannes 2003, his recent "experiments on [*sic*] emotion" had been merely "interesting" whereas the "sarcastic" mode *Dogville* had unleashed was much more than that; it was "very much me" (May 20, 2003). Recapitulating the trajectories of all three Gold Heart narratives only to reverse them in its stunning conclusion, *Dogville* may be read reflexively as a jaundiced travesty of Trier's previous oeuvre, one that pronounces Bess, Karen, and Selma foolish and "arrogant" in their martyrdom. A metaphorical immigrant who allows herself to be exploited, Grace is framed and punished, like Selma, for "crimes" of which she is innocent. Like Karen, she sacrifices her dignity for the sake of her (undeserving) adoptive community. Most of all, Kidman's Grace offers a sardonic corrective to *Breaking the Waves*. Where Bess's all-transcending love is associated with music and (missing) church bells, Grace is regulated by the mission house bell, which the film associates with the law as it warns of approaching police, proclaims votes, spaces out her shifts, mocks her sexual commodification, and marks her subjugation. Finally, *Dogville* reverses Bess's apotheosis-via-bells with the deus ex machina of the Big Man and perverse Father God. The religious allegory reinvested with sincerity in *Breaking the Waves* is deployed in *Dogville* with the equally didactic and subversive aim of satire, representing the final word on Sade's *Justine*. Grace enters the town seeking sanctuary, is systematically exploited, enslaved, raped, tortured, and subsequently punished for prostitution, escaping custody, and theft, becoming Tom's/Trier's perfect "illustration" for his sadomasochistic exemplum about virtue's failure.

Finally Trier travesties himself in Edison, Jr., his surrogate whose presumption to "philosophical" knowledge and a scientific gaze puts him in a position of power that is suspect from the beginning. Edison's name raises the specter of the father of cinema or, more specifically, the inventor of its apparatus and early entertainment film genres. As Trier reputedly uses his actresses (including Kidman), Edison uses Grace and Dogville for his experimental novel, implicating the Trier who plays Kidman's Hollywood superstar status against her richly nuanced performance as a victim. Introduced in an elegant, fox-fur-collared, full-length coat, the statuesque actress, fresh from her 2002 Academy Award, conveyed a privilege, beauty, and gravitas that transcended her role and provided its own *Verfremdungseffekt*. In conversation with P. T. Anderson, Trier stressed the "inhuman" mystique she brought to the role, describing her as "a more human character and a less human actress" than his previous heroines. The challenge was "to take this kind of size, and force it to break a little bit" and also "to take [Kidman's] ability and her professionalism and her willingness to work, which are all very positive things, and to try to break it up a little bit for the sake of the product" ("Cigarettes"). In calling Grace a "gift," it seems, the narrator speaks not only for Edison but for Trier about Kidman who worked for virtually nothing (in contrast to her usual fee) in exchange for Trier's acting "lessons" (figure 19).

In the concluding revelation, a final self-reflexive gesture on Trier's part, however, the film is exposed as something entirely different from what it seemed. Dogville (including Tom and, by implication Trier, the manipulative "player" he stands in for) is revealed to have been Grace's experiment in a test of the limits of Christian mercy (grace) that has miserably failed. Moreover, she has concealed not only her identity but her real purpose and the power at her disposal as in the final sequence between Grace and her father, the Big Man, we find ourselves in another narrative, another genre, another game entirely.

In terms of narrative strategy as established by conventional expectations, Grace has concealed her originating genre. With an ironic flourish, Trier's concluding chapter reverts from a Depression-era drama with resonances from The Grapes of Wrath, as Wim Staat has noted, into a variation on the American gangster film's theme of retributive violence. (The ending is a minimalist stylization of a Hollywood-scale bloodbath, with gangsters caricatured in comic-book style silhouettes and machine guns flashing jagged white light against a sanguine background dominated by a blood-red moon.) The gangster film provides the formula for Grace's motivation; she poses as a 1930s-era moll who undergoes a change of heart. But when the boss (Caan) is revealed as Grace's

Figure 19. *Dogville*. Paul Bettany and Nicole Kidman.

father, we fast-forward to *The Godfather* (1972, in which Caan played the ruthless Sonny Corleone) with Grace in the role of the boss's child returning to the gangster family (Staat 90). Above all, in the figure of the Big Man, whom Grace accuses of "plunder[ing] as if it were [his] God-given right," Trier alludes to Brecht's use of gangsters as metaphors for capitalism with its gloves off. As a final Brechtian device, the gangsters' return announces *Dogville*'s shift from the Gold Heart Trilogy's ethical concerns to the political, and in her final gesture, the newly armed and judgmental Grace becomes, among other probabilities, a caricature of the Bush administration's self-righteous militancy driven by misplaced idealism. In the production notes, Trier comments: "If you are strong, you also have to be just and good, and that's not something you see in America at all. I don't think that Americans are more evil than others but then again, I don't see them as less evil than the bandit states Mr. Bush has been talking so much about. . . . What can I say about America? Power corrupts."

In cathartic effect, *Dogville*'s conclusion topped Trier's previous provocations, rewarding and offending in equal measure. IMDb users were far more positive than critics, giving it a 7.9 (out of 10) ranking by 2009. Many loved or hated it as an art film variation on the rape-revenge genre, assuming that Grace's action simply reflected Trier's judgment of Dogville and small-town America. Advancing a similar interpretation in one of the more vitriolic mainstream reviews, *Variety*'s Todd McCarthy found that Trier had "judged America, found it wanting and therefore deserving of immediate annihilation," calling the identification between *Dogville* and the United States "total and unambiguous": Trier had "indict[ed] as being unfit to inhabit the earth a country that has surely attracted, and given opportunity to, more people onto its shores than any other in the history of the world."

In 2004, sounding oddly like McCarthy in a discursive context that could not have been more different, philosopher Jacques Rancière chose *Dogville* to exemplify what he terms an "ethical turn" in post-9/11 Western culture. Distinguished from a political perspective, in which each side of an ideological conflict is considered human and historically contingent, an "ethical" stance applies absolute moral standards and was epitomized by Bush's "war on terror" as an invocation of "infinite justice" on countries representing an "axis of evil" (Rancière 3). Grace thus deems Dogville "not good enough" to exist, a place the world would be better off without. Like Rancière, McCarthy overlooked the film's anti-illusionist and self-reflexive elements to take the conclusion at face value, equating Grace's judgment with Trier's. Neither considered the possibility that Bowie's "Young Americans" might include (or even refer *primarily* to) Grace.

As Trier told P. T. Anderson, when he selected the song—having rejected "Pirate Jenny" as "too obvious"—he thought the refrain "she wants the young American" said "she *was* the young American" ("Interview"; *italics mine*). Later he explained choosing the song because he "like[ed] this idea of America being very young"—"It's a very young country, historically, of course" (Thompson). On one hand, this "youth" suggests what Scott calls "willed innocence," and Mick LaSalle rightly notes how Trier "elucidates a peculiarly American strain of human pathology" in which "people with absolute, unshakable faith in their own rectitude" use it as "a license to commit grossly immoral acts." But it is Grace who epitomizes the "youthfully" fervent naïveté of the American character as embracing the binary extremes of self-sacrifice and "infinite justice." Her extremism characterizes American domestic and foreign policy, over the Bush years especially, as an alternation of grace with the messianic use of power. Grace's faith in her rightness is presented as equally if not more characteristically "American" (in the post-9/11 sense) than her initial pretense of grace as egalitarian tolerance. In its dialectic of ("arrogant") grace with the violence born out of ressentiment, the one making the other inevitable, the film ends not in synthesis but rupture, as Sinnerbrink points out, thus articulating the "deadlocks" of contemporary liberal democracy that are often "resolved" through violence.

Finally, Grace's retaliation represented a sweeping, genocidal enactment of the death penalty Trier had taken on in *Dancer in the Dark*, calling capital punishment "a sign of weakness in the state" because "revenge is a big part of it": "I don't think it will make a better world" (Filmmaker commentary). He would extend this critique in his screenplay *Dear Wendy* (2005) in which a group of antique gun fetishists (with "pacifist" principles) die in an orgasmic Western-style town-square shootout, parodying the Hollywood ending the audience is led to expect. This assessment of Grace's "justice" would be made unequivocal in *Manderlay*, where, backed by the gangsters' arsenal, she engages disastrously in what critics have compared to American liberal "do-gooderism" and neoconservative nation building alike. Far from representing an "ethical turn" to unilateral and "infinite justice" of the sort practiced by the Bush administration, *Dogville* was a satire *of* it. Most importantly, Sinnerbrink notes, *Dogville* used alienation effects to achieve and intensify the affect (ranging from shock, disbelief, and dismay to rage and disgust) that Brecht (and Trier's parents) had forbidden—in the interest of cultural enlightenment.

Rather than a simple Marxist critique, *Dogville* functions more like "a Nietzschean genealogy of morals," Sinnerbrink adds, a politically ambivalent unmasking or laying bare, through everything from stage design to affect, of the sadomasochistic power relations underlying the order of things, moral, social, and political. A similar strategy informed his mockery of Bush's mission in Iraq at Cannes 2005, where Trier announced his own campaign to "Liberate America," suggesting (with Althusser) that Americans were trapped in an ideology that tells them they are free—and moreover that this condition had become globally hegemonic. Trier's vision of the Bush years has been prescient. Synchronicity if nothing else ensured that these allegorical fantasies set during the Depression and derived from John Steinbeck, Dorothea Lange, Jacob Holdt, and Brecht would comment uncannily on the events of the next century as they were taking shape.

The accusations of anti-Americanism were leveled especially at the end credit sequence of archival U.S. Farm Security Administration photographs that McCarthy, for example, described as "emphatically vulgar" and "pointedly grim and grisly." A. O. Scott found the "sudden, gear-grinding shift" from allegory (from a film about any small town) to documentary the problem, accentuating a "tension between the universal and the specific" that made *Dogville* both fascinating and disturbing ("*Dogville*"). Worse, many such as Michael O'Sullivan concluded that Trier had used these photographs to indict the American *people.* Finally, as Holger Römers argued, Trier had displaced images that had lent dignity to the plight of impoverished rural people during the Depression and repositioned them in a grotesque context, producing something like the "surrealist montages" of *Wisconsin Death Trip* (1973).

But as *Manderlay* would make obvious, the end credit sequence was merely historical—if thinking forward in the direction of contemporary events. It insisted that events like those in *Dogville* had happened at several historical periods and nailed down associations that might be made between the film's ending and current American domestic and foreign policy. Thus a photograph accompanied Bowie's snide reference to "your President Nixon" and led directly into images from the civil rights era courtesy of Jacob Holdt's *American Pictures: A Personal Journey through the American Underclass* (1985), providing a bridge to *Manderlay,* whose end credits would begin where *Dogville's* left off, with far more devastating and specific references. Resonating uncannily with the harsh truths uncovered by Hurricane Katrina, capped with pictures of the World Trade Center towers and Bush at prayer, they revealed drug-infested ghettos, lynchings, Ku Klux Klan cross burnings, and hostile, gun-toting grannies.

Manderlay opens with a dazzling white screen that, zooming out, reveals the black outlines of a U.S. map and beetle-sized automobiles creeping over state lines, heading into the Deep South. In this fashion, Trier confirmed that *Dogville* had indeed been "about" America. More importantly, it informed that the trilogy would take a yet more geographically and historically specific turn. It is Alabama in 1933, and Grace (now Bryce Dallas Howard) and her father (now Willem Dafoe) stumble upon a cotton plantation practicing slavery seventy years after the Emancipation Proclamation. Expecting to be hailed as liberators— and against her father's expected protests (echoing the Southern states' rights mantra "It's a local matter")—she and her gunsels turn the community upside down and force "freedom" in the form of the unfamiliar system of democracy on the people (figure 20), with results that by 2005 were painfully predictable. Worse, her attempts to reverse these inherited abuses ultimately reinstate them.

From Trier's point of view, taking on the American equivalent of the Holocaust that had shaped his Europe Trilogy was merely logical, but the film disappointed critics who had found *Dogville* a masterpiece for its "universality" and vindicated others who had disparaged it as "anti-American." When read as a lesson about race, *Manderlay* was especially uncomfortable viewing, coming across as an insulting "history lesson" situated in relation to three centuries. It argued that slavery had been reinstated throughout the Reconstruction Era and its aftermath and continued in the present. Worse, it represented an outsider's perspec-

Figure 20. *Manderlay.* Bryce Dallas Howard enforcing democracy.

tive, that of a white male citizen of a Scandinavian welfare state who had still not visited the United States.

Others vilified or (often) championed the film as an allegory about present-day American interventionism and the invasion of Iraq (e.g., Tobias, Harsin), a reading encouraged by Trier's own statements and by posters and DVD covers flaunting the caption "Liberation, whether they want it or not!" Calling it "a return to our past that serves as a portrait of our present," Adam Balz praised its condemnation of "the America that presumes and meddles without second thought," and Trier conceded in November 2005 that "the parallels to Iraq are just begging to be drawn": "you can't simply do away with the old rules, introduce new ones and believe that it's all going to work. Moral traditions have to develop from within society" (Nicodemus). Since then, Trier has become slippery about making such connections, stressing that the script was written before the invasion. Regardless of intentions, Trier's vision of the history of U.S. race relations was bound to reflect his sense of the world's growing disillusionment with Bush-era diplomacy. Hedging, he told Jes Stein Pedersen of Danmarks Radio (DR2), "Because I work with clichés, the film is easy to transfer to other conflicts. . . . But it's a recurring situation."

The clichés created other issues. Long before the film opened, *Manderlay* encountered resistance. Casting was initially a struggle. African American actors shunned the film except for Danny Glover who, after initially turning it down, took the pivotal role of Wilhelm. Otherwise (other than French actor Isaach De Bankolé as Timothy), the black members of the cast were drawn from the British stage. As several critics remarked, the film blamed blacks as well as whites, teetering on the edge of reproducing the stereotypes it exposed and, as Jayson Harsin put it, might be construed by the unaware as "the most racist film since *Birth of a Nation*"—an allusion Trier no doubt had in mind.

The film's formal characteristics contributed to the antagonism. With its Brechtian mise-en-scène continued from *Dogville*, *Manderlay* had few formal innovations to flaunt and, at forty minutes shorter, had the discursive tone, sharp edges, and crude contrasts of a political cartoon. Trier was accused of "lecturing" (Kun) in a scolding professorial tone that his stance as a white outsider exacerbated. And where *Dogville*'s modulated sepia softened Brechtian didacticism with nostalgia, *Manderlay*'s starker (black and white) mise en scène, enhanced by Mantle's theatrical backlighting against a black scrim, complemented the film's running commentary on race, highlighting the black actors' positions, body language, and features—for example, casting long shadows as they trail bags of seed or cotton along invisible rows. The chiaroscuro aesthetic extends to a motif of texts, numbers, marks, and lashes that leads to the final revelations about the origins of "Mam's Law," which explains the ideology and operations of the plantation and whose centerpiece is a seven-category hierarchy designating where the characters stand at assembly under the mansion's balcony. Finally, in contrast to Dogville's rectangles, squares, and streets, each identified with a name and signifying private property, Manderlay (beyond the mansion dominating the bottom left) is circular, a point made by the donkey that plods around the central well. The film comes full circle as the newly freed slaves reinstate the former system that relieves them of responsibility for their abject state, and the unctuous house slave and elder Wilhelm confesses to having written Mam's Law. A devastating irony thus pervades the text's deep structure.

Among *Manderlay*'s more disconcerting surprises was its coolly sardonic and often comic tone. Where *Dogville*'s histrionics had distracted audiences from the intricacies of its political subtext, *Manderlay* holds its subject matter at an ironic distance, emotional high jinks are largely missing, and atrocities occur off-screen. But the most substantial departure from *Dogville* was the character of Grace, who had shrunken to fit the petulant gangster's daughter of that film's conclusion. When a schedule conflict made Kidman unavailable, Trier rewrote her around the much younger Bryce Dallas Howard, Hollywood director Ron Howard's daughter, whom he had spotted in the role of an angelic, blind seer in M. Night Shyamalan's allegorical thriller *The Village* (2004). Howard's Grace thus becomes a white, perky, and shallow All-American Girl stereotype who takes on the naive "Capra-corn" character of *Mr. Deeds Goes to Town* (1936) as well (Nochimson). With Lauren Bacall's cameo as the dying "Mam," Howard's performance sharpens Trier's ongoing satire on the Hollywoodized American Dream. Addressing the slaves in a discursive, rehearsed style, the new Grace exudes a schoolmarmish certainty and missionary zeal merely hinted at in *Dogville*'s conclusion, brilliantly embodying the rash "young" America of Europe's increasingly critical take on American interventionism. As he explained to Pedersen, "Her character behaves a bit cartoonishly," "jump[ing] directly from one film to the next. She doesn't evolve psychologically. She seems to take it rather lightly that she has just wiped out an entire town"—impishly adding, "But maybe that goes for the political leaders as well."

Manderlay's flat, Candide-like Grace signals Trier's return to a focus on (formerly male) idealists brought down by the power structures of which they are part. Epitomizing the blind arrogance the earlier Grace had masked, *Manderlay*'s protagonist repeats Leo Kessler's failed search for a context in which to "make the world a better place" and becomes Trier's most blatant caricature of America: "female" mercy backed by black-suited male power, democracy compelled by machine gun–wielding thugs. Characterized specifically as the liberal Northerner with a simplistic view of race relations, she is easily seduced by the film's *homme fatale*, Timothy, finds herself in over her head and manipulated unawares, her good intentions a catalyst for disaster. Her insistence to her father that she is "grown up now" underscores the threat represented by her certainty, providing another layer of irony.

As Bainbridge suggests, as a white liberal "social worker," the new Grace "unwittingly establishes another regime of power, reifying her position as that of 'the one who knows'" (*Cinema* 153). Her assumption of knowledge and mastery aligns her with Tom Edison, *Dogville*'s self-appointed social engineer, and ultimately with the plantation's former Mam, a position literalized in her vantage point throughout the film. This point is also emphasized by *Manderlay*'s frequently restricted point of view, manipulating Grace and the audience into skewed conclusions. At first, in contrast to *Dogville*'s transparent, gameboard-like set, *Manderlay* (although equally gamelike in other ways) is claustrophobic and shrouded in darkness, an enclave in which the practices of the past continue. The darkness also intensifies the sense in which Grace's "salvation army" represents an invasion. Striding through Manderlay's massive iron gates, their/our vision limited by a dramatic spotlight, surrounding and disarming the dying Mam, they are blind to the surrounding plantation, and the "late night deliberations" that go into dismantling and redrawing the community are conducted literally in the dark. *Manderlay*'s first overhead shot is not until scene 5, and Mantle notes in the DVD commentary that scene 16 is the first in which the whole plantation is revealed. Sound is similarly restricted (Trier and Mantle). Where *Dogville*'s "sounds that came from outside" encouraged the audience to imagine a landscape, *Manderlay* affected "a feeling of isolation: after all, Manderlay is a prison," Trier explained to Nicodemus. "All the sounds come only from inside."

In this context, Grace, armed with Mam's Law and assuming the omniscience of the overhead shot, gazes down on the freed slaves assembled on their marks, struggling to find clarity. Reinforced by the narrator, this "enlightened" perspective (identified with Trier's pleasure in visual mastery and games) also prompts her to raze the "Old Lady's Garden" to provide lumber and redistribute wealth while leaving the plantation vulnerable to dust storms. A similar motif emerges in Grace's short-sighted assessment of people. When Timothy accuses her of being uninterested in blacks as human beings, Grace retaliates by singling out Jim as artistic, only to discover she has confused him with his brother Jack. Her assessment, based on his features and body language, exposes its roots in racist nineteenth-century physiognomy and social Darwinism. In her final demoralization, her fundamental assumption that Mam's numbers refer to ideologically imposed stereotypes is reversed when Wilhelm reveals he wrote Mam's Law as a blueprint for survival in the "free" world.

For this premise, Trier drew on Danish socialist photographer Jacob Holdt, whose *American Pictures* had helped to shape the liberal European view of American race relations and poverty for more than twenty years. Holdt uncovered pockets of neo-slavery across the South (including "slave camps" often owned by corporations such as Minute Maid, Coca-Cola, Gulf, and Western) to indict American liberal democracy and unregulated free enterprise for creating huge economic and class disparities that sustained racial oppression.[10] Encapsulating Holdt's argument in its central metaphor and setting, *Manderlay* exposes the shortcomings of the conservative position that African Americans simply need to exercise freedoms granted by the Fourteenth Amendment. Writing the screenplay, Trier meditated on the meaning of *freedom* and decided the word was deceptive: "Maybe a slave who is subordinate to a man with a whip has more dignity than a slave who is held in check by economic forces. . . . In this world, it's your fault if you're black and poor, because you're free. Or at least what they call free" (Nicodemus). The film is therefore framed by the early "liberation" of Bert, whose body hangs from a tree outside Manderlay's gate in the concluding scene. It is punctuated by appearances of the predatory Dr. Hector (a memorable Zeljko Ivanek), who cheats blacks out of their money, returning 80 percent to their employers and keeping them dependent. Thus the end-credit photographs, which mirror *Dogville*'s and are identically accompanied by Bowie's "Young Americans," graphically illustrate the abuses of the post-Reconstruction: the rise of the Ku Klux Klan, debt peonage and the reemergence of Black Codes, the segregation of public facilities, and lynchings of African Americans. Targeting the liberal position that maintains that civil rights and education can equalize disparities, Trier indicts the American social welfare system that medicalizes and racializes African American poverty, sending in "stereotypically white, do-gooder social workers to rehabilitate poor African-Americans" (Harsin).

Following this paradigm, Grace attempts to teach the former slaves lessons in democracy, justice, and anger management. But democracy as Grace simplistically enforces it is a woefully inefficient, yet coercive and even vindictive, system. Without orders, work doesn't get done and planting deadlines go by unheeded. Once introduced, majority rule by vote determines everything including what time it is—finally causing Grace to miss, by fifteen minutes, an all-important meeting with her father. Instead of bringing real issues to the table, Manderlay's citizens vote about personal irritations such as Sammy's laughing at his own jokes. A dispute about the ownership of a rake is resolved by a vote that makes it Elisabeth's private property even though it must be shared collectively for the work to be done. When, during a period of scarcity, Old Wilma (Mona Hammond) steals food reserved for a dying child, all support the father's cry for her death. To prevent punishment from being performed as personal vengeance, Grace herself executes this woman with whom she has established a daughterly bond. When eventually, after these and other setbacks, Manderlay's economic experiment triumphs, the treasurer Timothy cannot resist the temptation of accumulating capital of his own and when Dr. Hector calls, steals the harvest money, plays the local stock market, and loses it.

Wilhelm's argument that neither Manderlay nor the world is "ready" for equality, echoing Booker T. Washington's accommodationist views, is supported by the ending in which the plantation reinstates slavery after the gangsters leave. Debunking all progressive readings, Trier leaves audiences with three equally negative alternatives: that of "the self-hating, frustrated liberal social worker, the accommodating African-American survivalist, [and] the conservative gangster-social Darwinist" (Harsin). As always, Trier exposes the problem in its depth and complexity, leaving solutions to the audience. In the narrator's final lines, having lost once again the struggle for independence from her cynical father, Grace lumps Manderlay with Dogville into the category of places the world would be better off without: "Manderlay had fossilized in a picture of this country that was far, far too negative. But 'not ready' to accept black people? You really could not say that. America had proffered its hand, discreetly perhaps, but if anybody refused to see a helping hand . . . he really only had himself to blame."

The film's clearest political point is that the "helping hand" of liberal individualism is anything but. A socialist like Holdt, Trier indicates a solution, if at all, in socialism's absence from this lineup, suggesting that in a context of unregulated capitalism, without the safety net that welfare-state socialism provides, pockets of abject poverty and slavery in its various contemporary forms will continue to exist under the radar until exposed, whether by activists or, as several critics pointed out in reference to the film, natural disasters such as Hurricane Katrina. "That's why I was not remotely surprised by what happened in New Orleans," Trier remarked to Nicodemus. "It was as if the storm had to come along to open the Americans' eyes. To show them the conditions in which the black population live."

In addition to Holdt, Trier returned to a yet more controversial source, "Happiness in Slavery," Jean Paulhan's critical introduction to Anne Desclos's (as Pauline Réage) *Story of O*, about an 1838 Barbados uprising in which some two hundred emancipated slaves confronted their former master with a list of grievances, begged to be taken back into bondage, and, when refused, massacred him and his family before returning to their customary habits (xxi). Much as "Pirate Jenny's Song" inspired *Dogville*'s ending, this anecdote provided *Manderlay*'s punchline: The film ends when Grace sends her gunsels away and the freed slaves revert to Mam's Law, forcing her to take on Mam's role.

But *Manderlay* departs from both Holdt's and Paulhan's perspectives, adding yet another turn of the screw, when it invokes (and subsequently revokes) Althusser's understanding of the subject's inculcation/interpellation by the Ideological State Apparatus (115–23) that *Dogville* dramatized in every frame: in the overhead shots of the town's citizens in their respective places (vis-à-vis the mission house) or the horizontal division of Grace's workday. Positioned like *Dogville*'s Tom Edison, *Manderlay*'s Grace analyzes the problem of slavery from the abstract height of "superior" knowledge literalized in her view from Mam's balcony while reading Mam's Law (figure 21). Following Althusserian logic, she assumes that "we made the Negroes what they are," and, consequently, that it is her white liberal responsibility "to right this great wrong." Wilhelm's revelation that *he* wrote Mam's Law exposes this as gross oversimplification and her eventual undoing, as her unwavering belief in it has blinded

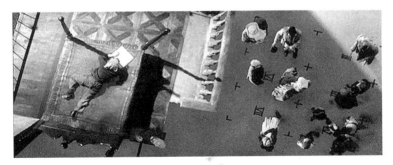

Figure 21. *Manderlay*. Bryce Dallas Howard
studying Mam's Law as the former slaves
assemble on their marks.

her to other, subtler forms and relations of power. *Manderlay* therefore supports Foucault's view in which power does not operate as a simple binary system (domination/oppression) but emanates from below and can take many diverse forms. Hegemony is negotiated and can even be productive, especially when manifested as resistance. Instead of the prescriptive "recipe for oppression and humiliation" Grace assumes it to be, Mam's Law is a metatext, a description of the discourses making up Manderlay's matrix of power relations. Harsin suggests along similar lines that *Manderlay* reflects scholarship by James C. Scott and others on "weapons of the weak" that are survival strategies in peasant societies. In the end, we find that Grace has been indoctrinating the slaves less than the slaves have been indoctrinating her—by using her power to manipulate her into a position where she is locked into their system. As her "liberator's" role leads incrementally to her enforcing their decisions and laws (such as capital punishment) against her will, she is groomed to serve as the new "Mam"—the old Mam now exposed as a figurehead and *their* slave.

Like *Dogville*, if not more so, *Manderlay* is metacinematic beginning with the name of the plantation, which alludes to the film's underlying mythologies and themes: especially Rudyard Kipling's colonialist orientalization of Burma in "On the Road to Mandalay," the doomed estate (Manderley) of Daphne du Maurier's Gothic romance *Rebecca* (1939), and Hitchcock's iconic film adaptation of 1940. Resonant of Scarlett O'Hara's Tara, Manderlay is a throwback, a trauma memory, and a haunting, an uncanny imprint in the cultural memory that will never be erased. But *Manderlay* has closest kinship with Richard Fleischer's *Mandingo* (1975), *Gone with the Wind*'s antithesis or parody, an explosive hybrid of exploitation, melodrama, and exposé of the economy of desire underlying slavery. ("Mandingo" refers to the African tribe that Trier translates into *Manderlay*'s "Munsi" mythology.)

The film's primary self-reflexive and thematic device, "Mam's Law," the tome that foregrounds the film's elements of performativity (and not incidentally recalls Trier's manifestos, rules, and limitations) is introduced by Mam on her deathbed as she pleads with Grace to burn it. Its core is a disturbingly familiar ranking of psychological types that, as Doughty (supported by studies such as David Bogle's *Blacks in American Film: Toms, Coons, Mulattos, Mammies and Bucks* [1988]) observes, are perpetuated by the film and television industry. Unveiling them from Grace's point of view, Hurt's narrator lingers on the word *nigger* as if relishing the taboo:

> Sammy was a group five, a "clownin' nigger." The formidable Victoria was, of course, a number four, a "hittin' nigger" . . . Wilma and Mark were "losin' niggers." Wilhelm was a two, a talkin' nigger. Flora was a weepin' nigger, et cetera, et cetera. There were "pleasin'" niggers and "crazy" niggers by the dozen. The final category, number one, "proudy niggers," consisted nowadays of Timothy as expected . . . and Elizabeth. No, . . . it said seven, not one. She was a "pleasin'" nigger also known as a "chameleon." A person of the kind who could transform herself into exactly the type the beholder wanted to see.

With stereotypes front and center, performed like blackface minstrel show, the film is contentious and reflexive. In *Counter-Racism*'s review of the film, Huggy Bear warns that "you know them already. Think of any other group of Negroes in a film":

> "Clownin Niggas": think Arnold from *Different Strokes*, JJ on *Good Times*, Rerun on *What's Happening!*, Richard Pryor in *The Toy*, Charles Barkley any time. "Hittin Niggas": Mister from *The Color Purple*, James Evans from *Good Times*, Andre Baptiste Sr. *Lord of War* or O-Dawg from *Menace II Society*. "Losin' Niggas"—Sams in *Lean on Me*, Booger in *He Got Game*, Halle Berry's obese child in *Monster's Ball*.

And so on. As Goss indignantly notes (whereas Huggy Bear gets the joke), these designations are derogatory (164)—with the questionable exception of "proudy" (encompassed by the overarching category of "losin'"). "Proud" Timothy, who is said to be an honest and upright "Munsi," is eventually exposed as a "pleasin'" (manipulative) "Mansi," cancelling out the film's sole positive example. And Wilhelm's "talkin' nigger" is profoundly ambiguous, suggesting qualities of leadership and intellect while finally underscoring his role as an Uncle Tom and Mam's Law's underhanded author.

A precursor that elicited a similarly mixed reception was Spike Lee's widely panned *Bamboozled* (2000), about a black television producer who, fed up with African American television stereotypes, creates a satirical variety show (set in an Alabama watermelon patch) in which black actors perform in blackface as characters such as "Mantan" and "Sleep 'n' Eat." When it becomes wildly successful with both industry professionals and audiences (who swallow it whole), everyone is bamboozled. Where Lee intended to indict black television comedies such as *The Jeffersons* and the postures of gangsta' rap, Grace indicts Manderlay's residents for performing the equivalent of blackface in the present day, having assimilated the postures, behaviors, and psychology of stereotypes handed down from slavery.

In a scene whose heavy handedness many critics disparaged, Grace punishes Mam's descendants by consigning them to hard labor and forcing them to wear blackface while serving and entertaining their former slaves. This convoluted variation on the minstrel show prepares us for Wilhelm's revelation that Mam's Law is a set of stage directions for an ironic blackface performance we have been watching half aware. Or as Leo Goldsmith suggests, *Manderlay* is Trier's variation on Genet's sardonic *The Blacks: A Clown Show* (1959) in which an all-black cast wear white greasepaint to play judges and queens. *Manderlay*'s masquerade of African American stereotypes (significantly by mostly non-American actors) denaturalizes and appropriates the dominant culture, subverting and utilizing it to undermine those in power, thus "mak[ing] over the terms of domination," as Judith Butler says of drag ball performance (348). This is far from saying that the "denaturalization" of race, any more than the denaturalization of gender implies liberation. In this artificially sustained enclave, these "slaves" defend themselves against the challenges of would-be scam artists like Dr. Hector, the Ku Klux Klan, lynch mobs, roving gangsters, and the horrors of ghetto life.

From the perspective of *Manderlay* as a game, a rather obvious one of masters and slaves, two characters are key avatars. A caricature familiar from Hollywood of the "quick-thinking, cunning African American," Timothy's "pleasin' nigger" descends from the trickster/rogue Zora Neale Hurston has traced back to West African oral literature. Through his appearance of weakness, he "manipulates and undermines figures of superiority" and empowers himself through their naïveté (Doughty 158), seducing Grace several times over—first through his "exotic accent" and proud defiance, then through his reversal into an inventive and courageous hero, and finally as he dominates her in a mock-African sexual ritual. Exposing her arrogance and naïveté, he subverts and destroys her regime, restores the status quo, and sends her packing. But if Timothy is the trickster in the most flamboyant senses, the subtler figure of Wilhelm operates as Trier's real surrogate. De Bankolé's/Timothy's seduction of Grace looms from the beginning, but Glover's "talkin' nigger" with the stoop and the hushed voice remains under the radar. His disclosure that he wrote Mam's Law reveals that all the "niggers" are in some sense "pleasin'" tricksters—in becoming "exactly the type that the beholder wants to see" as a means of gaining leverage.

Sustaining *Manderlay*'s hegemony/matrix is the sadomasochistic pleasure they take in their roles and moves, and it is no accident that one of Trier's two major sources was *Story of O*. Much as *Justine* underwrote *Breaking the Waves* and *Dogville, Manderlay* is inspired by Desclos's even more relentlessly sadomasochistic psychology. Victoria (Llewella Gideon), a "hittin' nigger," relishes maligning her subordinates and "discovering" a planted bottle of Rhenish wine under Timothy's saddle. Timothy relishes the pleasure of manipulating Grace into horsewhipping and "mastering" him, and as he spits her words ("You made us!") back at her at the film's conclusion, he exposes their true condescension.

Unsurprisingly, then, if to the chagrin of Nicodemus and others, what brings down Manderlay's experiment in democracy is "a hackneyed porn fantasy" in which a repressed white "Mam" is consensually raped by a black stud. That Trier foreshadows it in the film's first line, delivered offhandedly by Grace's chuckling father, suggests this scenario is anything but gratuitous: "Now, they will not admit it, but it's a fact, deep down inside, there isn't a woman alive who doesn't nurture these fantasies, whether they involve harems or being hunted through the jungle by torch-bearing natives. However much they go on and on about civilization and democracy, sexy it ain't." This opening volley precipitates Grace's move to disprove her father's thesis (by asserting her independence) and leads to her role as the film's central illustration of sadomasochistic psychology. In this way, Trier brings race and power politics into the same taboo areas he began to examine in *Breaking the Waves*.

Just as the fledgling community has equalized the races, established a functioning democracy and viable economy, and sent the troops home, he inserts the inevitable reversal and, with deliberate crudity, shifts the argument—this time to the level of desire—whence Manderlay's fragile balance of power collapses. As Grace's orientalized eroticization of Timothy (in a damning inversion of the white male gaze) becomes evident, Timothy responds by masquerading "Munsi" honor, "pleasin'" her to acquire authority and access to capital (the harvest money) but ultimately in the interest of sexual domination. There is even the hint that Grace's "liberation" of Manderlay in the first place had a gendered dimension inseparable from her will to power (beginning with her declaration of independence from the Oedipal father).

Accosted by Nicodemus for "mixing levels," Trier retorted that he believed it impossible "to separate the sexual and the political in the human consciousness," adding that "the desire for dominance and submission is part of our system of drives. I don't believe you can ignore these . . . if you are looking for a suitable way for people to live together. And you shouldn't forget the people in political power are sexual beings too. . . ." Confronted by Pedersen on the same issue, he argued that political theories are flawed by their refusal to acknowledge complex underlying "social and psychological facts." Thus returning to a theme that goes back to *The Night Porter*–haunted *Orchid Gardener*, *Manderlay* concurs not only with feminists such as Angela Carter and Maria Marcus (*A Taste of Pain*, 1981) but also with Foucault's analysis of the sadomasochism inherent in power relations, which are based, after all, in inequality. Accounting for the conversion of what would otherwise be painful into a source of pleasure, sadomasochism is the psychological mechanism that makes power productive in a libidinal sense. Thus in *The History of Sexuality*, volume 1, sadism and masochism are mutually inclusive positions that play off one another:

> The pleasure that comes of exercising a power that questions, monitors, watches, spies, searches out, palpates, brings to light; and on the other hand the pleasure that kindles at having to evade this power, flee from it, fool it, or travesty it. The power that lets itself be invaded by the pleasure it is pursuing; and opposite it, power asserting itself in the pleasure of showing off, scandalizing, or resisting. . . . these circular incitements have traced around bodies and sexes, not boundaries not to be crossed, but perpetual spirals of power and pleasure. (45)

If *Manderlay* has a "solution" other than democratic socialism, it may be a psychological one: an admission that we disavow the sadomasochism underlying power relations at our peril. The conclusion of the film is therefore a sadomasochistic application (on Trier's part) of that lesson, one designed to make spectators squirm.

But the squirm was (as it had to be) different. Where *Dogville*'s climactic deus ex machina released tension and provoked outrage, *Manderlay*'s big scene is the brutally sadomasochistic staging of intercourse between Grace and Timothy. Poised scandalously (as in *Mandingo*) between exploitation and critique, this orientalized, miscegenational, misogynistic rape fantasy provides the culminating taboo, and Trier displays it in full frontal nudity with stunning contrasts, black skin against white accented with the unsettling red of Howard's flame-colored hair. As the camera zooms out to reveal darkness, the sound of Grace's orgasmic scream carries over to the confusion of the next several images and scenes: the flicker of sporadic wildfires, Timothy's horse galloping in flames, and Wilhelm looking down at Sammy in a spreading pool of red. The scene of copulation that plays over (and partly facilitates) the violence outside displaces the usual histrionics: Sex replaces violence. The anarchy that leaves Sammy and Elisabeth dead and others wounded or missing occurs offstage in the darkness, left for us to imagine as Wilhelm and Mark, like tragic messengers, relay the information in hushed tones—that is, until multiplying accounts of what happened amass into a medley of sorrow, confusion, and outrage.

Manderlay's other poignant scenes are similarly dampered. The death and funeral of little Claire (in a glass-covered coffin that reflects the stars overhead, framed to recall *Dogville*'s iconic shot of Grace sleeping among the apples under the transparent canvas of Ben's wagon), is muted and brief. Old Wilma's execution, in contrast to Selma's, is presented as a mercy killing in which Grace shoots her discreetly in her sleep. Unlike the traumatic rupture that concluded *Dogville*, *Manderlay*'s ironic circularity underscores a refusal of the affect audiences had been trained to expect, making it the more didactic and Brechtian film. Reversing the film's opening, Grace horsewhips Timothy, grunting with each lash just as, in his display of power in Mam's bed, Timothy voiced brutal satisfaction with each thrust. Finally, because of *Manderlay*'s democratically fifteen-minutes-slow clock, Grace misses the escape proffered by her father and exits in an undignified huff in the direction of Washington, trailed as in her father's prophecy by torch-bearing "natives," and the film's mechanism locks with heavy irony into place.

However didactic in structure and tone, *Manderlay* lacked a simple political message and, like *Dogville,* made sense best as a Nietzschean and Foucauldian "genealogy" of power relations. But the film was ignored at the box office and, in contrast to the buzz surrounding *Dogville,* it provoked a relatively indifferent response. In a world weary of Bush's America and anti-Americanism alike, as Goss and the mainstream critical response suggest, Trier's "failed idealist" motif (having once inspired edgy and politically relevant films) had become tiresome and cynical (166). As opposition to American foreign policy became fashionable, however, the film has garnered a different response particularly in the "second life" of the blogosphere, where it is often read as an essential second installment in the director's analysis of the post-9/11 years and a benchmark for sheer audacity. Here is Sean Burns of the *Philadelphia Weekly Online:* "When the Danish cartoon controversy caught fire last month, I wondered if von Trier might be somehow disappointed, as he's no longer the most despised man in Denmark. You don't make a movie like *Manderlay* unless you really want people to hate your guts, but I daresay he's becoming modern cinema's most valuable asshole. Sure, Trier asks rude questions in a smarmy know-it-all tone, but at least someone's asking them."

The same issues that had made *Dogville* seem "anti-American" in 2003 made both films, but especially *Manderlay,* timely and relevant in the final years of the Bush administration, when a flurry of American antiwar films were released. For Burns, race relations are a "smokescreen" for a film whose real point is "the folly of recklessly forcing your worldview on an unfamiliar culture. At a time when the concept of 'freedom' is supposed to serve as an all-purpose panacea, *Manderlay* asks what liberation is really worth to . . . people . . . [whose] infrastructure has been so annihilated that nobody has anything to eat." From hindsight, in his latest incarnation of the misguided idealist, the unlikely and multifaceted character of Grace Margaret Mulligan, gangster's daughter, arrogant do-gooder, young American, and ardent sadomasochist, Trier had uncannily nailed the Bush era.

Comedy, Automavision, and *The Boss of It All*

At home in Denmark, the political landscape had changed in a rather different way. The controversy to which Burns referred (beginning in autumn 2005 when the conservative newspaper *Jyllands-Posten* published satirical images of the Islamic prophet Muhammad) threw Denmark into a political storm, exposed its increasingly polarized ideological climate and shook up the film community (Nilsson 102).[11] Bringing local race relations into the open, it problematized Trier's discussion of immigration and racism as American issues. As Peter Aalbæk Jensen explained in an interview on September 22, 2006, this was "a big wakeup" as, brought up to take pride in belonging to the world's "happiest" (Bordwell, "Cinema") and most tolerant of countries and now beleaguered with their own problems, Danes were regarded as less tolerant and "as mean as everybody else": "It was [once] all right to be offended about racial problems of the States, but now we have an extreme right-wing party and more than 50% of the country is rather right wing." Even before the crisis, in March 2004, Brendan Bernhard had called Trier on the issue: "[Dogville's] story is really happening in Europe, perhaps Denmark in particular, and yet you're projecting it into this big American narrative from a European point of view." Nor did *Manderlay*'s use of stereotypes go unnoted. Doughty writes that "Like the Danish cartoonist's satirical renditions," Trier could be accused of "inappropriate appropriation" (161) where another critic found that the "furore" over the cartoons made the film "all the more pertinent" in questioning whether one can impose freedom by force (Woolnough).

Trier had already decided to take a break from polemics. At the Cannes 2005 festival, he announced his postponement of *Wasington*, the trilogy's final installment, for lack of the "matur[ity]" necessary to make it (Higgins). Or was he too mature? March 2005 had marked the first decade of Dogme, and portentous turning points loomed. Shortly before turning fifty in May 2006, he released a "Statement of Revitality" that announced his intention to scale back in a quest to "rediscover my original enthusiasm for film," claiming to "have felt increasingly burdened by barren habits and expectations—my own and other people's. . . ." This meant a reduction in public relations and launches at "exotic, prestigious film festivals," a less structured routine, and time to develop scripts and fulfill "my own needs in terms of curiosity and play." Relinquishing (however temporarily) his role as cinema's reigning provocateur, he premiered his next film, a ninety-nine-minute Danish comedy, in September on his home turf, at the fledgling Copenhagen International Film Festival.

As "a comedy, and [being] harmless as such," he claimed in the opening voiceover, *The Boss of It All,* contained "[n]o preaching or swaying of opinion." Later he explained that "I had been criticized for being too political and maybe I criticized myself . . . for being too political[ly] correct, actually"—the slip referring to how his recent films had at times been understood as representing a European stereotype of Americans as racist, gun-toting imperialists. The new film was "not political, and I had fun doing it," he stressed, before adding that "of course the good comedies are not harmless" (McNab). In interviews, he mentioned screwball comedies—*Bringing Up Baby* (1938), *The Philadelphia Story* (1940), and *The Shop Around the Corner* (1940)—and the film is similarly replete with farcical sexual entanglements; smart, aggressive women; and passive-aggressive men. The humor is briskly paced, highly verbal, and punctuated with slapstick fistfights. But as usual, Trier had turned genre into his own game, lending it political reverberations and reflexive elements.

The screwball elements embellish and partly mask a trenchant corporate satire with an underlying, quite pessimistic, critique of capitalism. To provide another hook and/or distraction, the film was marketed as an office comedy that played off the current vogue initiated by Ricky Gervais's BBC television series *The Office* (2001–2003) and the NBC adaptation starring Steve Carell (2005–)—with Trier claiming to have seen neither. Employing "cringe" humor that bordered on repulsion, Gervais had laid bare the less-than-funny aspects of the corporate office—aspects that Stanley Aronowitz and Jonathan Cutler (*Post-Work,* 1998) and Jeremy Rifkin (*The End of Work,* 2000) envision in terms of a white-collar postindustrial, *post-work* culture besieged by downsizings, mergers, outsourcing, and offshoring. Or, as Tara Brabazon ventures, post-work work, being management, is a contradiction in terms, consisting essentially of spin or performance. *The Office* supports this concept in its mockumentary/reality-show premise (102) involving a TV crew shooting a workplace documentary and an attention-craving boss (Gervais) who aspires to being a stand-up comic, spends much of the workday mugging to the camera and regards his employees as an audience. *The Boss of It All* plays off a similar metaphor in which the workplace is conceived as bad (inept, vacuous, *and* irresponsible) theater.

In Trier's film, the boss in question isn't merely skiving off or acting out; in a sense, he doesn't exist. Ravn (Peter Gantzler), the owner of an unnamed information technology firm, has a pathological need to be accepted by his employees, having passed himself off for ten years as their recessive lawyer/colleague by inventing a fictional "boss of it all" (who resides in America) on whom he blames his unpopular decisions. This premise diagrams the contradiction inherent in corporate management style (which accumulates authority through a pretense of relinquishing it): He simply splits his identity. Posing as one of the guys, he retains trust, loyalty, and affection; performing behind the scenes as the anonymous, expatriate "boss of it all," he manipulates his employees without repercussions. The film begins as Ravn prepares to sell up and sell out his six senior managers, who are also his trustees. When the buyer, the irascible, Dane-hating Icelandic businessman Finnur (played by the legendary Icelandic director Fridrik Thor Fridriksson) demands to deal directly with the "boss of it all," Ravn hires a clueless, out-of-work but nevertheless self-important method actor, Kristoffer (Jens Albinus), to play the role, which requires surrendering power of attorney.

In one of several points that identify him as a surrogate for the auteur, Kristoffer is obsessed with one Antonio Gambini, a playwright, and his magnum opus *The Hanged Cat* (1969). This connection allows Trier to import (in place of Brechtian didacticism) elements from theater of the absurd (including absurdist humor directed at pretensions of theater of the absurd) to diffuse the satire. "Why not make fun of artsy fartsy culture?", Trier asks in voiceover as he introduces Kristoffer's obsession. At the same time, in a conflation of Harold Pinter (*The Birthday Party, The Dumb Waiter*), Eugene Ionesco (*The Bald Soprano*), and Luigi Pirandello (*Six Characters in Search of an Author*), Trier adds several layers to this tale of six employees in search of an illusory boss.

On the simplest level, unbeknownst to Kristoffer, the fictional boss has represented his sexual identity differently (via email) to two of the female employees, giving rise to a series of erotic intrigues, as Lisa's boss is gay, where Heidi A.'s is heterosexual and has proposed marriage. But like Pinter and Ionesco, Trier calls serious attention to the nonsensicality of language whether in the context of Kristoffer's meta-/fringe theater obsession (Gambini's virtuoso piece, a "Chimney Sweeper's Monologue" set in a "town without chimneys," consists of several minutes of silence) or in the high-tech world, where it plays off the central, unstated but everywhere implied paradox that information technology is an invisible, incomprehensible, nonexistent "product" that has the world in thrall. Tech meetings are ridden with nonsensical jargon, with no attempt to explain what the company produces. Technology rules in a cycle of information producing technology producing information ad infinitum, a process that becomes advantageous for Kristoffer. With few lines or cues from his devious "director" (he does not know his name or the name of the company much less anything about its product), but by uttering a couple of buzzwords—a formula he spots on a chart and the term *offshoring*—his character (his name eventually decided upon as "Svend") wings it, "passing" with ease, the point being that this level of management requires no special expertise: It is an act or an art. In his most brilliant move, when Ravn blames the decision to fire his employees on the boss of it all, Kristoffer/"Svend" invents a "boss of the boss of it all" and announces a bonding weekend at a resort. Thus he garners the affection Ravn had intended for himself and demonstrates a genius for passing the buck. In short, in inhabiting the role of the buck-passing boss of it all, he finds it suits him all too well and can't give it up. The complications multiply into farce and nonsense, but underlying it all is the nihilistic joke at the heart of the absurd and the perfect metaphor for empty-suit capitalism in which nothing is concrete (except hiring and firing), everything and everyone is at risk, and no one is responsible.

Punctuating the film with blatant sight gags, Trier infantilizes his characters and points out the childish nature of the proceedings. Meeting on "neutral ground," Ravn and Kristoffer (and Kristoffer and ex-wife Kisser [Sofie Gråbøl]) discuss strategy at a nursery (in winter), in a movie theater (where Ravn savors a lollipop), bobbing up and down on Tivoli merry-go-round horses, and at the monkey and elephant exhibits at the zoo—carnival settings that play against (while commenting on) the idlike and animal drives underlying the corporate world. One point is that when in positions of power with no strings attached, artists' inspirations and CEO's machinations are driven by the same infantile and territorial motives. Capping the metaphor is a sight gag featuring a teddy bear that sits in for the absent boss at meetings and is associated with the avuncular, bearlike Ravn—but ultimately with Trier, on whose lap it is conspicuously perched in publicity stills. Branding the film itself as "harmless" and funny, it also (sinisterly) links Trier with Gantzler's superficially cuddly, ultimately cutthroat boss, and the ethically challenged, narcissistic artist-as-child Kristoffer as well.

With such images and themes in play, *Boss* is as self-reflexive as anything by Trier. In the first shot, accompanied by an opening voiceover, a crane pans up a nondescript suburban office building to a window that reflects the director behind the camera in a trademark stocking cap reflected in the window. "If you look closely you can just see my reflection, but this film is not worth a moment's reflection," he puns. Reassuring the audience that there will be "no preaching or swaying of opinion," the voiceover uses a Brechtian technique to call attention to its supposed lack thereof, recovering memories of pompous and meddling narrators, hypnotists, and doomsayers of films past.

One level of reference is Trier's role as Zentropa's figurehead. Danish audiences are invited to read the film as *cinèma a clef,* with Ravn's direction of Kristoffer suggesting Trier's legendary struggles with actors while making comedy of the celebrated partnership of Peter Aalbæk Jensen and himself. "Life is a Dogme film. It's hard to hear but the words are important," one character quips. Publicizing *The Boss of It All* as another of Lars's stunts, the posters, press book, and Web site makes sure we know the joke (and the attention) is on the intrusive, imperious, unpredictable auteur and merchant of Zentropa. At the film's premiere on September 21, 2006, at Copenhagen's Imperial Theatre, mural sized posters that lined the two-story vestibule walls featured a bemused, fifteen-foot-tall Trier, dressed (atypically) in a black business suit, looking down at a diminutive Albinus in an identical black suit and a stocking cap identical to the one Trier wears in the opening crane shot.

For audiences in the know, Ravn's "direction" of Kristoffer is amusingly cryptic and familiar, consisting of two simplistic and contradictory instructions, the one sadistic and the other masochistic: "Subdue them [the unruly employees]" (which lands the feckless actor on the floor with a bloody nose)—and "Just say 'Yes'" (which leads to the aforementioned sexual intrigues and an unintended engagement). For Nordic audiences, several jokes were funniest on a national and cultural level. A running motif concerns avoidance of conflict as a Danish character trait. Hence, Ravn's arrangement is such that he can enjoy Danish "hygge" in which no one is better than anyone else and decisions are reached through consensus (except for those anonymous decrees from the "boss" in America). Or as Trier told McNab, Danes are "quite masochistic" and "love to hear that they are stupid." In contrast to the Danes, caricatured as given to emotionalism, long-winded sentimentality, and group hugs, are the openly competitive and easily incensed Icelanders, whose years under Danish rule have added zest to their embrace of free-market capitalism and the enthusiasm with which, as Trier noted in 2006, they had bought up much of Copenhagen (McNab; see also Interview, October 2007, n. 2, this volume)—before plunging, via the bank failures of late 2008, into economic and political crisis (Parker 39). The film's scene stealers are Fridriksson's volatile Finnur and his powerfully built translator (Benedikt Erlingsson) who renders his boss's tantrums into Danish with knifelike incisiveness. An ironic in-joke was the actual long-term collaboration of Trier and Fridriksson as prime movers in the Nordic new wave. (Fridriksson's Icelandic Film Corporation is Iceland's foremost production company.)

Included in the international satire is an all-important point: The expatriate Danish boss of it all's (and the boss of the boss of it all's) preferred residence suggests that Ravn like Finnur has shifted toward the American free-market model in which inequality and bloodshed, metaphorical or otherwise, are necessary to economic health. From this perspective, the film's vision of empty-suit capitalism's closest referent was perhaps neither screwball comedy nor *The Office* but the acclaimed Canadian documentary *The Corporation* (2002) whose titular "character," based on examples from IBM to Enron and analyzed by psychologists' diagnostic tools, is revealed as "a highly anti-social 'personality.'" "[S]elf-interested, inherently amoral, callous and deceitful," it "breaches social and legal standards to get its way; it does not suffer from guilt," yet mimics "human qualities of empathy, caring and altruism" ("The Film"). From this perspective, *Boss* had more in common with the USA Trilogy than it seemed to admit and may well be viewed, temporarily at least, as its third installment. As *Dogville* dismantled the ideologies underpinning a "typical" American town from hell, *The Boss of It All* decried the greed and deceit at the heart of the corporate workplace and the cutthroat aggression that informs the abstraction of its jargon, its medium, and its product—the big Ionescoesque joke being that medium and product (information technology) are the same, ensuring and replicating one another. As Trier acknowledged in 2007, "America has for me always to some degree stood for capitalism. And yes, I find many aspects of capitalism quite mean" (see Interview, October 2007, this volume), and casual allusions within the film support the association. When his ambitious ex-wife reveals she is Finnur's lawyer, Kristoffer quips, "Wow, capitalism. Weren't you going to use your degree to fight it?"—suggesting that she has gone over to the Icelanders' "American, winner-take-all" ways. Spelling out "HUMAN RESOURCES," HR officer Lise (Iben Hjejle) accuses "Svend"/Kristoffer of having "been in the states [so] long" as to have "forgotten what it means."

Filmed in an actual office building, the overlit depthlessness of the setting evokes the emptiness, dullness, redundancy, and cold impersonality of corporate culture, providing a deadpan, on-location variation on the Brechtian *Verfremdungseffekt*. Its complement is the film's credited cinematographer, Automavision. Except for the three narrative intrusions marked by zooms, and as advance publicity took pains to make known, *The Boss of It All* was shot via Dogme's opposite: a computer-operated fixed camera programmed to choose when to pan, tilt, zoom, and so forth. In the same way that Dogme's spastic camera work and Trier's holy foolishness were inseparable from *The Idiots,* and like them a source of off-the-wall humor, Automavision would say a great deal about *The Boss of It All* and vice versa. "I needed a form that suited the comedy" and a style that was not "human"—"freed of intention"—Trier told McNab. Described in the press book as "a principle of shooting developed with the intention of limiting human influence by inviting chance in from the cold," Automavision enforced randomness. Angles, colors, and sound levels jump erratically, and as Bordwell writes: "nearly every cut feels like an ellipsis," adding, by way of Trier's mantra that a film should be as irritating as "a pebble in your shoe" that the "abrasive tempo gives his comedy an anxious edge" (Bordwell, "Another"). The film looks "jarringly askance," Rich Cline remarks, and the method (or lack thereof) adds "a layer of depth," making the characters "cogs in the corporate machine," as their discourse is often blocked by coffee machines or computer monitors, and they are as likely as not to be left on the edge of the screen, halved, beheaded, or dropped from the frame altogether (figure 22). The film thrusts the characters' and actors' anxiety about finding their positions directly into the frame, forcing it on spectators who share their predicament by not knowing where to look. The metaphor is nailed with the character of "poor Mette" (Louise Mieritz), who screams when the copy machine turns on. (We learn that her husband was fired and hanged himself with a printer cable.) Automavision thus corresponds with the corporation as capitalist machine that, without regard for its human resources, and programmed for maximal efficiency, hires, fires, downsizes, and outsources by the numbers. Above all, it corresponds with the expatriate "boss of it all," a construct designed to take the blame from an abstract distance while the real boss absconds with the profits.

With obvious differences aside and as the polar opposite of Hollywood-style filmmaking, Automavision might also be read as a continuation of Dogme. The film is "ugly as sin to look at," claims Scott Foundas: "But it's all intentional on the part of von Trier, who once told an interviewer that moviemaking had become too easy because 'all you have to do is buy a computer and you have armies rampaging over mountains; you have dragons.' Now he's showing us how close we are to the time when movies will be directed by machines instead of artists. Perhaps he's telling us that we're already there."

Figure 22. *The Boss of It All.*
Jens Albinus upstaged by Automavision,
with Iben Hjejle and Mia Lyhne.

When confronted point-blank about what and how much Automavision "means," Trier refuses to (and perhaps cannot) say. Yet while avoiding the heavy didacticism he had been accused of in *Manderlay,* he had again managed to turn personal issues of control into a film with strong hints about sadomasochistic power relations under corporate capitalism. When read as a political or "accented" variation on twenty-first-century office comedy—as a metaphor for an unregulated corporate culture "running amok in its own insane rules" as Stephen Holden puts it—Trier had once again anticipated things to come. One wonders what the response would have been had it been released in late 2008 as the Bush era ended in economic collapse.

Automavision also shows him continuing to experiment with form and seeking audience interaction. As he speculated shortly before the film premiered, "70% of an audience will not even see it" (McNab) or would attribute it to some variation on Dogme style. The other 30 percent would presumably detect it, hear of or read about it, and learn to play the game—one in which spectators are challenged to discover (and in discovery create) continuity between takes. The randomness that "refreshes" the image and the sound every few seconds requires viewers to hunt for the subject or "meaning" within the frame, continually recovering their bearings and the film. To enhance this sport further, a few days before *The Boss of It All* was released in Danish theaters, Trier introduced a game he called *Lookey* that challenged viewers to spot (planted) "visual disturbances" in hopes of addressing film's "one great flaw": "it's a one-way media with a passive audience. As much as I love to dictate the storyline and control the experience I still wish that the audience could take an active part . . ." (Lundberg).

In *The Boss of It All,* Trier uses the machine as a paradoxical weapon in his ongoing struggle *against* the mechanical, a struggle to return to what is imperfect and human in the experience of cinema—in short, to give up control. Automavision was meant as a silly joke on himself but equally as a significant move: a complete break with the past. In a project originally announced as his second Dogme film, it marked another 180-degree turn; it forced him to relinquish the handheld camera that was Dogme's hallmark and that had remained throughout subsequent innovations his single crutch. Looking back yet further, and however ironic, Automavision was a total reversal of the match cuts, color coding, patinated textures, and intricately layered constructions that the young techno-wizard had obsessively applied—and to which he would return in perhaps the most notable reversal of his career.

Theatre of Cruelty: *Antichrist* (An Epilogue)

As a modest critical success in most of Europe and the United States, *The Boss of It All* once again demonstrated that Trier's audience was international and art house. In Denmark, whether in spite or because of its overt appeal to the local audience he had long since abandoned—or simply because it was too acerbic and self-reflexive for popular taste—it flopped. Theatrical distribution was limited (although IFC Films released it simultaneously to video on demand in the United States), and it was rarely seen until released on DVD. Thus, with the USA Trilogy's third installment indefinitely on hold and only two months after finishing his lightest film, the fifty-year-old Trier, no longer *L'Enfant* nor very *terrible*—and for whatever other reasons or none—plunged into a three-month depression. In May 2007, he resurfaced to announce to *Politiken* that his mind was "a blank sheet of paper" and that he despaired of making another film ("Depression"). Then, as he explained in the press book for *Antichrist,* "Six months later, just as an exercise, I wrote a script.[12] It was a kind of therapy, but also a search, a test to see if I would ever make another film." Noting that the script was made with "about half of my physical and intellectual capacity," he added that this, his most personal film, was the "most important" of his career. He claimed that it was virtually uncensored, that he had inserted images as they came to him, without logic or reason. In such fashion, and as his second attempt to put his stamp on a genre, Trier's "horror" film became his most controversial provocation yet.

Although publicized as a resuscitative, "emergency" film (Romer), *Antichrist* was not a new idea. In October 2004, Jensen had announced that before completing the USA Trilogy, Trier would make a film "for a wider audience, a horror film . . . in the style of *The Kingdom*"—"kind of an Antichrist . . . based on the theory that it was not God but Satan who created the world" (qtd. in "Von"). The choice of genre made perfect sense—horror could be adapted to psycho/melodrama and return to the dark expressionism of his earlier films, as he had a ready audience in

The Kingdom's paracinema and horror fans. When shortly thereafter the project was shelved (allegedly because of Jensen's plot leak), *The Boss of It All*, as a quite different take on a popular genre, had replaced it. Not until the press conference following *Boss*'s Copenhagen premiere (September 21, 2006) did Trier reannounce it under the title *Antichrist*.

The production history and distribution reveal a Hitchcockian level of calculation. Details were guarded and selectively released via internet. In February 2008, Zentropa's Trust Film Sales cryptically described the film as a "psychological thriller that evolves into a horror film": "A grieving couple retreat to 'Eden,' their isolated cabin in the woods, where they hope to repair their broken hearts and troubled marriage. But nature takes its course and things go from bad to worse." The cast remained unannounced until shooting started (August 18, 2008) in a forest near Cologne. Posed avuncularly between Willem Dafoe and Charlotte Ginsburg against a gigantic poster (the title spelled with the Venus/female symbol as the final "t"), Trier welcomed audiences to his nightmare: "I would like to invite you for a tiny glimpse behind the curtain, a glimpse into the dark world of my imagination: into the nature of my fears, into the nature of Antichrist" (Trust). Two weeks later, four more cast members, Fiona, Boniface, Blue, and No Name, were announced and depicted in thumbprints: a doe, a fox, and two ravens.

The Trust site also introduced the press book photo, an elaborate reinvention of Hitchcock's publicity photo for *The Birds* (in three-quarter profile with a crow perched on his shoulder in a nod to Poe's *The Raven*): Striking his predecessor's pose and deadpan expression, Trier appears in black and, in some kind of one-uppance, with a raven splayed dead at his foot (Longworth). From the moment this normally excessive director announced he had made a "horror" film as therapy for clinical depression, *Antichrist* became impossible to ignore. In late March, the first image, of the couple engaged in coitus amid the twisting roots of an ancient fairytale tree surreally intertwined with the hands of half-buried corpses, proliferated virally, with palpable excitement on sites such as Twitch, Freak Central, and CHUD; in mid-April, when the first trailer's blend of Boschian surrealism and gothic clichés appeared, the hype increased proportionally.

After the Cannes critics' screening on May 17 erupted into involuntary gasps, groans, yelps, laughter, and alleged fainting followed by hooting and booing amid scattered applause, *Antichrist* became the festival's defining moment, and as the first reviews appeared that evening, Cannes's biggest scandal in years—or ever. *Variety*'s Todd McCarthy led off, calling it "a great big art-film fart" ("*Antichrist*"). Jeffrey Wells followed, labeling it "an out-and-out disaster," a "major career embarrassment," lamenting that Trier had "lost his mind for the time being." A livid Wendy Ide fumed, "Lars von Trier, we get it. You really, really don't like women." If the dominant impression was shock and outrage, defenders emerged one by one. Poised between love and hate, Xan Brooks abruptly realized he loved it: Trier had "slapped" Cannes with "an astonishing, extraordinary picture—shocking and comical; a funhouse of terrors . . . that rattles the bones and fizzes the blood . . ." ("Mangy"). After calling it "the most despairing" film he had ever seen, a devastated Roger Ebert went on to herald it as "heroic" art, placing Trier with the "ecstatic giants" Bergman, Kurosawa, and Herzog ("Cannes #10"). "Do I believe his film 'works'? Would I 'recommend' it? Is it a 'good' film?" he asked before placing *Antichrist* beyond such questions: Trier "had the ideas and feelings, he saw into the pit, he made the film, and here it is" ("Cannes #6").

As always, yet as never before, the critics played into Trier's hands and created his platform. The frenzy mounted to hysteria when, opening the next morning's press conference, the *Daily Mail*'s Baz Bamigboye, demanded the director justify his work and Trier replied, after a beat, "I don't have to excuse myself. You are all my guests, not the other way around," adding "I don't make films for audiences. I make them for myself" before proclaiming himself "the best director in the world." (The same evening's premiere was "fantastic, a dream screening," Dafoe relates. "That d[id]n't get reported" [Nissim].) On the following Sunday, Gainsbourg won the best actress prize.

Antichrist surpassed already controversial expectations by drawing from pornography as well as horror, with extreme close-ups of penetration and genital mutilation (performed by stand-ins and prosthetics), and openly courted the misogyny charge that had followed him since *Breaking the Waves*. After speculation that it would never find U.K. or American distributors, the film was picked up on May 20 and 21 by IFC and Artificial Eye, respectively, who promised to release it intact.[13] The film next challenged the ratings systems, and when the British

Board of Film Classification awarded it an 18, the controversy flamed higher. As the United Kingdom's July 24 premiere approached, *TimeOut London* and the *Guardian* featured panel discussions from a range of demographics including feminist documentary filmmaker Kim Longinotto, a family counselor, and a token eighteen-year-old. In retort, the conservative press dredged up the "video nasties" controversy, and the *Daily Mail's* outbursts (see Hart's "What DOES It Take for a Film to Get Banned these Days?") reignited a longstanding class/culture war.

Selected by virtually every major festival, *Antichrist* opened around the world amid reports of more walkouts, vomiting (Toronto), a seizure (New York), and an unremitting onslaught of polarized reviews. In September, it momentarily found an empathetic audience at Austin's Fantastic Fest, where "Chaos reigns!," the line growled by a self-devouring fox to signal the shift into the frenzied final reel, became the festival catchword, with groups spontaneously bursting into chants and demanding t-shirts.[14] After protests and calls for bans in France and Poland, the hysteria reached a fever pitch with its U.S. opening on October 23 as conservative Christian media-watch groups demanded that the film, which IFC had released unrated, be submitted for an NC-17 rating and, that failing, to pressure the head of the Motion Picture Association of America to advise theaters to shun it (Unruh). Despite or because of its extremely limited theatrical release,[15] *Antichrist* had raised more hackles and issues than all of Trier's previous films combined including censorship in its many forms, the definition of pornography, the limits of film violence, and (invariably) misogyny—and more. Because Trier had pronounced his film a form of therapy, critics and bloggers debated whether it should be considered entertainment, art, primal scream, or stunt, with several concluding (with Ebert) that it was an event or experience beyond categorization or judgment. When several of its most vitriolic critics refused to screen it, film reviewing itself came under scrutiny and discussion.

For those who did see it, Trier opened debate by turning *Antichrist's* first moment into an extradiegetic joke: "Lars von Trier" is flashed on the screen followed by a shock chord and "ANTICHRIST" in a primitive red scrawl over a dingy green. What follows repeats *Dogville* and *Manderlay* in being divided into four allegorically resonant chapters—"Grief (Mourning)," "Pain (Chaos Reins)," "Despair (Gynocide)," and "The

Three Beggars"—framed by a prologue and an epilogue. These highlight the (fractured) fairy tale elements in the film in which a journey into the woods means confronting, one by one, a doe struggling to deliver a stillborn fawn; the self-devouring, speaking fox; and a half-buried crow that struggles sinisterly back to life. ("When the Three Beggars come, someone has to die.") In the narrative proper, a couple credited only as "He" and "She" is destroyed by the death of their child, the woman collapsing in despair, the man, a cognitive psychotherapist, retreating into clinical detachment. Taking over her therapy, He forces her to confront her fears of "nature" by returning to their woodland cabin where, the previous summer, she wrote her thesis on gynocidal witch hunts. Nature (external and internal) conspires in her (and increasingly his) derangement as the border between reality and the unconscious collapses, and they tear each other apart. On one level, Trier says, the film "sarcastically" represents his experience of cognitive exposure therapy, which declares Freudian psychoanalysis, with its Darwinian underpinnings and dreamwork, dead (Fanning).

On another level, *Antichrist was* therapy; of all of his films it was "closest to a scream" (Trier, qtd. in Romer). Abandoning the overscripted, conceptual cinema he had become known for, Trier returned to the oneiric logic, hypnotic expressionism, and technical virtuosity of his earliest films, with cinematographer Anthony Dod Mantle describing the work as the most challenging of his career (Pil). Where Trier's most recent films had featured a single (if radical) style, *Antichrist* blended his early and late styles and themes and was broken down into an intricate code. Contrasting sections produced dissonance, as it shifted from the hypnotic, hyperstylized black-and-white prologue (and epilogue) to the Dogme-style naturalism and deep blues and greens of the contemporary drama; this was fragmented by degraded close-ups (a pulsing throat, trembling hands) to express anxiety in haptic terms, distorted, high-contrast static images for hallucinatory "visualizations," and vérité body horror (Pil). "[R]eaching into the old toybox," Trier rediscovered, for example, slow motion (per *The Element of Crime),* slowed further with a Phantom HD camera. Accompanied in the prologue and epilogue by the exquisite Handel aria "Lascia ch'io pianga" ("Let me weep for my cruel fate, / and sigh for my lost freedom," from *Rinaldo*), it produced the stasis of extreme melancholia: sorrow, fear, paranoia (Romer). In contrast, the handheld footage of the film proper is accompanied by low-pitched Lynchean drones and alarmingly enhanced ambient, invariably natural, sounds: of the organic workings of the human body, the external environment (wind, trees stirring, acorns falling), the vast, encompassing cry of "all who are about to die."

Returning to the Tarkovskian ambience of his early monochromatic and color-coded films, Trier found a lifeline in cinematic allegiances of the past, drawing on Dreyer (*Day of Wrath,* 1943) and Bergman (*The Virgin Spring,* 1960, *Cries and Whispers,* 1972, *Scenes from a Marriage,* 1973), with many of the film's "metaphysical and monumental images," as Trier describes them, originating in the abandoned Wagner project ("Lars von Trier on *Antichrist*" 6). A dedication to Tarkovsky offered sincere homage to the artist whose metaphysical bent, meditative style, and vividly textured imagery marked Trier's earliest films and shaped his career. Before shooting, Trier had the actors screen *The Mirror* (Bo), Tarkovsky's most personal film, which was set in a cabin in a woodland setting, the home the exiled protagonist remembers sharing with his mother. Collapsing distinctions between characters and between past and present to convey the fluidity of identity, spatial experience, and psychological time, *Mirror* sustained a continuously subjective perspective. Populated by the archetypal "He" and "She," who simultaneously represent spouse, parent, and masculine and feminine aspects of the self, Trier's psychodrama similarly returns to the repressed and therefore mystical, space of "Eden." The Tarkovskian theme of nature encroaching on human life, central to the Europe Trilogy, re-emerges as they descend into a psychosexual and existential despair that, building to moments of nihilistic sublimity and terror, replaces Tarkovsky's spiritual certitude, whose lack Trier had always deeply felt.

Trier resists suggestions that the film's horrific content was therapeutic or even special, claiming the point was to have a genre whose "rules" allowed him to tell his story in a different way (Romer). Yet he also calls *Antichrist* "an investigation into all the forbidden things" (Fanning), which suggests how "horror" (in the broadest senses) offered a range and a vocabulary of understated frissons and excruciating extremes yet is capable of modulating from raw naturalism via the uncanny and the fantastic into surrealism, where all such distinctions might break down. Genre tropes (the isolated cabin and haunted forest) could merge with

Bergmanesque drama, shift into Lynchian sadomasochism, and from thence into Boschian grotesque and supernatural revenge, all the while playing off Freudian/Jungian archetypes to the extent that *Antichrist* (as Bordwell comments) imparts "the most unadulterated surge of emotion and mystical/mythical implication to be found in all [Trier's] work" ("Cinema"). Intrinsically voyeuristic and manipulative, "horror" provided a space for transforming personal trauma into its performative equivalent, primal scream into Theatre of Cruelty, Artaudesque shock therapy for complacent audiences. As Ebert writes, Trier draws on the genre's inherent violence "to inflict violence upon us, perhaps as a salutary experience" ("Cannes #5"). Finally, as what Trier calls a "horror film of substance" (Interview, October 2007, this volume), *Antichrist* comments self-reflexively on the traumatic aesthetic philosophy informing his cinema from the first.

In addition to genre films he admired from his youth (*The Exorcist, Carrie, The Shining,* and *Don't Look Now*) (Bordwell, "Cinema"), he mentions his recent fascination with Japanese horror films such as Hideo Nakata's *The Ring* (1998), adding that Asian cultures produce images "much different from what you are used to" (Schepelern, "Interview"). The fascination was with more than style. *Antichrist* returns to the trajectory of *Medea* and *Dogville* in which a gifted woman struggling against a repressive culture epitomized in a male antagonist avenges the crimes against her—with the revenge as unimaginable and apocalyptic as her powers have been suppressed. By 2006, Trier had become intrigued with the Asian avenging ghost story of a wraithlike woman with long dark hair associated both with female oppression and (as in *Medea*) the destructive aspect of primeval nature. *The Ring* and Takashi Miike's *Audition* (1999) feature suffering and avenging women with preternatural powers, and Nakata's *Dark Water* (2002) concerns an anxious mother and a child haunted by a cycle of parental abandonment. *Antichrist's* cycle of patriarchal condescension and female revenge evokes *The Ring*, in which a clairvoyant woman whom scientists scorn as a "freak" is avenged by her daughter, who inherits her powers tenfold and unleashes them on the world; associated with oceanic chaos, female power takes virally proliferating forms and destroys indiscriminately. But *Antichrist* has yet more in common with *Audition*, which shifts from a quiet family melodrama evocative of Ozu into the horror and shock/torture of "Asian extreme": A beautiful, melancholy woman seduces and renders men maimed, doglike wretches, cutting off their feet to avenge the abuse she suffered as a child and to keep them from leaving. Trier substitutes the equivalent Western mythology in which, as Nigel Andrews puts it, She is "finally driven to visit on the world the witching powers attributed to her sex through history."

When, in the last act, Trier switched genres, veering wildly from Bergmanesque melodrama to cosmic horror and from there into uncharted visceral and emotional territory, *Antichrist* also cannily/uncannily repeated the logic of sadomasochistic power relations explored (in comparatively abstract terms) in *Dogville* and *Manderlay,* to provoke outrage several times more intense and incoherent. With its "real" sex and (faked) genital mutilation, *Antichrist* ventured into an area restricted to pornography, the long-term interest at the core of Trier's most emotionally and intellectually challenging films (as well as some of Zentropa's riskier ventures).[16] The fusion of "pornography" with horror produced a sadomasochistic frisson intensified by Gainsbourg's visceral, taboo-breaking embodiment of aggressive female sexuality and was crowned by Trier's invitations to read the film as Strindbergian psychodrama. His "Director's Confession" refers to his youthful enthusiasm for the dramatist's "Inferno" crisis and concludes with the question—"was 'Antichrist' my Inferno Crisis? My affinity with Strindberg?" Like Nietzsche and the painter Edvard Munch, Strindberg had experienced not only creative psychosis but productively tumultuous relationships with women.[17] Reclaiming their collective insanity for his mature art, partly out of necessity, partly out of choice (and with more than a little irony), Trier gave up control in a more radical way than before.

The title is from *The Antichrist,* Nietzsche's "big showdown with Christianity" Trier claims to have kept on his bedside table since he was twelve (Romer), and transvaluation is behind the premise in which will to power rather than a merciful God is at the heart of life. Nietzsche's view of life as a struggle between weak and strong informed Strindberg's harrowing psychosexualized version of naturalism, featuring a battle of minds (*hjärnornas kamp*) between a man and a woman set on destroying one other, as in *Miss Julie* (1888) or *The Stronger* (1890). Waged in a naturalistic variation on Eden as nature red in tooth and claw, *Antichrist's* battle is between "male" reason and a "female" nature in which living beings procreate and suffer, kill, and die. In its final mutation into Boschian phantasmagoria merged with Grand Guignol,[18] the film might be compared to Strindberg's post-Inferno modulation into modernist expressionism, surrealism and overt psychodrama. In *A Dream Play* (1901), as Strindberg explained in his preface, "The characters split, double, multiply, evaporate, condense, dissolve and merge. But one consciousness rules them all: the dreamer's; for him there are no secrets, no inconsistencies, no scruples and no laws. He does not judge or acquit, he merely relates; and because a dream is usually painful rather than pleasant, a tone of melancholy and compassion for all living creatures permeates the rambling narrative."

Antichrist performs the repressed Strindbergian element in Trier's own personal/cinematic history of alleged misogyny with the wink and swagger of the title's culminating Venus symbol. Inconsolable in her grief, frantic for distraction and sexually insatiable, She becomes convinced of nature's evil and her participation in it and comes to embody sadomasochism in some ultimate form. The press invariably dwelt on the genital mutilations—hers especially but also the scene in which She bludgeons his genitals, masturbates him to a bloody climax, drills a hole through his calf, bolts it to a grindstone, and throws away the wrench (in an image that evokes Grace's humiliation in *Dogville*), castrating and "feminizing" him. Culminating only when He rids the world of her through strangulation and burning, an allusion to the mass execution of witches, *Antichrist* prompted the Ecumenical Jury, which normally honors a film for its spiritual value, to award it an "antiprize" for "the most misogynistic movie from the self-proclaimed biggest director in the world."

Yet the film is as often interpreted from the opposite perspective. As Heidi Laura, the film's credited "research[er] on misogyny," suggests, the real question is "why is it such a provocation . . . to be confronted with the image of woman as powerful, sexual and even brutal?" (Page). Thus, as Bordwell comments, when the "grieving mother rises into demonic fury by getting in touch with witchcraft," *Antichrist* can be taken "as a celebration of woman's primal energies" ("Cinema"). Thus read, the title supports the culminating vision of a pre-Christian, pagan Eden as, in the film's final moments, hordes of glowing, faceless (but otherwise ordinary, sturdy European) women surround and move past him and nature is restored to benignly indifferent fecundity. Supported by Gainsbourg's several interviews, Trier claims that She embodies his own psychological struggles, reminding Aftab that "I've always been the female character in all my films," adding that "the men tend to just be stupid, to have theories about things and to destroy everything" ("Lars"). Socialist-feminist historian Joanna Bourke finds *Antichrist* "more misanthropic than misogynistic. The man's violence is the heartlessness of rationality" that "sneers at the woman's research" and "bullies her into exposing her inner demons" (Brooks "*Antichrist*"). Contending that "a lot of male critics don't get it," Jessica Hopper reads *Antichrist* as a study of male hubris and compares Trier's vision of a world "in full masochistic flower" to radical/cultural feminist Andrea Dworkin's refusal to "look away from the relentless blunt force trauma of patriarchy."

Representing misogyny from both sides, *Antichrist* settles only as She, understanding female abjection all too well and pushed to the limit by masculine denial, internalizes and performs it on an apocalyptic scale, unleashing it (through reactive, ritualized *male* violence) once again throughout the world. Perhaps as per *Breaking the Waves,* Trier exploits and simultaneously confronts the taboo by unearthing a persistent, half-conscious misogyny that passes without comment in a glib, consumerist "post-feminist" era, exposing it for what it is. But *Antichrist* is equally and perhaps finally Trier repossessing his own unrepentant "misogyny"—taking on the label and shoving it in audiences' faces—in the most extreme manifestation of his trademark strategy of raising provocation to the level of metacommentary and metaculture. Whatever the case, the film confronts a misogyny unspeakable precisely because it is as ancient and ingrained as the distinction between self and other, "Man" and "Nature." As Erich Kuersten argues,

> If Lars is horrified when he gazes into the *vagina dentata* of the real chthonic nature ([w]here "chaos reigns"), at least he's not afraid to point his camera and shoot it. A true misogynist would just hide it in tight spandex and shoot it out of a wet t-shirt canon, . . . film[ing] it after the threat has been "subdued," i.e. objectified. . . . Expressing clear-eyed cognizance of masculine fear of women *cures* misogyny not creates it, that's the point of art and therapy. It's only when you need to prove you're *not* afraid, via sexual violence, winky objectification or smug condescension, that misogyny does its true damage.

A self-referential "Scandinavian" psychodrama from Lars von Trier at his most vulnerable and excessive—an expression of his "inferno" that represents his triumph over it—*Antichrist* demands psychological interpretation to salvage meaning. It is also about therapy's limitations, a hellish case study in cognitive exposure therapy in which patients confront and gain control over their fears—the method Trier had undergone for the last three years. The film's truer discourse, however, is that same therapy's nemesis, psychoanalysis, which fares considerably better in this grimmest of fairy tales in which self-cannibalizing foxes announce that "Chaos reigns!" The prologue is an extended allusion to Freud's primal scene: a three-year-old child calmly watches his parents' intercourse, slowly turns, and looks at the camera aligned with the open window from which he falls to his death (figure 23). The film then proceeds to validate the child's dying vision of a bestial, frantically sexualized world in which subject and family are destroyed. Elsewhere, audiences are invited to draw on various pre- and post-Freudian psychologies, mythologies, and practices including the Shamanic trances Trier claims to have undergone in his twenties. Set in a fairytale forest and cabin in which anima and animus battle it out—with the primal scene at one end and "torture-porn," the prescient Three Beggars, and chthonic witches at the other—it is a psychodrama that asks viewers to enter and play. The Hitchcockian allusions, for example, invite us to "discover" the auteur's struggle with Mother. When Karen Badt asked him point-blank if the

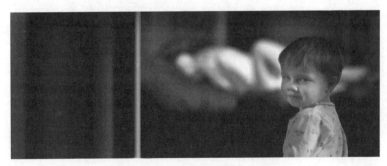

Figure 23. *Antichrist*. Storm Acheche Sahlstrom, Charlotte Gainsbourg, and Willem Dafoe staging the primal scene.

child who falls with arms outspread like an angel was himself, "Yes, that is it," he immediately responded, adding, "My mother didn't give me a childhood. She was magical to me of course. . . ." Later in the same interview he claimed that his Shamanic animal is the otter, often regarded as a trickster.

Although he claims he made the film without regard for logic or dramatic sense and some have found it a willful profusion of overdetermined symbols, he has also as always, but perhaps as never before, constructed a text that demands decoding. This is Trier's definitive performance in the context of a culture for whom trauma, confrontation, and confession are meaningful in some irreducible sense. Yet confession does not heal; what does is the filmmaking process and film itself as enabling, performative, provocative art.

Bordwell remarks that *Antichrist* "lacks the element of game-playing" found in the director's more "mathematical" projects ("Cinema"), which suggests that he may have missed the point. *Antichrist*—Trier's most reflexive game yet—challenged audiences to enter and battle his monsters, and many found it addictive. It was no wonder then in June 2009 when Zentropa announced *Eden, Antichrist*'s 2010 companion PC game, a first-person thriller/adventure that invites players (after uploading their fears, and with Dafoe's dulcet voiceover as a guide) to confront their own personal hells.

Notes

1. See Schepelern's *Lars von Triers Film—Tvang og befrielse* (Rosinante, 2000), *Lars von Triers Elementer—En filminstruktørs arbejde* (Rosinante, 1997), and Stevenson's *Lars von Trier* (BFI, 2002), the latter covering a vast amount of material previously unavailable in English including a deluge of tabloid journalism. Mette Hjort's several titles listed in the bibliography emphasize the strategic role and impact of Trier's public personality and cultural politics within Danish, Nordic, European, and global contexts. Finally, for an excellent range of theoretical approaches to Trier's work, see Caroline Bainbridge's work.

2. Among these new "performatists" Eshelman cites Jean-Pierre Jeunet (*Amélie*, 2001), Tom Tykwer (*Run, Lola, Run*, 1999), and Sam Mendes (*American Beauty*, 1999), with Trier and certain Dogme brothers leading the pack.

3. The bet was part of a strategy to obtain Danish Film Institute funding for *The Grand Mal*, a film about two gangster families in divided Berlin that Trier

had spent two years writing after *The Element of Crime*. Because the DFI awarded no more than five million kroner for a single film, Trier proposed making two films, one for nine million kroner and one (*Epidemic*) for one million. Although Trier obtained the one million and won the bet, neither *Epidemic,* a dismal box office failure, nor the screenplay for *The Grand Mal* convinced the DFI to fund the other nine million, and much of the material was subsequently incorporated into *Europa* (Björkman, *Trier* 85–6).

4. When the DFI balked at underwriting the first four Dogme films as a package, Zentropa and Nimbus, Vinterberg's production company, were joined by several media outlets (including Danmarks Radio) to foot the bill (Stevenson, *Lars* 77–78). Thus creating a precedent, Zentropa has continued to invent strategies to provide Danish filmmakers with a range of funding sources, technical resources, and ideas.

5. Dogme's impact on cultural politics continues in its role as an international initiative, public forum, and transmedia phenomenon rippling out through the arts and beyond. The term is now used to refer to at least five things: (1) the concept, as outlined by the manifesto and "rules" for making Dogme films; (2) the collective of four "Dogme brothers" and their films, designated by number and certified by a document that appears in place of the director's credit; (3) ten Danish-produced films and what Peter Schepelern estimates as forty to forty-five publicly distributed international features from fifteen to twenty countries ("Re: Dogme"); (4) Scandinavian and international Dogme-style films such as *Lilja 4-Ever* (Lucas Moodysson, Sweden, 2002), *Traffic* and *Full Frontal* (Steven Soderbergh, United States, 2000, 2002), and *Ten* (Abbas Kiarostami, Iran, 2002), or nearly any offbeat, low-tech film made offshore of Hollywood; and (5) global transmediary Dogme, or the plethora of initiatives across the arts and sciences that have adopted the concept. See Badley 90–92. In 2008, marking a decade of Dogme, the "brothers" were honored with the European Achievement in World Cinema Award.

6. The precedent nevertheless initiated a wave of art films featuring unsimulated sex including *Romance* (1999), *Baise-Moi* (2000), *Intimacy* (2001), *The Brown Bunny* (2003), *9 Songs* (2004), and *Shortbus* (2006).

7. The financing of *Breaking the Waves* thus provided a coproduction model for Trier's (and Zentropa's) subsequent projects.

8. Although Trier withdrew from the project in 2004 after having completed the plans (which he deemed impossible for a live production to pull off), he posted on Zentropa's Web site a detailed essay, titled "Deed of Conveyance," which, much like the Dogme Manifesto, offered his ideas to anyone who could use them. This has been reprinted in music newsletters and journals such as *Mostly Opera.*

9. Similarly Simons notes how the ancient tribal practice of potlatch, an elaborate expenditure of generosity, issues an implicit challenge to the recipient, leading to bankruptcy of both parties (*Playing* 109–11).

10. Trier's premise and Holdt's findings have been exhaustively supported by Douglas Blackmon's *Slavery by Another Name* (2008), which exposes a suppressed history of neo-slavery (the forced labor of hundreds of thousands of African Americans by corporations, mines, and plantations) extending to World War II.

11. Condemned as blasphemous, as they struck at Islamic laws that forbade depictions of the prophet, the cartoons were subsequently reprinted as a challenge to what was perceived as censorship in several European newspapers, and riots directed primarily at Denmark broke out in Muslim communities around the world. In defense, *Jyllands-Posten* referred to having sustained a precedent of open discussion in the fallout from the 2004 assassination of Dutch filmmaker Theo van Gogh.

12. As Trier explained in the Cannes press conference interview on May 18, he had collaborated with Anders Thomas Jensen on an earlier script that had been abandoned ("Press").

13. Zentropa had nevertheless provided what Peter Aalbæk Jensen called a "Catholic" (censored) version as well as the uncut "Protestant" one.

14. By December 2009, five different "Chaos Reigns" t-shirt designs were on the market and at least six different posters, three of them created for specific festivals.

15. In the United States, its widest theatrical release was nineteen venues, although five days after its premiere it was released on video on demand with record-breaking results. In Denmark, by contrast, it was an instant hit and eventually swept the major film academy awards.

16. In 1997, Trier and Zentropa founded Puzzy Power and, in 2001, Intimate Pictures, subsidiaries specializing in high-quality pornography, making Zentropa the first mainstream film company to produce adult features. Produced and directed primarily by women such as Lene Børglum and Lisbeth Lynghøft, the films were also allegedly made *for* women, as the Puzzy Power Manifesto states, and were extremely successful in Europe, especially *Constance* (1998), *Pink Prison* (1999), and *All About Anna* (2005). Their success influenced Norway's 2006 decision to legalize pornography. See Thomas Vilhelm's *Filmbyen* (Copenhagen: Ekstra Bladets Forlag, 2007).

17. Strindberg's correspondence with Nietzsche is well known, and in a *Figaro* interview, Trier mentions Strindberg's treatment by the Paris doctor who also treated Munch, whose painting *The Scream* (1883) Trier has brought up in several recent interviews (Wachthausen). Munch's equally iconic *Love and Pain* (1894, subsequently titled *Vampire*), in which a woman appears to smother her victim in her mass of blood-red hair, also comes to mind.

18. Hieronymus Bosch is also featured in a grotesquely funny sequence in *The Early Years: Erik Nietzsche Part 1* in which a lecturer presents a crazed illustrated meditation on the *Hell* panel of *The Garden of Earthly Delights* (c. 1504) in language similar to Trier's own description of *Antichrist*'s vision of chthonic nature in the October 2007 interview in this volume.

Interview, September 2006

On September 19, 2006, two days before *The Boss of It All*'s Copenhagen International Film Festival premiere, I interviewed Trier at Zentropa headquarters in Filmbyen, arriving with an impression gleaned from wandering the premises the weekend before. A twenty-minute train ride from the center of Copenhagen, Filmbyen lives up to its reputation as Hollywood's antithesis: Taking up the last row of low-rise, yellow-brick buildings separated by large, pothole-marked parking lots, the former military barracks look like a cross between a Soviet concentration camp and a hippie commune. Housing Zentropa's full-featured production company along with subsidiaries and collaborators, it has been officially declared "Open" by a manifesto-like statement issued in 1999. Since "the days when the moving image was equated with magic," Trier wrote, film production has been "shrouded in a veil of mystery," and Filmbyen offers a model of demystification, with community outreach programs based on an interactive/workshop model, writers' cabins, a hostel on the premises, and facilities given over to students in the evenings and on weekends ("Project" 224–5).

Trier and Jensen embrace a Danish tradition in which filmmaking is regarded as a collective art, enhancing it with a communist kitsch ambience that reflects their Marxist heritage. Hence, Jensen describes Zentropa as "an industrial enterprise with lots of machinery" but organized like a "guerilla network"—that is, horizontally rather than top-down—so its divisions "don't know what the others are doing," which encourages creativity (*A Small Film*). The main corridor of the editing building, painted in the same institutional green as *Dancer in the Dark*'s death row, is decorated with Maoist proverbs. (Inside, the equipment is cutting edge.) Following on Dogme's call for "films in uniform," Trier and Jensen have gone for militant names. The ominous "101 Storm Troopers" (children from all over Denmark) were given the digital cameras left over from making *Dancer in the Dark* and armed to make more films (Wakelin). Then followed Station Next, an outreach program for children and teenagers (a collaboration with Nordisk, the Danish Broadcasting Corporation, TV2, and Hvidovre Municipality) and a film school for teens. On Saturday, Jonas Jørgensen, a young Station Next post-graduate taking a break outside the editing rooms where he is finishing his film, talks about coming to Zentropa as a child on school trips and later, as a teenager, working alongside Denmark's foremost directors.[1] For serious would-be filmmakers, there are three-year apprenticeships in which one may advance from gopher to, say, assistant editor on a major project—or one's own film.

On the 19th, thirty minutes early for the interview, I stumble into the middle of Filmbyen lunch, which takes place in bustling buffet style inside the large main room of headquarters and spills over onto the picnic tables outside. When the crowd and tables are cleared, it all resembles a glorified Scout hutch with its dingy-cozy thrift-store furniture, drum set and keyboard, pinball machines, "trophy wall" (boasting the collective awards of the Zentropa family) in the center of which hangs a large, ugly stuffed fish. In a row of offices lining the left-hand side, fresh-faced assistants work the desks. The person who greets me, shyly smiling behind wire-rimmed glasses and tousled hair, looks nothing like the Lars von Trier legendary for deflecting tough questions with humor or turning them back on the interviewer—all of which he would carry off handily and with disarming charm. Soon we are zipping off on one of the ubiquitous golf carts to his office, a cabin nestled in Filmbyen's outskirts in a glade of overgrown bushes and trees. Inside, it looks like a living room, with an old piano, faded green sofa, books stacked on the floor, and a large desk next to a *Creature from the Black Lagoon–*themed pinball machine—all familiar from *The Five Obstructions,* the one film anyone thinking about interviewing Trier absolutely must see, for reasons that should become apparent.

"I should warn you that I'm not a reporter," I venture.

"Anything I say will be used against me," he quips.

Bristling with questions about the USA Trilogy's politics, Zentropa's communist ambience, and Filmbyen in relation to his role as an international auteur, I mention in introduction that I coedit a book series on world cinema, noting the recently published one on Japanese horror movies—and he stops me right there, throwing me completely off topic:

LARS VON TRIER: I'm very interested in Japanese horror movies. I'm watching a lot of them right now. Which ones are your favorites? Which ones are the most scary?

LINDA BADLEY: The *Ring* films, of course. *Pulse* was creepy. Have you seen that? Hmmm. *Audition?* There were rumors that you were going to do a horror film.

LvT: I'm still thinking about it. Before that I had never seen these films. Now that I have seen some I think it should be good fun to work with, and the horror genre gives opportunity [to work with] a lot of images and whatever. I just saw this *Dark Water.* It's beautiful, it really is. I thought it was beautiful.

LB: *Epidemic* was a horror film of sorts, wasn't it?

LvT: It was a horror! One million Danish kroner.

LB: And it came long before *Blair Witch Project!* But seriously [pause] in this book I thought I would emphasize your recent, more political projects, especially the USA Trilogy. Then you decided to do *The Boss of It All* and threw off the whole idea! Can you tell me anything about the film?

LvT: I felt like I needed some time off for a tiny nice project that wasn't too hard to do. So it's a Danish film. And it's about a man who has a company but has not told the employees that it is his. He's said that he has a boss—he is trying to avoid unpleasant things—and if he has to fire somebody he can blame it on the boss. And when he wants to sell the company he needs a boss for just one day and hires an actor who has to stay on, and that is problematic because he doesn't know what's been going on for ten years. Yeah, it's complicated. Actually I've been told that it's a screwball comedy. I was always fond of these comedies like *Bringing up Baby* and *The Philadelphia Story.* I like them very much. I'm very fond of Katherine Hepburn. So it's a little in that tradition.

LB: In those screwball comedies there's always a romance between this rather aggressive woman and a man who is less so and usually lower class, and they always fight and talk a lot.

LvT: Yeah, they talk, talk, talk. Still Katherine Hepburn always turns out to be very—what do you say, feminist—correct, would you say; she's always the boss, wouldn't you say? But the whole thing about this female-male thing was best put at the end of *Annie Get Your Gun.* She's supposed to shoot at something, and then there is the guy she wants to marry. And this old Indian finally destroys the whole aiming thing on the gun, so she can't win. She says, "So then I can't win." And he says, "But you can win him." And so she misses, and then they get married.

LB: Yes, it always ends like that. So, since *The Boss of It All* is a screwball comedy, do you have the male-female thing going on in it?

LvT: Yes, actually, yes, but that's not the main story. This director [boss] is. And then there's a moral story in it also about how much you should kind of exploit your employees.

LB: Should or shouldn't?

LvT: Yeah, you shouldn't. Most of all it's about an actor, because I know some, this terrible, egocentric actor who is crazy about some Italian absurd writer—like Harold Pinter or whatever—and it's of course very confusing for everybody since that's not what he's there for.

LB: Absurdist comedy about theater of the absurd?

LvT: Oh, no, no, it's light, and. . . .

LB: Okay so no political or philosophical commentary. And you've said that it's lighter than your previous, certainly your most recent, films. But you have comedy in most of your films.

LvT: But somehow I tried to stick to . . . [pauses]. This is a real comedy. But I would say the other films I have made have never been real genre films. Hopefully when people see that it says it's a comedy that they *see* it as a comedy. For entertainment! See it!

LB: You mean that you are compromising your great ideals?

LvT: Yeah, yeah, but I would love to compromise. It's harder for me, but I would like to learn to compromise. For me as a person it would be very nice.

LB: You think it would make you . . .

LvT: Happier? Yes.

LB: You at one time said that it would be a Dogme film.

LvT: No, it's not a Dogme film. I changed it again. No, this is actually kind of interesting. Now I've invented a new set of rules. This is only for the camera. The other rules were for the actors and stuff. This is for the camera and for the sound. We have invented this thing called Automavision. And that is that when I film I put up the [fixed] camera, I make the shot that I want, and then I press the button on the computer, and that gives us 8 or 9 offsets. And that means that the camera moves 10 meters to the side or up, or whatever. . . . And that means that the whole film—the framing of the film—is of course different. When you see a normal film there [are] maybe only two places in the frame that you have to look at. That's how you frame normally. But here the main action can be going on anywhere in the frame. I myself could make strange framing, but here there's no use in that. The whole idea here is that there's not an idea behind it. It's random. It's the same with the sound. You start with the sound man putting up a mike here as he would have, and then he presses the button, but the computer says you have to cut here or here. And so it makes the film very imprecise because you are limited by these ideas that the computer gives, this randomization. But I think it's very lively to see because it jumps anywhere in the frame. The big work was to put the limitations in the formula—you know, the camera should be able to move a half a meter to the left or right or so— but if you had just had the randomization—without the limitations—it would be impossible to work, so actually it's just making things more imprecise. It's Automavision!

LB: Is it in any way a continuation of your project of pointing instead of framing, of refusing to frame?

LvT: Yeah, you can say that because these frames are all fixed shots.

LB: Well that certainly sounds appropriate for the subject of the film—[laughs] the business aspect of it. I was just sitting at a lunch table with a group of set painters who said you filmed it on location at some actual corporation.

LVT: Yeah. That was the easiest way to do it. But I tried to find, as you say, a very dull place to do it.

LB: How do you feel about opening the film at the Copenhagen International Film Festival? Of course I've read your "Statement of Revitality."

LVT: But I'm so happy that I don't have to go to Cannes. I'm sure that one day that it could be fun to go to Cannes again but right now I am so pleased that I don't have to do that.

LB: I wonder if you could talk a little about your sources of inspiration. Your first three films were influenced greatly by other films, and after that it seems you've been influenced by anything *but* film, and you've suggested that you've quit watching new films—except for Japanese horror films, of course [laughs].

LVT: Yes, but these Japanese horror films are the most recent films I've seen for many years.

LB: I'll have to tell my horror film students about that. They'll love it.

LVT: Could you do me a favor and ask them maybe what their favorites are? And maybe mail me about which ones these are. It would be very interesting for me because I am planning this one now. So I will look at what they think. And about what is scary.

LB: I would be happy to. [Pause.] But back to influences. The USA and Gold Heart trilogies have been influenced by literary sources. You mention *Story of O* in connection with *Manderlay,* and further back, with *Menthe.* Do you read a lot?

LVT: Oh, I'm terrible, I don't see films and I don't read. I don't do anything. I don't know what I do with my time. Of course, I have four children and that takes a lot of time. And . . . I am tiptoeing through life in the sense that I have all these . . . [anxieties]. I don't know what I do—I can't read because it gets me started thinking about other things, and films are not too great to see. My problem is that seeing a film is not as fantastic as it was when I was young. And it *was* fantastic to see a new great film [pause]. It was great to see *Barry Lyndon*—I just saw that again. Fantastic film, it really is. But to see new films—[pause]. The newest film

I've seen [recently] is *Mulholland Drive*. I thought that was very good. But normally I'm not too crazy about David Lynch, for some reason.

LB: I thought Lynch influenced *The Kingdom* . . .

LVT: Oh yes, I liked *Twin Peaks* very much, but his feature films I haven't [liked so much]. The beginning of *Twin Peaks* was masterly. Once I was about to meet David Lynch. He was here at a meeting about TM—you know he is into transcendental meditation—and I was going to lunch with him and with some TM types, and they were all sitting at this table, and I got into the room and got afraid and I went away. So I never met him.

LB: I can't believe it! You were afraid of David Lynch?

LVT: I was afraid of the whole thing. If it had only been just David Lynch, but it was just too much. They were all in suits. It was scary.

LB: Back to the sources of inspiration. It seems that the literary inspiration goes back to something that has real emotional or psychological power like the connection between Brecht and your mother. And *Story of O* goes way back [to the student film *Menthe* (1979)].

LVT: But everything that I'm doing is based on stuff from way back. So no wonder that everything looks the same. It all comes from the same [sources].

LB: I use a psychoanalytic film theory in my classes and force my students to work with it, but they're often very intolerant of Freud. Some of your statements suggest that you "believe" in it or at least take it seriously.

LVT: I don't know if I believe it is the way to get rid of your problems. I don't know . . . [pause]. Yes I know of it, and I believe there is something to it. And it makes sense to me. But as the best way to help sick people, I don't think so. I know a lot of people who are less [than] nice to be around who spend a lot of time on the couch. It's still very popular in France, you know.

LB: You've commented about being influenced by games. Zentropa's Web site has that Pong game. And the rules you come up with are part of what might be called a game you're playing. At one point you said you play video games a lot, and people have commented on their influence on films like *Dogville*. Are you still doing that?

LVT: Yes, well the game I was inspired by was *Silent Hill*. The first time it was . . . wonderful.

LB: Horror again?!

LvT: Well, it's kind of a cozy horror.

LB: It has a map, doesn't it?

LvT: Most of those adventure games have maps. *Silent Hill* was fantastic. Also they had this very good thing with the fog in the town so you could only [see a limited amount]. It was very scary, and you run around, and there were all of these monsters.

LB: To the extent that you are influenced by sources other than film, do you ever think film as a medium is at a dead end? Or do you see your experimentation with film as a new beginning?

LvT: When I've made a film, and just after, I'm generally very satisfied with the film. And that's a reason for doing it. Of course it would be very nice if somebody would use some of these little things that I've been experimenting with. But I'm sure film changes rather quickly, you know I saw *Alien*[3] recently and it looked exactly like *The Element of Crime*—the locations whatever, exactly the same. And I don't know how much, ten years or so between. So you know everything changes all the time. And yeah, it would be fine if they used it in changing things.

LB: I am interested in how you see yourself as an auteur. Peter Schepelern has argued that your work can be seen as a "prototypical auteurist initiative"—you aim "not simply to make films but to construct Lars von Trier, the auteur filmmaker." And you've mentioned your admiration of David Bowie, who does much the same thing. This easily supports the conventional notion of the auteur. But you also seem to want to be a sort of "anti-auteur" in making 180-degree turns—from the Europe Trilogy, for example.

LvT: I don't think there's really a plan behind anything, but when things are going too steadily, then I get upset, and it's really like I need some—[pause]—I feel like a horse, a hungry horse who needs some different things to eat—[laughs]—I don't know why I said "horse." I need some food and then when it gets kind of dull I need some other kind of food. I am contradicting myself a lot—that is part of my technique, you see.

LB: That's your signature?

LvT: That's my signature, that I am always trying to see things from quite another point of view. And that's what I do when I choose projects, and when I write, and whatever. If it's too easy to read, or too *convenient*—I would say is a better word—then I get [pause, sighs]. I am both.

LB: You've said that the USA Trilogy was an attempt to stick to the same subject?

LvT: Yeah, well. But that was true at the time. All that I say is true at the time when I say it.

LB: You are very good at making provocative statements.

LvT: But on the other hand [in reference to] Peter Schepelern and David Bowie and all that, it's the films that are the things that I need to do. I need to do these films, otherwise I would become more crazy than I am, and to create a part for myself and all is not important. It might happen that I was fond of David Bowie, but later on even David Bowie has said it was not in his hand, really, what happened.

LB: Is that true of you?

LvT: Yeah, It's in that same line. I'm not planning things very carefully, not at all. I'm trying not to. For some time I've been trying to not to. I've been trying for some time to get in my own way. Yeah, I think that's my technique.

LB: I'm fascinated with Filmbyen and Zentropa and this whole communist, communalist inflection you have here. And the initiatives like Dogme where you deny the director credit, or collaborative arrangements such as Advance Party. Are you trying to redefine the auteur's role?

LvT: I know, and if it sounds messy then it is because I am messy. I just want to argue all the time. You know when you have a standpoint, then it is good to argue.

LB: The film towns you and Peter have been helping to found—do you have much to do with Trollhättan, for instance?

LvT: Yes, but that's mostly Peter. Yeah, the reason we made the company was to make my films—to produce and control them. And then we had to take in and produce some other films, and it has turned out some other way. But that is not my main occupation, to take care of the company. It's Peter's. Oh, we discuss it now and then.

LB: But you were making rules for other filmmakers. What about your agreement with Sigma Films, for instance? Did they approach you or did you approach them? Didn't you make the rules for the three directors—you know, nine actors, filming in Glasgow, and so on?

LvT: Yeah, yeah, yes, I probably did—oh, yes, rules come so easy to me [laughs]. Yes, yes, we should have had a concentration camp here. No gassing after dark. But seriously we try all the time to do stuff that makes it a little different to produce here, than with other production companies, and I talk to other directors—the directors talk [to each other] all the time—which I think is good.

LB: Yes, when I got here, Thomas Vinterberg, Anthony Dod Mantle, Peter, and everybody else were gathered and having lunch [in the main hall]. And you have rules that the actors and crew have to eat together, and so forth. That's not just Peter, is it?

LvT: Yes, and I think that's important. But of course that's just very Danish.

LB: Usually when you've been asked if you have political intentions, you've said no.

LvT: Political intentions? It depends on what you mean by that.

LB: It seems that in the USA Trilogy and your [other recent] films set in America you have been more and more engaged with politics—or at the very least with the clash between ethics and pragmatics. And most Americans seem to have interpreted your recent films as political. *Manderlay* was seen as taking on the Bush administration, and the posters and DVD covers featured the words "Liberation whether they want it or not."

LvT: But the funny thing is that the film was written a long time before Iraq.

LB: So who played on that connection? You didn't intend any of that?

LvT: No, that wasn't me. I'm not crazy about Bush but. . . . You know, if I wanted to do things with politics . . . [pause]. I don't believe that you can do that in films. You know, someone like Ken Loach, he believes it can work, which is beautiful, and I admire him very much, but I don't think that is the way you can do things. But if you make the films personal, then that will also of course reflect your political point of view. I would like to put things that way rather than say that these [films] are made for political reasons or have political intentions.

LB: That certainly makes sense with *Dogville*. But *Manderlay* is a very researched film and if it doesn't have anything to do with Iraq and Bush, it certainly has to do with slavery. How is *Manderlay* personal?

LvT: In what way is it personal? [chuckles] That's a good question.

It's not personal in the sense that I have been to the States or that I have a lot of colored friends. I was asked in one of these conferences on the Internet with somebody in New York, and he asked if I had any colored friends, and I said "One person, but we don't talk any more." But, no [pause]. How it is personal? I believe that it is. But how it is . . . ?

LB: But what about the character of Grace? Who changes a whole lot from *Dogville*.

LVT: I still can follow her. I think she's me very much. She wasn't me so much in *Dogville* when she killed the whole town, but I could understand her. But in *Manderlay*, I understand her all the way.

LB: How so, specifically?

LVT: No, it's just very much how I would react.

LB: You would go in there and make some rules?

LVT: Yes, go in there and make some rules, and if they wouldn't play my game then I would be totally hysterical [chuckles].

LB: [laughs] Yes, make some rules requiring they be free. So it was an experiment in which you could see how it would turn out in a situation like that?

LVT: Oh, yes. But that is actually a very good exercise—to kind of put yourself in a very difficult situation and see how things will turn out.

LB: In that respect, a film is a little like a video or computer game except that you create the set, the situation?

LVT: Hmmm. But I was trying to see how much I could push myself if I was Grace, what situation could [push her that far]. I started of course, as I've said before, with the end, that she would kill everybody or ask for everybody to be killed. And then see how I could make a story that could make it possible. That was typical.

LB: Grace's uncompromising nature strikes me as, er, familiar. I read *Dogville* as being a comment on American idealism as naive and extremist—her initial tolerance versus her eventual "blow-'em-all-away" attitude, which struck me as a view of how the current administration sees things. It's based in a kind of puritanism. Is Grace a Puritan?

LVT: Yes. Oh, yes, black or white. That's a problem you have when you see everything in black or white. No, she doesn't know how to have fun.

LB: I think it is fantastic that you make films about the U.S. and haven't gone there—it's as if you are reflecting America in a European mirror, reflecting it back to the world from a European perspective, and maybe trying to reflect the U.S. back to the U.S. But who is your audience?

LvT: That is also a good question.

LB: Did you intend to reach Americans? Or anyone else?

LvT: [pause] I don't know. It's not really . . . —it's not made *for* Americans. But still I think that some Americans could maybe find it interesting to see it from this perspective that you talk about. My problem is maybe that I don't have an audience in my mind, so I do not have an audience. I don't think about them if they are there. I don't work for an audience; I work for myself. That's the only way I can do it. I was in the commercial business for a few years to make some money, and I don't think that you can allow people to say that they know what an audience wants and what they should have, blah, blah, blah. I think that's crap. I don't think anybody can do that. But if you want to do something good you have to do it for yourself and then afterwards there's hope that other people also will benefit, or see, or whatever. Anyway that's the only way I can work.

LB: At Cannes you called yourself 60 or 80 percent American. Since I've been in Denmark I see what you mean. Looking at Danish television, so much of the programming is from the States. . . .

LvT: I think that today's television shows what is popular in America—*Desperate Housewives* and whatever. I think it's even worse in Sweden, actually.

LB: . . . and [at Cannes in 2005] you were all riled up about that. You implied that it was about time someone from outside made a film about America. Wasn't that political? Weren't you making a serious statement about globalization?

LvT: Somehow that is political, but it doesn't have to have a political aim to do it—but by being comfortable by [being] who we are.

LB: You referred to Dogme [in the Manifesto] as involving an attempt to reach some kind of truth. I'd like to know what you meant by "truth."

LvT: I don't know if "truth" is the right word. For me it can be a revelation. One scene of a film can come up and say it all. The instant of the film was worth going along to fight for rather than the whole, and that was what you were trying to find. And that was what we were trying to find through all these rules.

LB: Do you like Japanese horror films because they get to the truth?

LVT: Yes. Somehow they do because they are not so story fixed. A lot of absurd things can happen in them, and you don't care because it's within in the framework of this genre film. As long as it's scary we don't care. It's a much freer form of film I think somehow.

LB: Are you still going to make the third part of the USA Trilogy?

LVT: The third part of the trilogy I'll do, maybe in America. But please let me know what your students think about these horror films.

Interview, October 2007

This excerpt, from a Skype interview of October 3, 2007, follows up the discussion of *The Boss of It All* begun at Zentropa approximately one year previously.

LB: *The Boss of It All* is one of your most Danish films. What are some of the jokes about Denmark, Iceland, and so on that Americans might not get?

LVT: Iceland used to be a Danish colony. And that's why of course they hate us very much, which they are entitled to do. But it's quite funny that right now we have a lot of Icelandic people who are buying up most of Copenhagen. You know, for some reason they are very rich, all these [corporations] in Iceland. I don't know why, but they buy up everything that is considered to be very Danish, I think to teach us a lesson, which, yeah, is good enough. But it's significant.[2]

LB: You included jokes about Danish sentimentality and the boss's need for acceptance by his subordinates. Is that a commentary on any cultural trait?

LVT: In the Danish national character there lies a fear of conflict in any way, so to hire a Dane to be a bad guy is very difficult. If somebody wants to be a bad guy, they all want to be smiling and friendly, and I think that's maybe typical for a small country. But it is very typical that you can't really hire anybody to be a bad guy. And actually we talk about [the issue] in the film a lot because, whenever we produce with a lot of

American and British actors, it is of course important that there is—even in my strange way of shooting films—some discipline somewhere, and of course it's a very good thing if the discipline doesn't come directly from the director but from some producer or somebody who says "Now you have to [do the job]. Now you have talked enough, now you have to shoot for a while." To be the "bad guy" is important but you cannot get it from a Dane normally. From any other country you could easily get people who would be bad guys. Anyway in the film industry, that's for sure. Whenever we want somebody who is really good [at being "bad"], we will buy them from England or America or whatever.

LB: Is it a coincidence that the "boss of it all"—and also the boss of "the boss of it all"—lives in America?

LvT: Yeah, that's very—that's interesting, yeah. I hadn't thought about it. That must be, yeah. I'm sorry—it's very childish, I can see that. Of course America has for me always to some degree stood for capitalism, which is completely true. And yes, I find many aspects of capitalism quite mean but, yeah. So maybe that's why. I haven't thought about it that much.

LB: Do you see differences between European and American capitalism?

LvT: Capitalism is capitalism if it's European or American. I don't think there's any difference in that, but the Americans—and there are so many [of them]—for some reason are very good at it. But then again I wouldn't be able to talk about that. I don't know America or Americans to that degree.

LB: As narrator you say that it's a "harmless" comedy, but is it? Do you ever see yourself as a satirist?

LvT: Well a little bit, yeah.

LB: If you were not afraid of flying would you be tempted like Susanne Bier to make films in the U.S.?

LvT: I doubt it. No I don't think so. I'm good where I am. Early in my career I made quite a lot of commercials and you don't have much freedom there, and I don't think I would have a lot of freedom in America—or [rather] I know I wouldn't. I'm good where I am, I have never dreamt of going to Hollywood.

LB: Automavision . . . Do you remember how you got the idea for it?

LvT: The idea came because I was so much opposed to framing a picture. It's difficult to completely control any image, and [the reasoning was that] since it is [nearly] impossible then you shouldn't try at all. In my first films I framed a lot, and we made a lot of rules about tracking shots, craning shots, and no pans and whatever, and after I had done that so much I was very happy [to use] the handheld camera because you didn't frame—you were merely looking at some action when framing it. And then after working with handheld camera for a long time I thought it [would be] interesting if you could find another way of not having to frame. And then of course it was that it should be chance that framed, so that we made the computer decide the framing to some degree.

LB: You said at one point that you devised the form to fit the content of the film. *How* does Automavision fit *The Boss of It All?*

LvT: I don't know [pause]. It feels right, yeah. It feels right, I feel good about it, but I can't explain why.

LB: In the press book interview, you said something about men being funnier than women in the film?

LvT: There can be funny women also, but I think it's somehow not funny if the woman is just stupid. Maybe it's because of how we are taught that you should look at women, but somehow it's not funny. I don't find it funny anyway. But whereas men who are stupid can be very funny. There are a lot of things women can do that are funny but somehow not being stupid, no. But I think that is actually something that could be investigated into—that is, what do we find funny, because don't you agree that it is different, that it has to do with gender also?

LB: Kisser reminded me of Katharine Hepburn characters in the old screwball comedies. You seem to make her smart and "good" when she could have been turned into a pretentious character.

LvT: Yes, but you know, my mother, even though she was Communist, she loved Katharine Hepburn. She was crazy about her, because she also stood for some kind of freedom for a woman. I'm probably influenced by her quite a lot.

LB: Your last films have had increasingly stronger female characters. Are your films moving more in the direction of women characters more like your mother admired?

LvT: Yes. Yes, probably. But I don't want her to steer anything. She should not be allowed to steer anything but of course she is—but please don't tell me if she is, you know. Because it's none of her business. She's dead—and she should stay that way—many years ago. She has nothing to do with the life I'm leading any more. Of course she has, but I don't want to see it.

The stronger female characters of Trier's recent films would take new form and resonance in *Antichrist*. Besides revealing that his mother still had plenty to do with the life he was leading, the film would confront "her" more directly than before—in part by adapting the horror genre for its age-old function of providing a controlled environment for exorcising (and exercising) fears and desires.

For three weeks after the Copenhagen trip of fall 2006, I followed up on Trier's parting request for students' viewpoints. The class blog raged with debate among j-horror fans striving to show their chops. *Audition* (1999), *The Eye* (2002), *Dark Water* (2002), *Ju-on* (2003), *A Tale of Two Sisters* (2003), *Suicide Club* (2003), *The Three Extremes*, and cross-genre films such as *Battle Royale* (2000) and *Ichi the Killer* (2001) were at the top of their lists, which I emailed to Trier with their discussion in mid-October. Two months later, Trier plunged into the depression for which making *Antichrist* was to become a form of therapy. The interview excerpt that follows, also from the Skype interview of October 3, 2007, seems to have been similarly therapeutic, as I found him, in the late afternoon and after a bit of coaxing, in nearly characteristic form.[3] As our conversation moved to his current work, he was, as before, keener on quizzing me about horror movies than on deflecting questions about his political views and more engaged with topics such as fear, cruelty, and catharsis than the discussion of *The Boss of It All* I had prepared for. Being in process and at risk, the film's status lent the game unique elements of performativity: questions teetered on the edge of possibility; a response might be a prediction, a decision, or a diversion.

LB: When I talked to you last year, you mentioned you were attempting to compromise. I chided you about abandoning your commitment to reinventing the medium, and you talked about your interest in making genre films. Where are you now in relation to this issue?

LVT: Well, first of all, I've come to a time in my life where I'm mostly trying to survive, so there're not so many thoughts about compromising or reinventing anything. I work very little or less than I would have liked to because I'm still kind of . . . I think I suffer a little from the aftershocks of the depression that I had [pause]. Compromising, yeah, I would like to pull in other people more, yes. If that's what you mean by compromising, yes, I'm trying to do that [pause]. It would be good.

LB: So what are you working on now? *Antichrist?*

LvT: I just wrote the first draft. And I went to Germany to research a little because we probably will shoot it in a forest in Germany. They are very good forests, in Germany.

LB: They have very good forests, and they also have very good history for this sort of thing, don't they? So will you be returning to some of the themes of the Europe Trilogy?

LvT: No . . . I don't know. I think I've written a horror film but let's see, maybe it's not. Maybe it's only horrific in the concept of the film [pause]. I am trying anyway, you know, but every time I try to [make a genre film] people tell me that it's not, but I'm trying, I'm trying.

LB: Why did you choose horror this time? You chose comedy before. Why horror now?

LvT: Yeah, yeah, that's a very good question. It's also because, or partly because [pause] all this anxiety that, you know, I deal with every day or do not deal with is something that I can use in this film. And of course it's better to use it than to suffer from it.

LB: In *The Kingdom* for example, you used your phobias. . . .

LvT: It's a little the same, but it's a genre where—I don't know how to put [this] in English—I've seen it in some Japanese horror films, and we talked about [how Asian horror is] actually one of the most open forms of films in the sense that the storytelling is not as important as it is in other films. You know, actually, if you changed the music to non–horror film music then they could be seen as art films [as] they can be very slow. . . . This genre—some of the films anyway—I like very much. I'm very fond of the genre. There are of course things that I think [are] too popular, but I tried to take a Tarkovsky film the other day and just put horror music on, and then it became a horror film. You know, it's actually a forgiving genre. And very open in the sense that there are of course some things that you have to do in the right "horror" way, but then you are free to do a lot of things that you can do any way you like.

LB: Which Tarkovsky film was it?

LvT: It was *The Mirror*. It's really very, very scary if you change the music.

LB: Have you seen *Solaris?*

LvT: Oh yes. Oh yes. I liked it, I just saw it again. Have you seen the new *Solaris* also? How is that?

LB: It's good. . . . It's of course shorter and has George Clooney in it [laughs]. It works pretty well as an American remake, but of course it's nothing like the original. It's [directed by] Steven Soderbergh—who's been quite influenced by you, you know.

LvT: No, no, but I talked to Jeremy Davies. He was about to do the [Soderbergh] film, but I made a long [reference] to the director when we went through a tunnel in our camper and Jeremy was driving for me. I made a little joke about [Tarkovsky's] *Solaris* because I thought it was such an odd choice for a commercial film. If some of the money people had ever seen the original *Solaris,* they would have never gone into a new one. I can't think of anything less commercial than the original.[4]

LB: Right, but Soderbergh is interesting for alternating between art films and Hollywood films—like *Kafka* and *Ocean's 12*—he makes a Hollywood blockbuster and then does whatever he wants.

LvT: Yes, I think absolutely he's a very interesting character.

LB: Back to your horror film. When I teach horror, one point I start out with is that it's a very discredited genre—in the States anyway—it's a bottom feeder—the only genre "lower" is pornography. . . .

LvT: Really . . ., well that is what I want to do also, so . . . [laughs].

LB: . . . and we talk about how both pornography and horror and, to some extent, melodrama are "body" genres in that they provoke extremely physical reactions as well as emotions. Does that attract you to the genre?

LvT: Yes, yes, yes.

LB: How do or did you go about writing a horror film?

LvT: I don't know. I'm just looking at the film now because it's on my wall down here—and [in] lots of little notes. I paint on the wall a long line and then I put all the scenes on there on the wall so I can see them. But when you ask me how I did it I'm not really sure. Hopefully in some original way.

LB: You've spoken of rules of comedy in *The Boss of It All*. So what are the rules of horror?

LvT: No, no, no, but it's just difficult to [say]. What are the rules of horror? This is kind of my—me—trying to make a horror film. I don't know how other people [make horror films]. I hope it works, it's a very, very short script, that's all I can say, it's forty-seven pages.[5] Normally I write two hundred pages or so. I think *Dogville* was a hundred and eighty or something like that.

LB: Okay, so no rules of horror.

LvT: No, no.

LB: You like horror because it's open territory. Which is totally the opposite of the way you usually talk.

LvT: Yes. Yes. But of course I will now apply some rules. That's called the style of the film. [Also] it's a very intimate film. It's only two persons.

LB: When I last talked to you, you were watching Asian horror, and you mentioned *Dark Water* in particular. Do you have a new favorite now?

LvT: No, no, I still think that was one of the best. It's very interesting with how the Japanese always have something to do with the hair. It's very strange because that's not very dramatic in the Western world. Do you know why this is? Is it something Japanese?

LB: Yes, it has to do partly with gender roles in Japanese culture. The film often focuses on a woman who has been wronged and is involved in some sort of curse. She's both a victim and a victimizer, and her victimization has to do partly with her being part of a traditional culture in which she can't fully express her feelings. A good example would be *The Ring*, where the hair suggests repression and also something primal. Have you seen *Audition*?

LvT: Yes. I saw that.

LB: That's a good example. The woman with the hair is at first a completely passive person and then she takes her revenge, which is disturbing because the guy actually is fairly nice. [The film is] typical in that the woman is a victim and yet she's terrifying and tortures him far beyond what the crime [seems to deserve]. Usually my students bring up this issue: "Did he really deserve that?"

LVT: That may be the same thing about *Dogville.* The punishment is, yeah.

LB: Yeah, it's very like *Dogville.* So, there's a paradox where her victimization produces an even worse victimization, and it just goes on in a vicious, never-ending cycle.

LVT: Yeah. But [*Audition*] was very hard to watch.

LB: Why?

LVT: Oh, it was just very cruel.

LB: But people often call you cruel.

LVT: Ah. Yeah, yeah, yeah. I would like to be cruel. I'm not cruel enough. Let's see what you say after [you see] this film that I have on my wall here.

LB: Yeah, get some cruelty into it—that would be fun.

LVT: I'll try [laughs]. I'm working on it.

LB: Have you seen much international horror other than Asian—Italian, for example?

LVT: . . . I've seen, I think you mentioned it also, this Australian film [*Wolf Creek*]? There's a guy out in the middle of nowhere and these young people in a car and they are trying to escape and he's torturing them. Yeah, that's a nasty one. But that's the whole idea isn't it, that they should be nasty?

LB: Yeah, right [laughs]. But *The Kingdom* was scary and surreal and hilarious too. Is *Antichrist* going to be funny?

LVT: No. It might be funny when you see it but that is not the idea. I'm doing a serious horror film.

LB: Have you seen *The Texas Chain Saw Massacre*?

LVT: No, but wasn't that supposed to be funny when they did it?

LB: Yes and no. It sort of mixes over-the-top performances and absurdist humor with horror. It can be really nerve-wracking when these two impulses to laugh and to scream at the same time are present.

LVT: I saw—what is it called? *Nightmare on Elm Street.* That is funny and scary.

LB: You defined *The Five Obstructions* as "therapy" [for Jørgen Leth]—so do you think a genre film—say, a horror film—can be therapeutic?

LVT: Yeah. I'm quite sure it can. A good thing about genre films is that every [genre is] kind of closed. They [genres] are a very closed definition of what a film is, and because of that every time you open a new genre it's very interesting because you are so limited, in a way, and then it opens up a completely new area every time you delve into [it]. I find that very inspiring and therapeutic also. Yeah of course it's therapeutic in the sense that if I'm making a film I can't be so scared myself; that's one thing. But it's also therapeutic in the way that—if you see it as becoming better at making films.

LB: "Occupations," your entry for the Cannes . . . [60th Anniversary Tribute] . . .

LVT: Yeah, you saw that?

LB: I saw it and thought it was hilarious. That's a horror film isn't it?

LVT: Well, he only got what he deserved.

LB: [laughs] It's kind of a joke and a horror film. It combines horror and humor—but it is mostly a joke I guess?

LVT: Oh, yes.

LB: But it's very gratifying to the audience when you beat the guy into a bloody pulp. Is it just because he's talking a lot?

LVT: Well, yeah, but I was just thinking about, how every time you have an opening in Cannes there's some idiot sitting talking, and normally it's a reviewer of the film, so when they just sit talking instead of watching that's always irritating.

LB: What he was talking about was kind of interesting, you know, about how many cars he has and the leather industry—"Buy cheap and sell high," he advises you. Why the leather industry?

LVT: [laughs] I think I met somebody who talked about the leather industry.

LB: [laughs] I want to make something out of that, of course.

LVT: That's a problem with the horror genre—that you know there will automatically be so many symbols in the film . . . that it's impossible not to interpret it, what is it called, to decode the film.

LB: I think that's one reason I like it. A [good] horror film invites decoding, as your films always do. This film is called *Antichrist.* What is the Antichrist, or who is the Antichrist?

LVT: But you have to see the film to kind of figure that out. That I can't tell you.

LB: Oh, phooey.

LVT: But it's a good title. And Mr. Nietzsche also wrote a book called *Antichrist*.[6]

LB: Yes! And you have said that *Antichrist* [the film] postulates that the world was created by Satan rather than God. Are you sticking with this premise?

LVT: Oh, yes!

LB: Well, that's what I've always thought. [Laughs.] No surprise there!

LVT: No, no, there is no surprise in anything. But it's only the way we—we're not surprised when somebody dies, the only thing that can be surprising is the way he dies, right?

LB: Uh huh. [Pause.] So, who is Satan?

LVT: Yeah. It's a little . . . —please I would be happy to hear what you think about the film when it's done.

LB: Okay, but you can answer this one: Do you believe in Satan?

LVT: Do I believe in Satan? I believe as much in Satan as I believe in God.

LB: Baudelaire and others have suggested that it's easier to believe in evil or Satan than it is to believe in God. Or do you see the universe as Manichean—an opposition of good versus evil, black and white, God versus Satan? Or is this [title, *Antichrist*] just a nod to the genre?

LVT: Well [pause] it's based on me looking at plants and whatever, living things and how much they suffer. It is as you also have thought from the same conclusion that it's really a nasty idea, life. And especially human life, because—I think we talked about this—but [it's] one thing to be an animal and tortured and made to suffer your whole life and then to die in the end, but being a man, it's . . . much worse, because first of all, the man knows that he's going to die, and furthermore he knows that it's morally not right to kill other beings—or anyway there can be some emotional problems—and to know that for every step we take we kill a lot of animals, or plants, or whatever, and for every breath we take we kill. So it's really . . . that being a human is really a nasty joke. There's nothing new in that, but when you talk about drama it's . . . [pauses] really, it's very . . . [long sigh]. If it were a film—life—a very well written film, that is . . . now, that would really be a horror film of substance.

LB: [Pause]. I had some questions from my students that I don't know if we have time for . . .

LvT: Yeah—let's go for one or two of these.

LB: This is a hard one, from Nancy, who is tough: "Obviously you're interested in the act of sacrifice since in your films one character often sacrifices everything for another. What would you sacrifice for your art?"

LvT: More than most people. [Pause.] Actually, I've thought about that and I think that I'm willing to sacrifice more than most people, yes. I thought about it actually a couple of days ago. I'm willing to go quite a long way. But even if I was filming I would still run into a burning house if my family was there. But would I sacrifice? Yes, quite a lot. It's not that you have to feel that I want to be pitied for that, not at all, but I'm sure that's how it is.

LB: She follows with "What would you sacrifice for your children?" And I guess you answered that.

LvT: Yeah, well, I would sacrifice a lot for my children also. Thank God it has not been a question of if I should do films or, you know, be with my children. It has not been that, because I'm with my children quite a lot, normally, so I would of course sacrifice a lot for them. I don't see myself as a monster, you know.

LB: Nancy is just being tough. And she has another tough one: "In your film *The Five Obstructions* you state 'There are just a few areas in life on which I think I'm an expert. One of them is Jørgen Leth.' What are the others?"

LvT: That I'm an expert in? [laughs] That is, yeah, that's very good. Yeah. Probably it's only Leth that I'm an expert in—it's always easier to be an expert on somebody else. [laughs] If I'm an expert in anything then it must have something to do with filmmaking because that's what I've, you know, used most of my life for. I have to think about that. Yeah, yeah. No, I can't. Yeah, she's a tough one. If I find out I'll write you.

LB: Aaron asks, "Where is your favorite place to be in the world?" Now that's a nice question, isn't it?

LvT: Yes. Right. I have a little spot in a Danish wood that I once visited when I was a child. It was definitely my favorite spot. It was a place with wild strawberries, and there was nobody else there and the sun was shining and there was a little river and it was fantastic. I was all alone.

LB: Sounds wonderful.

LvT: [laughs] Yeah, doesn't it?

LB: [laughs]

LvT: Now I actually have to pick my children up. You don't want them to suffer.

LB: No, no, and yes, you must go pick your children up. I was just going to ask if that place—your favorite place—was in any of your films, but you don't have to answer that.

LvT: To some degree. Maybe in the one I'm writing now.

LB: In a horror film, huh?

LvT: Yeah. Yeah, I think.

LB: Well, don't destroy it—the place, I mean [laughs].

LvT: No, no, no, I'll keep it for myself also.[7]

Notes

1. Peter Aalbæk Jensen explained in an interview of September 22, 2006, that Zentropa puts "7,500 kids through that film school per year. Here they come for a weekly course together with the school class, and they can stay out here in a youth hostel." At the end of the week, each student premieres a film.

2. Within one year after this interview, the situation had reversed. Beginning in the 1990s, Iceland's increasingly privatized and risk-oriented economy had made the country one of the world's wealthiest by 2007, but with the international economic crisis and the collapse in October 2008 of all three of its major banks, it plunged into bankruptcy (Pierce; Parker 39). Much of Iceland's banking trade had been with the United Kingdom and the United States. In contrast, the Nordic welfare states including Denmark, Norway, Sweden, and Finland remained relatively stable. Reuters reports on June 16, 2009, that as "the financial crisis has shown," their welfare systems "also serve as a kind of insurance policy for the broad economy," as people who lose their jobs have a guaranteed income, which feeds back into the economy (Moskwa).

3. Originally scheduled for September 17, 2007, the interview had to be postponed after Trier had left work early after a panic attack, one of (apparently) many such aftershocks of his depression.

4. Trier refers to the tunnel sequence in Tarkovsky's *Solaris,* shot in Tokyo, which has been celebrated for its (creative and economical) use of real settings to create futuristic effects, much as Godard did in *Alphaville.* In an allusion to that sequence in *Epidemic,* the filmmakers drive through a tunnel at night.

Similarly, *Epidemic* cheaply uses the urban wasteland of the Ruhrgebiet to haunting effect.

5. The draft eventually grew to seventy-two pages (Iarussi).

6. "Mr. Nietzsche" refers back to a warm-up discussion that began with a few questions about the recently released *The Early Years: Erik Nietzsche Part 1*, the thinly disguised Trier-scripted comedy/autobiography based on his experience at the Danish Film School. I was especially interested in the title, named for the protagonist/Trier. "Why 'Erik'? Why 'Nietzsche'?" I asked. He replied, "That [Nietzsche] is the most interesting one. Well, when I was very young I read quite a lot of Nietzsche and was very fond of this funny fellow Erik. . . . I thought [the name] sounded really stupid."

7. The woods-as-favorite space brings together Trier's earliest and latest films. In his graduation project, *Images of a Relief*, in a scene that the director describes as exemplifying "some sort of nature poetry," Leo returns to his childhood refuge, an image of a lost Eden imagined as a Tarkovskian forest where he talks to the birds, alerts enemies lying in ambush, and is mortally stabbed by his mistress as chthonic manifestations of life continue all around. *Antichrist* reimagined the chthonic, exposing the horror and absurdity inherent in its lush beauty. "Eden" became a performative space in which he could express his trauma while flouting his deepest taboos. There "Nature" is a fecund bloodbath in which nestlings and acorns fall to infanticidal deaths, animals disembowel themselves, and even plants strangle one another to survive.

Orchidégartneren (The Orchid Gardener, 1977)
Denmark
Format: 16mm
Running time: 37 minutes
Language: Danish
Presentation: Black and white
Production company: Film Gruppe 16
Director: Lars von Trier
Screenplay: Lars von Trier
Photography: Hartvig Jensen, Helge Kaj, Peter Nørgaard, Mogens Svane, Lars von Trier
Editor: Lars von Trier
Cast: Lars von Trier (Victor Morse), Inger Hivdtfeldt (Eliza), Karen Oksbjerg (Eliza's friend), Brigitte Pelissier (third girl), Martin Drouzy (the gardener), Yvonne Levy, Carl-Henrik Trier (old Jew), Jesper Hoffmeyer (the narrator)

Menthe-la bienheureuse (Menthe—The Blissful, 1979)
Denmark
Format: 16mm
Running time: 31 minutes
Language: French
Presentation: Black and white
Production company: Film Gruppe 16
Director: Lars von Trier
Screenplay: Lars von Trier, Pauline Réage (novel)
Photography: Hartvig Jensen, Lars von Trier
Editor: Lars von Trier
Cast: Inger Hvidtfeldt (the woman), Annette Linnet (Menthe), Carl-Henrik Trier (the gardener), Lars von Trier (driver), Jenni Dick (the old lady)

Nocturne (1980)
Denmark
Format: 16mm
Running time: 8 minutes
Language: Danish
Presentation: Color and black and white
Production company: Det Danske Filmskole
Director: Lars von Trier
Screenplay: Lars von Trier, Tom Elling (uncredited)
Photography: Tom Elling
Editor: Tómas Gislason
Cast: Yvette (the woman), Solbjørg Højfeldt (telephone voice), Anne-Lise
    Gabold (the woman/voice)

Sidste detalje, Den (*The Last Detail,* 1981)
Denmark
Format: 35mm
Running time: 31 minutes
Language: Danish
Presentation: Black and white
Production company: Det Danske Filmskole
Director: Lars von Trier
Screenplay: Rumle Hammerich
Photography: Tom Elling
Editor: Tómas Gislason
Cast: Otto Brandenburg (Danny), Torben Zeller (Frank), Gitte Pelle (the
    woman), Ib Hansen (gangster boss), Michael Simpson (assistant)

Befrielsesbilleder (*Images of a Relief,* 1982)
Denmark
Format: 35mm
Running time: 57 minutes
Language: Danish
Presentation: Color
Production company: Danmarks Radio, Det Dankst Filmskole
Director: Lars von Trier
Screenplay: Lars von Trier, Tom Elling
Photography: Tom Elling
Music: Pierre de la Rue
Editor: Tómas Gislason
Cast: Edward Fleming (German officer Leo Mendel), Kirsten Olesen (his
    mistress)

Forbrydelsens element (*The Element of Crime*, 1984)
Denmark
Format: 35mm
Running time: 104 minutes
Language: English
Presentation: Color and black and white
Production company: Det Danske Filminstitut, Per Holst Filmproduktion
Producer: Per Holst
Director: Lars von Trier
Screenplay: Lars von Trier, Niels Vørsel
Photography: Tom Elling
Music: Bo Holten
Editor: Tómas Gislason
Cast: Michael Elphick (Fisher), Esmond Knight (Osborne), Me Me Lai
    (Kim), Jerold Wells (Police Chief Kramer), Ahmed El Shenawi (therapist),
    Astrid Henning-Jensen (housekeeper), János Herskó (coroner), Stig
    Larsson (coroner's assistant), Lars von Trier (Schmuck of Ages)

Epidemic (1987)
Denmark
Format: 16mm and 35mm
Running time: 106 minutes
Language: Danish, English
Presentation: Black and white
Production company: Det Danske Filminstitut
Producer: Jacob Eriksen
Director: Lars von Trier
Screenplay: Lars von Trier, Niels Vørsel
Photography: Henning Bendtsen
Music: Peter Bach
Editor: Thomas Krag, Lars von Trier
Cast: Lars von Trier (Lars, Dr. Mesmer), Niels Vørsel (Niels), Michael
    Simpson (cabbie, priest), Susanne Ottesen (herself), Cæcilia Holbek Trier
    (nurse), Leif Sabro (pilot), Udo Kier (himself), Claes Kastholm Hansen
    (himself), Svend Ali Hamann (hypnotist), Gitte Lind (hypnotized girl)

Medea (1988, TV)
Denmark
Format: Shot on video, copied onto film, copied back to video
Running time: 75 minutes
Language: Danish
Presentation: Color
Production company: Danmarks Radio
Director: Lars von Trier

Screenplay: Euripides, Carl Theodor Dreyer, Preben Thomsen, Lars von
Trier
Photography: Sejr Brockmann
Music: Joachim Holbek
Editor: Finnur Sveinsson
Cast: Udo Kier (Jason), Kirsten Olesen (Medea), Henning Jensen (Kreon),
Solbjørg Højfeldt (nurse), Preben Lerdorff Rye (teacher), Baard Owe
(Aigeus), Ludmilla Glinska (Glauce)

Europa (*Zentropa*, 1991)
Denmark, Sweden, France, Germany, Switzerland
Format: 35mm CinemaScope
Running time: 112 minutes
Language: English, German
Presentation: Black and white, color
Production companies: Nordisk Film, Det Danske Filminstitut, Svenska
Filminstitutet, Eurimages, Fund of the Council of Europe, Sofinergie 1,
Sofinergie 2, UGC, Institut suisse du film, Gunnar Obel, WMG, Gérard
Mital Productions, Alicéléo
Producer: Peter Aalbæk Jensen, Bo Christensen
Director: Lars von Trier
Assistant director: Tómas Gislason
Screenplay: Lars von Trier, Niels Vørsel
Photography: Henning Bendtsen, Edward Klosinski, Jean-Paul Meurisse
Music: Joachim Holbek
Editor: Hervé Schneid
Cast: Jean-Marc Barr (Leopold Kessler), Barbara Sukowa (Katharina
Hartmann), Udo Kier (Larry Hartmann), Ernst-Hugo Järegård (Uncle
Kessler), Erik Mørk (Pater), Jørgen Reenberg (Max Hartmann), Henning
Jensen (Siggy), Eddie Constantine (Colonel Harris), Max von Sydow
(narrator), Holger Perfort (Mayor Ravenstein)

Riget (*The Kingdom,* 1994, TV miniseries)
Denmark
Format: 16mm and video (blown up to 35mm for theatrical release)
Running time: 286 minutes
Language: Danish, Swedish
Presentation: Color
Production companies: Zentropa Entertainments, Danmarks Radio, Arte,
Swedish Television, Greco, The Coproduction Office, Westdeutscher
Rundfunk, TV Collaboration Fund, Nederlandse Omroepstichting
Producer: Sven Abrahamsen, Peter Aalbæk Jensen, Ole Reim, Ib Tardini
Director: Lars von Trier

Assistant director: Morten Arnfred
Screenplay: Lars von Trier, Niels Vørsel, Tómas Gislasen
Photography: Eric Kress, Henrik Harpelund
Music: Joachim Holbek
Editor: Molly Marlene Stensgård, Jacob Thueson
Cast: Ernst-Hugo Järegård (Stig Helmer), Kirsten Rolffes (Mrs. Drusse),
   Ghita Norby (Rigmor), Søren Pilmark (Jørgen Krogshøj), Holger Juul
   Hansen (Moesgaard), Annevig Schelde Ebbe (Mary), Jens Okking
   (Bulder), Otto Brandenburg (Porter Hansen), Baard Owe (Bondo),
   Solbjørg Højfeldt (Camilla), Birgitte Raabjerg (Judith), Louise Fribo
   (Sanne), Peter Mygind (Mogge), Vita Jensen (Dishwasher 1), Morten
   Rotne Leffers (Dishwasher 2), Michael Simpson (Man from Haiti), Dick
   Kayso (Security Manager), Mette Munk Plum (Mona's Mother), Laura
   Christensen (Mona), Udo Kier (Aage Krüger), Ulrik Cold (Narrator)

Breaking the Waves (1996)
Denmark, Sweden, France, Netherlands, Norway, Iceland
Format: 35mm
Running time: 159 minutes
Language: English
Presentation: Color
Production companies: Zentropa Entertainments; in coproduction with Argus
   Films, Arte, Canal+, CoBo Funds, Eurimages, Det Danske Filminstitut,
   European Script Fund, Finnish Film Foundation, Icelandic Film, La
   Sept Cinéma, Memfis Film, Lucky Red, Liberator Productions, Media
   Investment Group, Nederlands Fonds voor de Film, Nordisk Film and
   TV Fonds, YLE, Northern Lights, Norwegian Films, October Films, Trust
   Film Svenska, Svenska Filminstitutet, STV Drama, Philippe Bober, ZDF
Producer: Peter Aalbæk Jensen, Vibeke Windeløv
Director: Lars von Trier
Assistant director: Morten Arnfred
Screenplay: Lars von Trier, Peter Asmussen, David Pirie
Photography: Robby Müller
Editor: Anders Refn
Cast: Emily Watson (Bess McNeill), Stellan Skarsgård (Jan Nyman), Katrin
   Cartlidge (Dodo McNeill), Jean-Marc Barr (Terry), Adrian Rawlins (Dr.
   Richardson), Jonathan Hackett (Minister), Sandra Voe (Mother), Udo Kier
   (sadistic sailor), Phil McCall (Grandfather), Robert Robertson (Chairman)

Riget II (*The Kingdom II*, 1997, TV miniseries)
Denmark
Format: 16mm
Running time: 286 minutes

Language: Danish, Swedish
Presentation: Color
Production companies: Zentropa Entertainments, Det Danske Filminstitut,
    Danmarks Radio, La Sept-Arte, Liberator Productions, Norsk
    Rikskringkasting, Radiotelevisione Italiana, Sveriges Television
Producer: Vibeke Windeløv, Svend Abrahamsen
Director: Lars von Trier
Assistant director: Morten Arnfred
Screenplay: Lars von Trier and Niels Vørsel
Photography: Eric Kress
Music: Joachim Holbek
Editor: Pernille Bech Christensen, Molly Marlene Stensgård
Cast: Ernst-Hugo Järegård (Stig Helmer), Kirsten Rolffes (Mrs. Drusse),
    Holger Juul Hansen (Dr. Einar Moesgaard), Søren Pilmark (Jørgen
    Krogshøj), Ghita Norby (Rigmor), Jens Okking (Bulder), Birthe Neumann
    (Miss Svendsen), Otto Brandenburg (Hansen), Erik Wedersoe (Ole),
    Baard Owe (Bondo), Birgitte Raaberg (Judith), Solbjørg Højfeldt
    (Camilla), Peter Mygind (Mogge), Vita Jensen (Dishwasher 1), Morten
    Rotne Leffers (Dishwasher 2), Udo Kier (Little Brother/Aage Krüger),
    Louise Fribo (Sanne), Ole Boisen (Christian), Thomas Stender (Student),
    Claus Nissen (Madsen), Thomas Bo Larsen (Falcon), Laura Christensen
    (Mona), Mette Munk Plum (Mona's Mother), Michael Simpson (Man from
    Haiti), Fash Shodeinde (Philip Marco), Annevig Shelde Ebbe (Mary),
    Ulrik Cold (Narrator)

Dogme #2—Idioterne (The Idiots, 1998)
Denmark, Sweden, France, Netherlands, Italy
Format: 35mm
Running time: 117 minutes
Language: Danish
Presentation: Color
Production companies: Zentropa Entertainments, Danmarks Radio; in
    coproduction with Liberator Pictures, La Sept Cinéma, Argus Film
    Produktie, Vrijzinnig Protestantse Radio Omroep; in collaboration or
    association with other companies
Producer: Vibeke Windeløv
Director: Lars von Trier (uncredited)
Screenplay: Lars von Trier
Photography: Lars von Trier
Editor: Molly Marlene Stensgård
Cast: Bodil Jørgensen (Karen), Jens Albinus (Stoffer), Anne Louise Hassing
    (Susanne), Nikolaj Lie Kaas (Jeppe), Louise Mieritz (Josephine), Troels
    Lyby (Henrik), Henrik Prip (Ped), Luis Mesonero (Miguel), Knud Romer

Jørgensen (Axel), Trine Michelsen (Nana), Anne-Grethe Bjarup Riis (Katrine), Paprika Steen (high class lady), Erik Wedersøe (Stoffer's uncle), Michael Moritzen (man from Municipality), Anders Hove (Josephine's father), Hans Henrik Clemensen (Karen's husband), Lars von Trier (interviewer)

D-Dag (*D-Day*, 2000, TV)
Denmark
Format: Digital video
Running time: 70 minutes
Language: Danish
Presentation: Color
Production companies: Nimbus Film, Zentropa Entertainments, Danmarks
    Radio, TV2, TV3, TV Danmark
Directors: Søren Kragh-Jacobsen, Kristian Levring, Thomas Vinterberg, Lars
    von Trier Photography: Anthony Dod Mantle, Jesper Jargil, Eric Kress,
    Henrik Lundø, Jens Schlosser
Music: Flemming Nordkrog
Editor: Valdis Óskarsdóttir
Cast: Charlotte Sachs Bostrup (Lise), Dejan Cukic (Boris), Nicolaj
    Kopernikus (Niels-Henning), Bjarne Henriksen (Carl), Stellan Skarsgård
    (Lise's husband), Alexander Skarsgård (Lise's papsøn), Louise Mieritz
    (Lise's sister), Jesper Asholt (Jørgen), Helle Dolleris (Carl's wife), Klaus
    Bondam (receptionist)

Dancer in the Dark (2000)
Denmark, Germany, Netherlands, Italy, United States, France, United
    Kingdom, Sweden, Finland, Iceland, Norway
Format: 35mm
Running time: 140 minutes
Language: English
Presentation: Color
Production companies: Zentropa Entertainments, Film i Väst, Trust Film
    Svenska, Liberator Productions; in coproduction with Pain Unlimited
    GmbH, Cinematograph A/S, What Else? B.V., Icelandic Film, Blind Spot
    Pictures Oy, Danmarks Radio, STV Drama, Arte France, France 3, Arte,
    Good Machine; in collaboration or association with other companies
Producer: Vibeke Windeløv
Director: Lars von Trier
Screenplay: Lars von Trier
Photography: Robby Müller
Composer: Björk
Lyrics: Sjón Sigurdsson, Lars Von Trier, Björk

Choreography: Vincent Paterson
Editor: Francois Gédigier, Molly Marlene Stensgård
Cast: Björk (Selma), Catherine Deneuve (Cathy), David Morse (Bill
    Houston), Peter Stormare (Jeff), Joel Grey (Oldrich Novy), Cara Seymour
    (Linda Houston), Vladica Kostic (Gene), Jean-Marc Barr (Norman),
    Vincent Paterson (Samuel), Siobhan Fallon (Brenda), Zeljko Ivanek
    (District Attorney), Udo Kier (Doctor), Jens Albinus (Morty), Reathel
    Bean (Judge), Mette Bergreen (Receptionist)

Dogville (2003)
Denmark, Sweden, Norway, Finland, United Kingdom, France, Germany,
    Netherlands, Italy
Format: 35mm
Running time: 178 minutes
Language: English
Presentation: Color
Production companies: Zentropa Entertainments; in coproduction with
    Film i Väst, Trollhättan Film AB, Sigma Films, Pain Unlimited GmbH,
    Slot Machine, Liberator Pictures, 4 1/2, Arte France, France 3, Trust
    Film Svenska, Memfis Film and Television, Danmarks Radio, Sveriges
    Television, Something Else B.V., Isabella Films International B.V.,
    Westdeutscher Rundfunk, Norsk TV2 AS, Filmmek, NPS Television, YLI
    TV1, Arte; in collaboration or association with other companies
Producer: Vibeke Windeløv, Lars Jönsson
Director: Lars von Trier
Screenplay: Lars von Trier
Photography: Anthony Dod Mantle
Editor: Molly Marlene Stensgård
Cast: Nicole Kidman (Grace), Paul Bettany (Tom Edison, Jr.), James Caan
    (Big Man/Grace's father), John Hurt (Narrator), Harriet Andersson
    (Gloria), Lauren Bacall (Ma Ginger), Jean-Marc Barr (man with big hat),
    Blair Brown (Mrs. Henson), Patricia Clarkson (Vera), Jeremy Davies (Bill
    Henson), Ben Gazzara (Jack McKay), Philip Baker Hall (Tom Edison, Sr.),
    Siobhan Fallon (Martha), Zeljko Ivanek (Ben), Udo Kier (gangster), Cleo
    King (Olivia), Miles Purinton (Jason), Bill Raymond (Mr. Henson), Chloë
    Sevigny (Liz Henson), Shauna Sim (June), Stellan Skarsgård (Chuck)

De Fem benspænd (The Five Obstructions, 2003)
Denmark, Switzerland, Belgium, France
Format: 35mm
Running time: 90 minutes
Language: Danish, English, French, Spanish
Presentation: Color and black and white

Production companies: Zentropa Real, Almaz Film Productions S.A., Panic
    Productions, Wajnbrosse Productions
Producers: Vibeke Windeløv and Carsten Holst
Directors: Lars von Trier and Jørgen Leth
Screenplay: Lars von Trier and Jørgen Leth, with Asger Leth and Sophie
    Destin
Photography: Kim Hattesen, Dan Holmberg
Animation: Bob Sabiston
Editors: Daniel Dencik, Morten Højbjerg, and Camilla Skousen
Cast: Claus Nissen (the Man, *The Perfect Human*; the Man, "Obstruction
    #4), Lars von Trier (himself/obstructor, "The Conversations"), Jørgen
    Leth (himself/filmmaker; narrator, *The Perfect Human*, "Obstruction #5";
    the Man, "Obstruction #2"), Daniel Hernandez Rodriguez (the Man,
    "Obstruction #1"); Jacqueline Arenal (the Woman, "Obstruction #1"),
    Vivien Rosa (second woman, "Obstruction #1"), Patrick Bauchau (the Man,
    "Obstruction #3"), Alexandra Vandernoot (the Woman, "Obstruction #3"),
    Bob Sabiston (himself)

Manderlay (2005)
Denmark, Sweden, Netherlands, France, Germany, United Kingdom
Format: 35mm
Running time: 139 minutes
Language: English
Presentation: Color
Production company: Zentropa Entertainments; in coproduction with
    Isabella Films B.V., Manderlay, Film i Väst, Ognon Pictures, Sigma
    Films, Pain Unlimited GmbH, Arte France, France 3, Arte, Memfis
    Film, Danmarks Radio, Sveriges Television, NPS Television, YLE Co-
    Productions; in collaboration or association with other companies
Director: Lars von Trier
Screenplay: Lars von Trier
Photography: Anthony Dod Mantle
Music: Joachim Holbek
Editor: Bodil Kjærhauge and Molly Marlene Stensgård
Cast: Bryce Dallas Howard (Grace), Isaach De Bankolé (Timothy), Danny
    Glover (Wilhelm), Willem Dafoe (Grace's father), John Hurt (Narrator),
    Michael Abiteboul (Thomas), Lauren Bacall (Mam), Jean-Marc Barr
    (Mr. Robinson), Geoffrey Bateman (Bertie), Virgile Bramly (Edward),
    Ruben Brinkman (Bingo), Doña Croll (Venus), Jeremy Davies (Niels),
    Llewella Gideon (Victoria), Mona Hammond (Old Wilma), Ginny Holder
    (Elisabeth), Emmanuel Idowu (Jim), Zeljko Ivanek (Dr. Hector), Teddy
    Kempner (Joseph), Udo Kier (Mr. Kirspe), Rik Launspach (Stanley
    Mays), Suzette Llewellyn (Flora), Charles Maquignon (Bruno), Joseph

Mydell (Mark), Javone Prince (Jack), Clive Rowe (Sammy), Chloë Sevigny (Philomena), Nina Sosanya (Rose)

Dear Wendy (2005)
Denmark, France, Germany, United Kingdom
Format: 35mm
Running time: 105 minutes
Language: English
Presentation: Color
Production companies: Nimbus Films, Zentropa Entertainments, Lucky Punch I/S, in coproduction with TV2 Danmark
Producer: Sisse Graum Jørgensen
Director: Thomas Vinterberg
Screenplay: Lars von Trier
Photography: Anthony Dod Mantle
Editor: Mikkel E. G. Nielsen
Cast: Jamie Bell (Dick), Bill Pullman (Krugsby), Michael Angarano (Freddie), Danso Gordon (Sebastian), Novella Nelson (Clarabelle), Chris Owen (Huey), Alison Pill (Susan), Mark Webber (Stevie), Trevor Cooper (Dick's father)

Direktøren for det hele (*The Boss of It All*, 2006)
Denmark, Sweden, Iceland, Italy, France, Norway, Finland, Germany
Format: 35mm
Running time: 99 minutes
Language: Danish, Icelandic, English, Russian
Presentation: Color
Production companies: Zentropa Entertainments; in coproduction with Memfis Film, Slot Machine, Lucky Red, Pain Unlimited GmbH, Trollhättan Film AB, Orione Cinematografica, Det Danske Filminstitut, Sveriges Television, Film i Väst, Filmstiftung Nordrhein-Westfalen, Nordisk Film and TV Fond, Icelandic Film Center; in collaboration or association with other companies
Producer: Meta Louise Foldager
Director: Lars von Trier
Screenplay: Lars von Trier
Visual effects: Peter Hjorth
Editor: Molly Marlene Stensgård
Cast: Jens Albinus (Kristoffer), Peter Gantzler (Ravn), Fridrik Thor Fridriksson (Finnur), Benedikt Erlingsson (Tolk), Iben Hjejle (Lise), Henrik Prip (Arne), Mia Lyhne (Heidi A.), Casper Christensen (Gorm), Louise Mieritz (Mette), Jean-Marc Barr (Spencer), Sofie Gråbøl (Kisser), Anders Hove (Jokumsen), Lars von Trier (Narrator)

"Occupations" (segment, *Chacun son cinéma ou Ce petit coup au coeur quand la lumière s'éteint et que le film commence/To Each His Own Cinema*, 2007)
France
Format: 35mm
Running time: 3 minutes
Language: English
Presentation: Color
Production company: Cannes Film Festival, Elzévir Films
Producer: Gilles Jacob
Director: Lars von Trier
Screenplay: Lars von Trier
Editor: Bodil Kjæhauge
Visual effects: Peter Hjorth
Cast: Lars von Trier (the filmmaker), Jacques Frantz (obnoxious businessman)

De unge år: Nietzsche sagaen del 1 (*The Early Years: Erik Nietzsche Part 1*, 2007)
Denmark, Italy, Sweden, Austria, France
Format: 35mm
Running time: 100 minutes
Language: Danish
Presentation: Color
Production companies: Zentropa Entertainments, Det Danske Filminstitut, DR TV International, Eurimages, Sveriges Television, The Swedish Film Institute, Film i Väst, Lucky Red, Trollhättan Film, Film i Väst, Memfis Film, Pappagallo Film, Australian Film Institute, Danmarks Radio, Les Films du Losange, Dor Film Produktionsgesellschaft
Producer: Sesse Graum Jørgensen
Director: Jacob Thueson
Screenplay: Lars von Trier (as Erik Nietzsche)
Photography: Sebastian Blenkov
Editor: Per K. Kierkegaard
Cast: Jonatan Spang (Erik), Jens Albinus (Trois), Troels Lyby (Bent), Nikolaj Coster Waldau (Sammy), David Dencik (Zelko), Søren Pilmark (Mads), Thomas Bendixen (Thorvald), Kristian Boland (Husejer), Marie Brolin Tani (Stine), Hans Henrik Clemensen (Carsten Virén), Lars von Trier (narrator)

Antichrist (2009)
Denmark, Germany, France, Sweden, Italy, Poland
Format: 35mm CinemaScope

Running time: 104 minutes
Language: English
Presentation: Color and black and white
Production companies: Zentropa Entertainments; in coproduction with
    Zentropa International Köln, Zentropa International Poland, Memfis
    Film, Slot Machine, Arte France Cinéma, ZDF-Arte, STV, Film i Väst,
    The Danish Film Institute, The Swedish Film Institute, The Polish Film
    Institute, Nordisk Film and TV-Fond, Trollhättan Film AB, Lucky Red; in
    cooperation with other production companies
Producer: Meta Louise Foldager
Director: Lars von Trier
Screenplay: Lars von Trier
Photography: Anthony Dod Mantle
Sound: Kristen Eidnes Andersen
Editor: Anders Refn, Åsa Mossberg
Cast: Willem Dafoe (He), Charlotte Gainsbourg (She), Storm Acheche
    Sahlström (Nic)

Melancholia (forthcoming, 2011)
Denmark
Language: English
Production companies: Zentropa Entertainments; in coproduction with
    Zentropa International Köln, Memfis Film, Slot Machine, Trollhättan Film
    AB, Arte France Cinéma
Producer: Meta Louise Foldager
Director: Lars von Trier
Screenplay: Lars von Trier
Photography: Manuel Alberto Claro
Cast: Kiefer Sutherland (John), Alexander Skarsgård (Michael), Kirsten Dunst
    (Justine), Stellan Skarsgård (Jack), Charlotte Gainsbourg (Claire), Charlotte
    Rampling (Gaby), Udo Kier (wedding planner), John Hurt (Dexter), Brady
    Corbet (Tim)

Aftab, Kaleem. "Lars von Trier—'It's Good that People Boo.'" *Independent* May 29, 2009. Web. June 1, 2009. http://www.independent.co.uk/.

Ago, Allesandro. "Once Upon a Time in Amerika: *Dancer in the Dark* and Contemporary European Cinema." *Spectactor—The University of Southern California Journal of Film and Television* 23.2 (2003): 32–43. Print.

Althusser, Louis. *Lenin and Philosophy and Other Essays.* Trans. Ben Brewster. New York: Monthly Review Press, 2001. Print.

Altman, Rick. *The American Film Musical.* Bloomington: Indiana University Press, 1987. Print.

Andersen, Lars K. "A Stone-Turner from Lynby." 1994. Lumholdt, *Lars* 88–105.

Andrews, Nigel. "Beauty and the Unspeakable." *Financial Times* July 22, 2009. Web. July 22, 2009. http://www.ft.com/.

———. "Maniacal Iconoclast of Film Tradition." 1991. Lumholdt, *Lars* 81–83.

Ansen, David. "God, Sex, and Sacrifice." *Newsweek* December 9, 1996. Web. May 17, 2010. http://www.newsweek.com/.

Aronowitz, Stanley, and Jonathan Cutler, eds. *Post-Work.* New York: Routledge, 1998. Print.

Arroyo, Jose. "How Do You Solve a Problem like Lars von Trier?" *Sight and Sound* 10.9 (2000): 14–16. Print.

Austin, J. L. *How to Do Things with Words.* Oxford: Clarendon, 1962. Print.

Avinger, Charles. "*The Kingdom* I and II." *DVD Maniacs* October 11, 2001. Web. May 1, 2008. http://www.dvdmaniacs.net/.

Badley, Linda. "Danish Dogma: 'Truth' and Cultural Politics." *Traditions in World Cinema.* Eds. Linda Badley, Steven Jay Schneider, and R. Barton Palmer. Edinburgh: Edinburgh University Press, 2006. 80–94.

Badt, Karin. "Most Hated Director at Cannes: Lars von Trier as Antichrist or Shaman?" *Huffington Post* May 29, 2009. Web. June 19, 2009. http://www.huffingtonpost.com/.

Bainbridge, Caroline. *The Cinema of Lars von Trier: Authenticity and Artifice.* London: Wallflower Press, 2007. Print.

―――. "Just Looking? Traumatic Affect, Film Form and Spectatorship in the Work of Lars von Trier." *Screen* 45.4 (2004): 391–400. Print.

―――. "Making Waves: Trauma and Ethics in the Work of Lars von Trier." *Journal for Cultural Research* 8.3 (2004): 353–69. Print.

Bakhtin, Mikhail. "Forms of Time and of the Chronotope in the Novel: Notes toward a Historical Poetics." *The Dialogic Imagination: Four Essays.* Ed. Michael Holquist. Austin: University of Texas Press, 1982. 84–258. Print.

―――. *Rabelais and His World.* Bloomington: Indiana University Press, 1984. Print.

Balz, Adam Terry. "*Manderlay.*" *Plume Noir* 2005. Web. April 30, 2010. http://www.plume-noire.com/.

Barthes, Roland. *Mythologies.* Trans. Annette Lavers. London: Vintage, 1972. Print.

Bell, Emma. "Lars von Trier: Anti-American? Me?" *Independent* October 21, 2005. Web. January 12, 2009. http://www.independent.co.uk/.

Benjamin, Walter. *The Arcades Project.* Ed. Rolf Tiedemann. Cambridge, Mass.: Harvard University Press, 2002. Print.

Bernhard, Brendan. "Lars Attacks!" *LA Weekly* March 25, 2004. Web. June 22, 2006. http://www.laweekly.com/.

Björkman, Stig. "Naked Miracles." *Sight and Sound* 6.10 (1996): 11–14. Print.

―――, ed. *Trier on von Trier.* Trans. Neil Smith. London: Faber and Faber, 2003. Print.

Blackmon, Douglas. *Slavery by Another Name: The Re-Enslavement of Black Americans from the Civil War to World War II.* New York: Doubleday, 2008. Print.

Bo, Michael. "De overlevede Antikrist—og von Trier." *Politiken* May 23, 2009. Web. June 5, 2009. http://politiken.dk/.

Bogle, David. *Blacks in American Film: Toms, Coons, Mulattos, Mammies and Bucks.* New York: Garland, 1988. Print.

Bordwell, David. "Another Pebble in Your Shoe." *Observations on Film Art. David Bordwell's Website on Cinema.* Posted December 13, 2006. Last modified December 31, 2006. Web. April 29, 2009. http://www.davidbordwell.net/blog/.

―――. "Cinema in the World's Happiest Place." *Observations on Film Art. David Bordwell's Website on Cinema.* Posted July 2, 2009. Web. July 3, 2009. http://www.davidbordwell.net/blog/.

―――. "Risk and Renewal in Danish Film." Film # 57. *The Danish Film Institute* February 2007: 16–19. Web. December 12, 2008. http://www.dfi.dk/.

The Boss of It All: A Comedy by Lars von Trier. Official Web site. 2006. March 3, 2010. http://www.direktorenfordethele.dk/.

Brabazon, Tara. "What Have You Ever Done on the Telly?" *International Journal of Cultural Studies* 8.1 (2005): 101–17. Print.

Brecht, Bertolt. *Poems 1913–1956*. Ed. John Willett and Ralph Manheim with the co-operation of Erich Fried. New York: Methuen, 1976. Print.

Brooks, Xan. "*Antichrist:* A Work of Genius or the Sickest Film in the History of Cinema?" *Guardian* July 16, 2009. Web. July 21, 2009. http://www.guardian .co.uk/film.

———. "Mangy Foxes and Fake Firs: The Reel Chaos at the Cannes Film Festival." Review of *Antichrist*. *Guardian* May 18, 2009. Web. June 6, 2009. http://www.guardian.co.uk/film.

Burns, Sean. "Lars Rover." *Philadelphia Weekly Online* March 15, 2006. Web. April 9, 2009. http://www.philadelphiaweekly.com/.

Butler, Judith. "Gender Is Burning: Questions of Appropriation and Subversion." *Bodies that Matter: On the Discursive Limits of "Sex."* Rpt. in *Feminist Film Theory: A Reader*. Ed. Sue Thornham. New York: New York University Press, 1999. 336–49. Print

Carter, Angela. *The Sadeian Woman and the Ideology of Pornography*. New York: Pantheon Books, 1978. Print.

Christensen, Claus. "Documentary Gets the Dogma Treatment." Hjort and MacKenzie, *Purity and Provocation* 183–88.

Christensen, Ove. "Spastic Aesthetics—*The Idiots.*" *p.o.v.: A Danish Journal of Film Studies* 10 (2000). Web. May 2, 2008. http://pov.imv.au.dk/.

Chu, Jeff. "Great Dane." *Time* May 11, 2003. Web. June 3, 2007. http://www .time.com/time/magazine/.

Cline, Rich. "*The Boss of It All.*" *Shadows on the Wall* October 15, 2006. Web. May 6, 2009. http://www.shadowsonthewall.co.uk/.

Corliss, Richard. "*Breaking the Waves.*" *Time* 148.25 (1996): 81. Print.

Creeber, Glen. "Surveying *The Kingdom:* Explorations of Medicine, Memory and Modernity in Lars von Trier's *The Kingdom* (1994)." *European Journal of Cultural Studies* 5.4 (2002): 387–407. Print.

"Depression Threatens von Trier's Career." *Reuters* May 12, 2007. Web. August 18, 2008. http://www.reuters.com/.

Derrida, Jacques. *Given Time 1: Counterfeit Money*. Chicago: University of Chicago Press, 1995. Print.

Doane, Mary Ann. "Film and the Masquerade: Theorising the Female Spectator." *Screen* 23.3–4 (1982): 74–87. Rpt. in *Feminist Film Theory: A Reader*. Ed. Sue Thornham. New York: New York University Press, 1999. 131–45. Print.

Dogville Confessions. Dir. Sami Saif. *Dogville*. Dir. Lars von Trier. Disc 2. Nordisk, 2003. DVD.

Doughty, Ruth. "*Manderlay* (2005): Lars von Trier's Narrative of Passing." *New Cinemas* 5. 2 (2007): 153–61. Print.

Durovičová, Nataša, and Jonathan Rosenbaum. "Movies Go Multinational." Rosenbaum and Martin 141–49.

East Side Story. Dir. Dana Ranga. Kino International, 1997. Kino Video, 2000. DVD.

Ebert, Roger. "Cannes #5, 'For Even Now Already It Is in the World.'" *Roger Ebert's Journal. Chicago Sun-Times* May 17, 2009. Web. May 24, 2009. http:// blogs.suntimes.com/ebert/.

———. "Cannes #6, A Devil's Advocate for 'Antichrist.'" *Roger Ebert's Journal. Chicago Sun-Times* May 19, 2009. Web. May 24, 2009. http://blogs.suntimes .com/ebert/.

———. "Cannes #10, 'And, at Last, the Winners Are . . .'" *Roger Ebert's Journal. Chicago Sun-Times* May 24, 2009. Web. May 24, 2009. http://blogs.suntimes .com/ebert/.

———. "Dancer in the Dark." *Roger.ebert.com. Chicago Sun-Times* October 20, 2000. Web. May 12, 2009. http://rogerebert.suntimes.com/.

———. "Zentropa." *Roger.ebert.com. Chicago Sun-Times* July 3, 1992. Web. May 2, 2009. http://rogerebert.suntimes.com/.

Eisenstein, Sergei M. "The Montage of Film Attractions."1924. *The Eisenstein Reader.* Ed. Richard Taylor. London: British Film Institute, 1998. Print.

Elley, Derek. *"Dancer in the Dark." Variety* May 22, 2000. Web. July 6, 2009. http://www.variety.com/.

Elsaesser, Thomas. *European Cinema: Face to Face with Hollywood.* Amsterdam: Amsterdam University Press, 2005. Print.

Eshelman, Raoul. "Performatism, or the End of Postmodernism." *Anthropoetics* 6.2 (Fall/Winter 2000). Web. November 6, 2008. http://www.anthropoetics .ucla.edu/.

Faber, Alyda. "Redeeming Sexual Violence?: A Feminist Reading of *Breaking the Waves." Literature and Theology* 17.1 (2003): 59–75. Print.

Fanning, Evan. *"Antichrist* was Lars' 'Fun' Way of Treating Depression." *Independent.ie* July 26, 2009. Web. July 26, 2009. http://www.independent.ie/.

Feuer, Jane. *The Hollywood Musical.* London: British Film Institute, 1982. Print.

"The Film: Synopsis." *The Corporation.com* 6 (Spring 2009). Web. May 6, 2009. http://www.thecorporation.com/.

Forbert, Katia, dir. *Von Trier's 100 Eyes (von Trier's 100 øjne).* Zentropa Real, 2000. Film.

Foster, Hal. *The Return of the Real: The Avant-Garde at the End of the Century.* Cambridge, Mass.: The Massachusetts Institute of Technology Press, 1966. Print.

Foucault, Michel. *The Birth of the Clinic: An Archaeology of Medical Perception.* Trans. A. M. Sheridan Smith. New York: Vintage-Random House, 1975. Print.

———. *The History of Sexuality, Vol. 1. An Introduction.* New York: Random House, 1978. Print.

Foundas, Scott. "Who's the Boss?" *Village Voice* May 15, 2007. Web. January 12, 2008. http://www.villagevoice.com/.

Fuller, Graham. "See Emily Play—Actress Emily Watson—Interview." *Interview* December 1996. Web. May 25, 2008. http://findarticles.com/.

Gade, Rune, and Anne Jerslev. "Introduction." Gade and Jerslev, *Performative* 7–17.

———, eds. *Performative Realism: Interdisciplinary Studies in Art and Media.* University of Copenhagen: Museum Tusculanum Press, 2005. Print.

Galt, Rosalind. *The New European Cinema: Redrawing the Map.* New York: Columbia University Press, 2006. Print.

Giralt, Gabriel. "The Existential Framework of *Zentropa*'s Narrative: A Clash of Two National Identities." *Kinema: A Journal for Film and Audiovisual Media* Spring 2001. Web. December 4, 2009. http://www.kinema.uwaterloo.ca/.

Goldsmith, Leo. "*Manderlay.*" *Not Coming to a Theatre Near You* October 6, 2005. Web. May 1, 2009. http://www.notcoming.com/.

Gordon, Suzy. "*Breaking the Waves* and the Negativity of Melanie Klein: Re-thinking 'the Female Spectator.'" *Screen* 45.3 (2004): 206–25. Print.

Goss, Brian Michael. *Global Auteurs: Politics in the Films of Almodóvar, von Trier, and Winterbottom.* New York: Peter Lang, 2009. Print.

Harsin, Jayson. "Von Trier's Brechtian Gamble." *Bright Lights Film Journal* 51 (February 2006). Web. March 12, 2009. http://www.brightlightsfilm.com/.

Hart, Christopher. "What DOES It Take for a Film to Get Banned these Days?" *Mail Online* July 20, 2009. Web. January 10, 2010. http://www.dailymail.co.uk/.

Haskell, Molly. *From Reverence to Rape: The Treatment of Women in the Movies.* 2nd ed. Chicago: University of Chicago Press, 1987. Print.

Heath, Stephen. "God, Faith and Film: *Breaking the Waves.*" *Literature & Theology* 12.1 (March 1998): 93–107. *Project Muse.* Web. December 10, 2009. http://muse.jhu.edu/.

Higgins, Charlotte. "Lars von Trier Acts as a Slave to Controversy." *Guardian* May 17, 2005. Web. November 2, 2006. http://www.guardian.co.uk/.

Hilderbrand, Lucas. "Les Miserables, or, It's Oh So Björk." *PopMatters* 2000. Web. July 2008. http://www.popmatters.com/film/reviews/.

"The History." *Zentropa* (official site). April 24, 2009. Web. May 2, 2009. http://www.zentropa.dk/about/historie.

Hjort, Mette. *Dekalog¹: On The Five Obstructions.* Guest Ed. Mette Hjort. London: Wallflower, 2008. Print.

———. "Dogma 95: A Small Nation's Response to Globalisation." Hjort and MacKenzie, *Purity and Provocation* 31–47.

———. "The Globalisation of Dogma: The Dynamics of Metaculture and Counter-Publicity." Hjort and MacKenzie, *Purity and Provocation* 133–57.

———. *Small Nation, Global Cinema: The New Danish Cinema.* Minneapolis: University of Minnesota Press, 2005. Print.

Hjort, Mette, and Ib Bondebjerg, eds. *The Danish Directors: Dialogues on a Contemporary National Cinema.* Bristol, United Kingdom: Intellect Books, 2001. Print.

Hjort, Mette, and Scott MacKenzie, eds. *Purity and Provocation: Dogma 95.* London: British Film Institute, 2003. Print.

Hjort, Mette, and Duncan Petrie, eds. "Denmark." *The Cinema of Small Nations.* Bloomington: Indiana University Press, 2007. 23–42. Print.

Hoberman, J. "Darkness Visible." *Village Voice* September 19, 2000. Web. June 30, 2008. http://www.villagevoice.com/.

Holden, Stephen. "It's Not That the Boss Seems Distant. It's Just That He Doesn't Exist." Rev. of *The Boss of It All. New York Times* May 23, 2007. Web. May 1, 2009. http://movies.nytimes.com/.

Holdt, Jacob. *American Pictures: A Personal Journey through the American Underclass.* Copenhagen: American Pictures Foundation, 1986. Print.

———. *American Pictures.* 1997. Web. April 12, 2009. http://www.american-pictures.com/.

Hopper, Jessica. "In Which Nature Is Lars von Trier's Satanic Church." *This Recording* October 27, 2009. Web. December 1, 2009. http://thisrecording .com/.

Huggy Bear. "*Manderlay.*" *Counter-Racism* 2003–2007. Web. March 2, 2009. http://www.counter-racism.com/.

The Humiliated. (De ydmygede). Dir. Jesper Jargil. 1998. *Idioterne. Dogme Kollektion 1–4.* Disc 2. Electric Parc, 2005. DVD.

Iarussi, Signe (Assistant to Lars von Trier). "Lars von Trier Interview Permissions Signature." Message to the author. June 19, 2009. Email.

Ide, Wendy. "Antichrist at the Cannes Film Festival." *Times Online* May 18, 2009. Web. July 21, 2009. http://entertainment.timesonline.co.uk/.

In Lars von Trier's Kingdom (I Lars von Triers Rige). Dir. Ole Koster. TV2 documentary, 1999. *Riget II.* Disc 1. Zentropa Kollektion #15. Electric Parc, 2004. DVD.

"Interview with Lars von Trier and Paul Thomas Anderson." *BlackBook Magazine.* Winter 2004. Web. June 3, 2008. http://www.cigarettesandredvines .com/.

James, Gareth, and Gardar Eide Einarsson. *Lars von Trier.* American Fine Arts Co. New York 22.5–6.7. 2002. Exhibitions. *Artfacts.net* July 6, 2002. Web. January 4, 2008. http://www.e-flux.com/.

Jameson, Fredric. *Signatures of the Visible.* New York: Routledge, 1992. Print.

Jappe, Anselm. *Guy Debord.* Trans. Donald Nicholson-Smith. Berkeley: University of California Press, 1999. Print.

Jensen, Bo Green. *A Conversation with Lars von Trier. Hypnotic Features. Lars von Trier's E-Trilogy.* Disc 4. Tartan, 2005. DVD.

Jensen, Peter Aalbæk. Personal interview, Zentropa, Filmbyen 22. September 22, 2006.

Jerslev, Anne. "Dogma 95, Lars von Trier's *The Idiots,* and the 'Idiot Project.'" *Realism and Reality in Film and Media.* Ed. Run Gade and Anne Jerslev.

Northern Lights: Film and Media Studies Yearbook 2002. University of Copenhagen: Museum Tusculanum Press, 2002. 41–65. Print.

Kaufman, Anthony. "Lars von Trier Comes out of the Dark." Interview with Lars von Trier. *IndieWIRE* 2001. Lumholdt, *Lars* 153–58.

Kehr, Dave. "From the Voice of Dogma Comes the Sound of Music." *New York Times* September 10, 2000. Web. June 12, 2008. http://www.nytimes.com/.

Kelly, Richard. *The Name of This Book Is Dogme95.* London: Faber and Faber, 2001. Print.

Kidman, Nicole. "My Favorite Year: 1996." *Entertainment Weekly* June 27/July 4 (Summer Double Issue) 2008: 34. Print.

"The *Kingdom (Riget)*." *Time Out Film Guide 2009.* London: Ebury, 2008. 569. Print.

The Kingdom II (Riget II), 1997. Disc 1. Zentropa Kollektion #15, Electric Parc, 2004. DVD.

Kirkeby, Per. "The Pictures Between the Chapters in *Breaking the Waves.*" *Breaking the Waves.* By Lars von Trier. London: Faber and Faber, 1996. 12–14. Print.

Knudsen, Peter Øvig. "The Man Who Would Give Up Control. *Weekendknavisen* May 11, 1998. Lumholdt, *Lars* 117–124. Print.

Koster, Ole. Interview with Lars von Trier. TV2. Cannes May 20, 2003. *Dogville.* Disc 2. Nordisk, 2003. DVD.

———. Interview with Lars von Trier. TV2. Cannes May 23, 2003. *Dogville.* Disc 2. Nordisk, 2003. DVD.

Kristeva, Julia. *Powers of Horror: An Essay on Abjection.* Trans. Leon S. Roudiez. New York: Columbia University Press, 1982. Print.

Kuersten, Erich. "Acid's Greatest Horror #1: *Antichrist* (2009)." *Acidemic: Journal of Film and Media* November 13, 2009. Web. November 28, 2009. http://acidemic.blogspot.com/.

Kun, Josh. "Movie Review: *Manderlay.*" *LA Times* February 3, 2005. Web. April 3, 2009. http://www.latimes.com/.

"Lars von Trier—Genius or Fraud?" *Arts diary. Guardian.co.uk* May 20, 2009. Web. June 1, 2009. http://www.guardian.co.uk/.

"Lars von Trier on *Antichrist.*" Transcript of Q & A with participants. *7th International Conference of the Society for Cognitive Studies of the Moving Image* June 26, 2009. Web. May 30, 2010. http://scsmi09.mef.ku.dk/.

Larsen, Jan Kornum. "A Conversation between Jan Kornum Larsen and Lars von Trier." *Kosmorama* 167 (1984). Lumholdt, *Lars* 32–46.

Longworth, Karina. "*Antichrist* Review." *Spout Blog* May 23, 2009. Web. August 23, 2009. http://blog.spout.com/.

Luckhurst, Roger. "Trauma Culture." *New Formations* 50 (2003): 28–47. Print.

Lumholdt, Jan. "There Will Be No Fun-Poking Today." Interview with Lars von Trier. *Filmhälftet* February 2000. Lumholdt, *Lars* 159–69.

———, ed. *Lars von Trier: Interviews.* Jackson: University of Mississippi Press, 2003. Print.

Lundberg, Pia. "Von Trier Unveils 'Lookey.'" *Variety* December 6, 2006. Web. February 1, 2009. http://www.variety.com/.

Makarushka, Irena S. M. "Transgressing Goodness in *Breaking the Waves.*" *Journal of Religion and Film* 2.1 (April 1998). Web. November 5, 2009. http://www.unomaha.edu/jrf/.

Martin, Adrian. "Musical Mutations: Before, Beyond and Against Hollywood." Rosenbaum and Martin, *Movie Mutations* 94–108.

Marx, Karl. *Capital: A Critique of Political Economy.* Vol. 1. 1867. Introduction. Ernest Mandel. Trans. Ben Fowkes. Harmondsworth, United Kingdom: Penguin, 1992. Print.

McCarthy, Todd. "*Antichrist.*" *Variety* May 17, 2009. Web. July 21, 2009. http://www.variety.com/.

———. "*Dogville.*" *Variety* May 19, 2003. Web. April 22, 2009. http://www.variety.com/.

McGwin, Kevin. "Cream of Culture for Some Is Sour." *Copenhagen Post* February 3–9, 2006. Web. June 9, 2009. http://www.in-other-words.dk/background/clippings/.

McMillan, Brian. "Complicitous Critique: *Dancer in the Dark* as Postmodern Musical." *Discourses in Music* 5.2 (Fall 2004). Web. June 6, 2008. http://www.discourses.ca/.

McNab, Geoffrey. "Interview with Lars von Trier." *The Boss of It All* Press Booklet. 2006. Print.

"Meeting the Danish Press." Press conference, Cannes 2003. *Dogville.* Disc 2. Nordisk, 2005. DVD.

Merin, Jennifer. "Interview: Lars von Trier." *New York Press* February 1, 2006. Web. April 2, 2009. http://www.nypress.com/.

Michelsen, Ole. "Passion Is the Lifeblood of Cinema." Interview with Lars von Trier. *Tusind Øjne* #54 August 1982. Lumholdt, *Lars* 5–12.

Modleski, Tania. *The Women Who Knew Too Much.* London: Methuen. 1988. Print.

Moskwa, Wojciech. "Crisis Impact: Nordic Welfare State Coping Well, So Far." *Guardian* June 16, 2009. Web. June 17, 2009. http://www.guardian.co.uk/.

Mulvey, Laura. "*Visual Pleasure* and Narrative Cinema." *Screen* 16.3 (Autumn 1975): 6–18. Print.

Naficy, Hamid. *An Accented Cinema: Exilic and Diasporic Filmmaking.* Princeton: Princeton University Press, 2001. Print.

The Name of This Film Is Dogme 95. Dir. Saul Metzstein, writ. Richard Kelly. Minerva Pictures, United Kingdom, 2000. Film.

Nelson, Victoria. *The Secret Life of Puppets.* Cambridge, Mass.: Harvard University Press, 2001. Print.

Nicodemus, Katja. "I Am an American Woman." Interview with Lars von Trier. *Sign and Sight.com* November 17, 2005. Web. January 10, 2008. http://www.signandsight.com/.

Nielsen, Dorothy Kirkgaard. "Zentropa Family." *FILM* #66. *Det Danske Filminstitut* May 2009. Web. June 16, 2009. http://www.dfi.dk/.

Nilsson, Jonas Langvad. "Danish Movies Rebel against Dogma." *Copenhagen Exclusive* #01. Copenhagen: MPH Communications, 2006. 98–102. Print.

Nissim, Mayer. "Willem Dafoe (*Antichrist*)." *Digital Spy* July 21, 2009. Web. July 26, 2009. http://www.digitalspy.com/.

Nochimson, Martha. "Movies and the America of the Mind: New York Film Festival 2005 Report (Part One)." *Film-Philosophy* 9.44 (November 2005). Web. May 18, 2010. http://www.film-philosophy.com/.

Ogden, Perry. "Dogmatic." Interview with Anthony Dod Mantle. *FilmIreland* 96 (February 2004). Web. March 6, 2008. http://www.filmireland.net/.

100 Cameras: Capturing Lars von Trier's Vision. Dir. Vincent Paterson. *Dancer in the Dark.* New Line, 2001. DVD.

Ostrowska, Dorota. "Zentropa and von Trier: A Marriage Made in Heaven." *Studies in European Cinema* 2.3 (December 2005): 185–98. Print.

O'Sullivan, Michael. "Dogville: A Biting American Tale." *Washington Post* April 9, 2004: 41. Print.

Page, Nicholas. "Her Dark Materials: Antichrist's 'Mysogyny [sic] Consultant' Interviewed." *The Big Picture* August 6, 2009. Web. May 30, 2010. http://www.thebigpicturemagazine.com/.

Parker, Ian. "Letter from Reykjavik." *New Yorker* March 9, 2009: 39. Print.

Paterson, Vincent. Choreographer commentary. *Dancer in the Dark.* New Line Home Entertainment, 2001. DVD.

Paulhan, Jean. "Happiness in Slavery." *Story of O.* By Pauline Réage. 1954. Trans. Sabine d'Estrée. New York: Ballantine, 1965. xxi–xxxvi. Print.

Peden, Knox. "The Threepenny Shot." *Critical Sense* Spring 2005: 119–29. PDF.

Pedersen, Jes Stein. "Ān den vej fil *Manderlay*." Interview with Lars von Trier. *2.Sektion Deadline. Manderlay.* Dir. Lars von Trier. Disc 2. Zentropa Productions, 2005. DVD.

Penner, Todd, and Caroline Stichele. "Accenting the Other: Rhetorical Constructions of Identity and Difference in the Films of Lars von Trier." *Queen: A Journal of Rhetoric and Power.* Special Issue 5. Conference paper. The Rhetorics of Identity: Place, Race, Sex and the Person. University of Redlands, Redlands, Calif. January 20–22, 2005. PDF.

Perkins, Claire. "Your Friends and Neighbors: The American Smart Film." Diss. Monash University, September 2008. Print.

Pierce, Andrew. "Financial Crisis: Iceland's Dreams Go Up in Smoke." *Telegraph* October 6, 2008. Web. June 17, 2009. http://www.telegraph.co.uk/.

Pil, Morten. "Kindred Spirits." Interview with Anthony Dod Mantle. *FILM* #66 *Det DanskeFilminstitut* May 2009. Web. June 2, 2009. http://www.dfi.dk/.

Powers, Ann. "FILM; Making a Tragedy with a Happy Ending." *Interview with Björk. New York Times* September 17, 2000. Web. July 8, 2008. http://www.nytimes.com/.

"Press Conference: *Antichrist*." With Lars von Trier, Willem Dafoe, and Charlotte Gainsbourg. *Festival de Cannes 2009* May 18, 2009. Web. March 4, 2010. Streaming video. http://www.festival-cannes.fr/en/.

The Purified (De Lutrede). Dir. Jesper Jargil. Jesper Jargil Film/Danish Film Institute, Denmark, 2002. Film.

"The Puzzy Power Manifesto: Statement on Women and Sexuality." *Puzzy Power Presents Constance*. Intimate Pictures 1998. Web. March 3, 2010. http://www.innocentpictures.com/.

Rafferty, Terrence. "Breaking the Waves." *New Yorker* November 25, 1996. Web. March 2, 2009. http://www.newyorker.com/.

Rancière, Jacques. "The Ethical Turn of Aesthetics and Politics." *Critical Horizons* 7.1 (2006): 1–20. Print.

Rifkin, Jeremy. *The End of Work*. Rev. ed. London: Penguin, 2000. Print.

———. *The European Dream: How Europe's Vision of The Future Is Quietly Eclipsing the American Dream*. New York: Tarcher/Penguin, 2004. Print.

Rockwell, John. *The Idiots*. London: British Film Institute, 2003. Print.

———. "Von Trier and Wagner, a Bond Sealed in Emotion." *New York Times* April 8, 2001. Web. April 29, 2006. http://www.nytimes.com/.

Rombes, Nicholas, ed. *New Punk Cinema*. Edinburgh: Edinburgh University Press, 2005.

Romer, Knud. "A Hearse Heading Home." Interview with Lars von Trier. *FILM* #66. *Det Danske Filminstitut* May 2009. Web. June 14, 2009. http://www.dfi.dk/.

Römers, Holger. "'Colorado Death Trip': The Surrealist Recontextualisation of Farm Security Administration Photos in *Dogville*." *Senses of Cinema* October 2004. Web. April 2009. http://archive.sensesofcinema.com/.

Rosenbaum, Jonathan. "Mixed Emotions." Rev. of *Breaking the Waves. Chicago Reader* 1997. Web. June 6, 2008. http://www.chicagoreader.com/.

Rosenbaum, Jonathan, and Adrian Martin, eds. *Movie Mutations: The Changing Face of World Cinephilia*. London: British Film Institute, 2003. Print.

Ruland, Richard. "The American Plays of Bertolt Brecht." *American Quarterly* 15. 3 (Autumn 1963): 371–89. *JSTOR*. Web. March 2, 2010. http://www.jstor.org/.

Sade, Marquis de. *Justine, or Good Conduct Well Chastised*. 1791. *The Marquis de Sade: Justine, Philosophy in the Bedroom, and Other Writings*. Comp., trans. Richard Seaver and Austryn Wainhouse. New York: Grove, 1965. 447–743. Print.

Schepelern, Peter. "Film According to Dogme: Restrictions, Obstructions and Liberations." *Dogme95*. n.d. Web. May 29, 2009. http://www.dogme95.dk.

———. "Interview with Lars von Trier." *Antichrist*. Official Web site. May 14, 2009. Web. June 2, 2009. http://www.antichristthemovie.com/.

———. "The Making of an Auteur: Notes on the Auteur Theory and Lars von Trier." *Visual Authorship: Creativity and Intentionality in Media*. Ed. Torben Grodal, Bente Larsen, and Iben Thorving Laursen. Copenhagen: University of Copenhagen, Museum Tusculanum Press, 2005. 103–27. Print.

———. "Re: Dogme films (a quick question)." Message to the author. March 16, 2010. Email.

Schepelern, Peter, and Stig Björkman. Commentary. *The Idiots* (*Idioterne*). *Dogme Kollektion 1–4*. Disc 2. Electric Parc, 2005. DVD.

Schwander, Lars. "We Need More Intoxicants in Danish Cinema." *Levende Billeder* June 1983. Lumholdt, *Lars* 13–23.

Schwarzbaum, Lisa. "French Foreign Legions." *Entertainment Weekly* June 2, 2000. Web. July 3, 2009. http://www.ew.com/.

Schweitzer, Vivien. "Björk Film 'Dancer in the Dark' to Hit Denmark Stage as an Opera." *Playbill* May 25, 2007.Web. June 14, 2008. http://www.playbill.com/.

Scott, A. O. "*Dogville*: It Fakes a Village." *New York Times* March 21, 2004. Web. February 12, 2009. http://www.nytimes.com/.

Scott, James C. *Weapons of the Weak: Everyday Forms of Peasant Resistance*. New Haven, Conn.: Yale University Press, 1983. Print.

Seltzer, Mark. *Serial Killers: Death and Life in America's Wound Culture*. New York: Routledge, 1998. Print.

Simons, Jan. *Playing the Waves: Lars von Trier's Game Cinema*. Amsterdam: Amsterdam University Press, 2007. Print.

———. "Von Trier's Cinematic Games." *Journal of Film and Video* 60.1 (Spring 2008): 3–13. Print.

Sinnerbrink, Robert. "Grace and Violence: Questioning Politics and Desire in Lars von Trier's *Dogville*." *Film as Philosophy: SCAN/ Journal of Media Arts Culture* 4.2 (August 2007). Web. July 30, 2008. http://scan.net.au/scan/journal/.

A Small Film about a Big Company. Dir. Carsten Bramsen. Zentropa Productions, 2007. *Zentropa*. Web. May 20, 2010. http://www.zentropa.dk/.

Smith, Gavin. "Imitation of Life: Gavin Smith Interviews the Great Dane." *Film Comment* September–October 2000: 22–26. Print.

Staat, Wim. "*Dogville* Characterized by *The Grapes of Wrath*: European Identity Construction through American Genre Conventions." *Framework* 48.1 (Spring 2007): 79–96. *Project Muse*. Web. February 12, 2009. http://muse.jhu.edu/.

Stevenson, Jack. *Dogme Uncut: Lars von Trier, Thomas Vinterberg, and the Gang that Took on Hollywood*. Santa Monica, Calif.: Santa Monica Press, 2003. Print.

———. "Lars von Trier: Pornographer?" *Bright Lights Film Journal* 43 (February 2003). Web. June 30, 2008. http://www.brightlightsfilm.com/.

————. *Lars von Trier.* World Directors. London: British Film Institute, 2002. Print.

————. "The Wave Breaks." *Bright Lights Film Journal* 41 (August 2003). Web. May 20, 2008. http://www.brightlightsfilm.com/.

"A Story about People and Emotions." *Breaking the Waves.* By Lars von Trier. London: Faber and Faber, 1996.15–19. Print.

Strindberg, August. "Preface." *A Dream Play.* 1901. *Miss Julie and Other Plays.* By August Strindberg. Trans. Michael Robinson. Oxford: Oxford University Press, 1998. 176. Print.

Sutton, Martin. "Patterns of Meaning in the Musical." *Genre: The Musical: A Reader.* Ed. Rick Altman. London: Routledge and Kegan Paul, 1981: 190–96. Print.

Sweet, Matthew. "The Cruel and Crazy World of Lars von Trier." *Independent* May 5, 2000. Web. January 12, 2009. http://www.independent.co.uk/.

Tangherlini, Timothy R. "Ghost in the Machine: Supernatural Threat and the State in Lars von Trier's *Riget.*" *Scandinavian Studies* 73.1 (2001): 1–25. Print.

Tapper, Michael. "A Romance in Decomposition." *Chaplin* #2, 1991. Lumholdt, *Lars* 71–80.

Tate, Greg. "Björk's Second Act: Existential Soul Sister Björk on 'Dancer in the Dark' and the Changing Face of Her Music." *Papermag* October 1, 2000. Web. March 2, 2010. http://www.papermag.com/.

Thomas, Dana. "Meet the Punisher: Lars von Trier Devastates Audiences—and Actresses." Interview with Lars von Trier. *Newsweek* April 5, 2004. *HighBeam Research.* Web. December 8, 2008. http://www.highbeam.com.

Thompson, Matt. "Director in the Dark: Depressed Danish Filmmaker Gets Happy." *Radar Online* June 4, 2007. Web. February 29, 2009. http://www.radaronline.com/.

Thomsen, Christian Braad. "Control and Chaos." *Politiken* July 5, 1996. Lumholdt, *Lars* 106–16.

Thomson, Philip. *The Grotesque.* Critical Idiom. London: Methuen, 1972. Print.

Tobias, Scott. "*Manderlay.*" *A.V. Club* January 25, 2006. Web. May 12, 2009. http://www.avclub.com/.

Tocqueville, Alexis de. *Democracy in America.* Bk. II. Ed. Francis Bowen. Trans. Henry Reeve. 3rd ed. 1835. Cambridge: Sever and Francis, 1863. Print.

Tranceformer—A Portrait of Lars von Trier. Dir./writ. Stig Björkman. 1997. *Lars von Trier's E-Trilogy.* Disc 4. Tartan, 2005. DVD.

Trier, Lars von. "Automavision—Shooting Concept for *The Boss of It All.*" *The Boss of It All* Press book. Zentropa Entertainments. May 8, 2006. Print.

————. *Breaking the Waves.* London: Faber and Faber, 1996. Print.

————. *Dancer in the Dark.* London: FilmFour Books, 2000. Print.

————. "Deed of Conveyance." *Zentropa.* Web. May 20, 2010. http://www.zentropa.dk/.

————. "Director's Confession." *Antichrist.* Official Web site. May 18, 2009. Web. May 22, 2009. http://www.antichristthemovie.com/.

————."Director's Note—This Film Is about 'Good.'" *Breaking the Waves.* By Lars von Trier. London: Faber and Faber, 1996. 20–22. Print.

————. "Dogme95 Manifesto and the 'Vow of Chastity.'" March 13,1995. Web. January 10, 2009. http://www.dogme95.dk.

————. *Dogville* Production Notes. 2003. Web. January 5, 2005. http:// www .dogville.dk.

————. "Lars von Trier on Making Dancer in the Dark." Production Notes. *Dancer in the Dark.* Official Web site. Fine Line Features. Web. June 20, 2008. http://www.dancerinthedarkmovie.com/.

————. "Project 'Open Film Town': Visions in Connection with the Film Town in Avedøre." Hjort and Bondebjerg 224–27.

————. "Selma's Manifesto." *Dancer in the Dark.* Official Web site. Fine Line Features. 2000. Web. June 18, 2008. www.dancerinthedarkmovie.com/.

————. "Statement of Revitality." Rpt. in "What, Me Dogmatic?" By Adam Dawtrey. *Variety* February 10, 2006. Web. May 6, 2009. http://www.variety .com/.

Trier, Lars von, and Jens Albinus. Commentary. *The Idiots (Idioterne). Dogme Kollektion 1–4.* Disc 2. Electric Parc, 2005. DVD.

Trier, Lars von, Tom Elling, and Tómas Gislasen. Commentary. *The Element of Crime. Lars von Trier's E-Trilogy.* Disc 1. Tartan, 2005. DVD.

Trier, Lars von, and Tómas Gislasen. Commentary. *Nocturne. The Element of Crime. Lars von Trier's E-Trilogy.* Disc 1. Tartan, 2005. DVD.

Trier, Lars von, and Anthony Dod Mantle. Commentary. *Manderlay.* Nordisk Film, 2005. DVD.

Trier, Lars von, and Niels Vørsel. Commentary. *Epidemic. Lars von Trier's E-Trilogy.* Disc 2. Tartan, 2005. DVD.

————. Commentary. *The Kingdom II (Riget II).* Disc 2. Zentropa Kollektion, Electric Parc, 2004. DVD.

Trier, Lars von, Vibecke Windelov, Peter Hjorth, and Per Kirkeby. Filmmaker commentary. *Dancer in the Dark.* New Line Home Entertainment, 2001. DVD.

"Trier on von Trier." *Editorial Reviews. Amazon.* 2005. Web. April 4, 2010. http://www.amazon.com.

Trust Film Sales. "Lars von Trier Shoots *Antichrist* in Eden." *Trust Film Sales* August 18, 2008. Web. June 19, 2009. http://www.trust-film.dk/.

Unruh, Bob. "Theater Operators Could Be Warned over 'Antichrist.'" *WorldNet Daily* November 4, 2009. Web. December 2, 2009. http://www.wnd.com/.

van De Walle, Mark. "Heaven's Weight." *Artform* 35.3 (November 1996): 82–88. Print.

"Von Trier Preps Antichrist Film." *Filmmaker: The Magazine of Independent Film* October 27, 2004. Web. May 16, 2010. http://filmmakermagazine .com/.

Wachthausen, Jean-Luc. "Lars von Trier: '*Antichrist* est ma thérapie.'" Interview. *Le Figaro* May 18, 2009. Web. June 2, 2009. http://www.lefigaro.fr/.

Wakelin, Simon. "Zentropa's Revolutionary Appeal." *Boards* September 1, 2000. Web. June 9, 2009. http://www.boardsmag.com/.

Wall, James M. "*Breaking the Waves.*" *The Christian Century* 114.5 (February 5, 1997): 115–17. Print.

Walters, Tim. "Reconsidering *The Idiots:* Dogme95, Lars von Trier, and the Cinema of Subversion?" *The Velvet Light Trap* 53 (2004): 40–54. Print.

Wells, Jeffrey. "*Antichrist* = Fartbomb." *Hollywood Elsewhere* 2009. Web. July 21, 2009. http://www.hollywood-elsewhere.com/.

Williams, Linda. "Film Bodies: Gender, Genre and Excess." *Film Quarterly* 44.4 (1991): 2–13. Rpt. in *Feminist Film Theory: A Reader.* Ed. Sue Thornham. New York: New York University Press, 1999. 267–81. Print.

Woodgate, Ken. "'Gotta' Dance' (in the Dark): Lars von Trier's Critique of the Musical Genre." *The Play within the Play: The Performance of Meta-Theatre and Self-Reflection.* Ed. Gerhard Fischer and Bernhard Greiner. Amsterdam: Rodopi, 2007. 393–402. Print.

Woolnough, Tara P. "*Manderlay.*" *Spannered* March 14, 2006. Web. April 1, 2009. http://www.spannered.org/.

Zinn, Howard. *A People's History of the United States.* New York: HarperCollins, 2005. Print.

Žižek, Slavoj. "Death and the Maiden." *The Žižek Reader.* Ed. Elizabeth Wright and Edmund Wright. Oxford: Blackwell, 1999. 206–21. Print.

———. "Why Is a *Woman* a Symptom of a Man?" *Enjoy Your Symptom!* New York: Routledge, 1992. 36–67. Print.

identity politics, 7, 13, 70, 101–2; immigration and, 101, 102, 111, 131; race
and, 102, 116–30; transnationalism,
2–3; the United States and, 93–97,
99–103, 105–30, 157, 158, 163–66. *See
also* capitalism
pornography, 3, 65, 73, 78–79, 82, 127,
142, 143, 147, 153n6, 153n16, 172
postmodernism, 3, 7–13, 15–16, 35, 36,
45, 56, 59, 67, 73, 74, 85, 91
psychoanalysis, 6, 13, 76, 133, 150, 161
psychodrama: 4, 7, 13, 57, 59, 70, 91,
145–46, 147, 148, 150
Psykomobile #1: The World Clock, 14
Purinton, Miles, 108
Puzzy Power, 153n16

Raaberg, Birgette, 49
race, 102, 116–30, 131, 165
Rancière, Jacques, 113–14
Reed, Carol, *The Third Man*, 24–25, 27,
36
Reenberg, Jørgen, 37, 46
religion, 8, 39, 51, 72–75, 82–87, 88
Rigshospital (Copenhagen), 32, 47, 48
Rodriguez, Robert, 56
Rolffes, Kirsten, 49
Ruders, Poul, 89

Sade, Marquis de (*Justine*), 73, 78, 81–83,
84, 111
sadomasochism, 17, 78, 106–8, 111, 115,
127–30, 139, 146–48
Safety Last (Newmeyer and Taylor), 43
Sahlström, Storm Acheche, 150
Sandemose, Aksel. See *Jantelovn*
satire, 2, 6, 10, 16, 43–45, 52, 59, 82,
102–3, 109–11, 115, 119, 132–33,
136–39, 144
"Sauna," 47
Scherfig, Lone, 57, 59
science fiction, 3, 22, 28, 48
self-fashioning, 7, 12, 60
self-reflexivity: *Antichrist*, 150; *The Boss
of It All*, 134–36, 140; *Breaking the
Waves*, 77, 81; *Dancer in the Dark*,
92; *Dogville*, 105, 112, 114; *Epidemic*,
28–35; *Europa*, 36, 37, 40–41; *The*

Idiots, 62, 67–68; *Manderlay*, 124–26.
See also Dogme95: metacinema
Seven Brides for Seven Brothers
(Donen), 96
Sevigny, Chloë, 107
Shop Around the Corner, The (Lubitsch),
132
Shortbus (Mitchell), 68
Sigma Films, 12, 163
Silver Dust (Armand and Room), 95
Simpson, Michael, 29, 32
Sirk, Douglas, 76
situationism (Debord), 14, 58
Skarsgård, Stellan, 72, 107, 108
Smith, Kevin, 56
socialism, 58–59, 91, 95–97, 120, 122,
129, 149
Soderbergh, Steven, 172; *Full Frontal*,
68, 152n5; *Kafka*, 172; *Ocean's 12*, 172;
Solaris, 172; *Traffic*, 152n5
Sound of Music, The (Rogers and Ham-
merstein), 91–92
speech act theory (Austin), 15
"Statement of Revitality," 131–32, 160
Station Next (film school), 156, 178n1
Sternberg, Josef von, 9
Stormare, Peter, 88
Strindberg, August: "Inferno" crisis and
Antichrist, 147–48; influence on Trier,
4, 9; and Nietzsche, Munch, 153n17
Strindberg, August, works of: *A Dream
Play*, 148; *Miss Julie*, 9, 147; *The Stron-
ger*, 147
Stroheim, Erich von, 9
student films, 10, 16–21, 26, 35, 36, 128,
179n7
sublime, the, 6, 15, 52–54, 80–81
Sukowa, Barbara, 36, 38, 44
surrealism, 23, 44, 54, 115, 141, 145–46,
148, 174

Tarantino, Quentin, 56
Tarkovsky, Andrei, 3, 17, 18, 19, 22, 23,
32, 35, 47, 145, 179
Tarkovsky, Andrei, films of: *The Mirror*,
19, 145, 171–72; *Solaris*, 172, 178n4
Texas Chain Saw Massacre, The
(Hooper), 174

Linda Badley is a professor of English
at Middle Tennessee State University. She is the author
of *Film, Horror, and the Body Fantastic* and *Writing
Horror and the Body: The Fiction of Stephen King,
Anne Rice, and Clive Barker* and the coeditor
of *Traditions in World Cinema.*

Books in the series
Contemporary Film Directors

The University of Illinois Press
is a founding member of the
Association of American University Presses.

Composed in 10/13 New Caledonia
with Helvetica Neue Std display
at the University of Illinois Press
Manufactured by Cushing-Malloy, Inc.

University of Illinois Press
1325 South Oak Street
Champaign, IL 61820-6903
www.press.uillinois.edu